# Industry 4.0 Transformation Towards Industry 5.0 Paradigm - Challenges, Opportunities and Practices

*Edited by Ibrahim Yitmen and Amjad Almusaed*

Published in London, United Kingdom

Industry 4.0 Transformation Towards Industry 5.0 Paradigm - Challenges, Opportunities and Practices
http://dx.doi.org/10.5772/intechopen.1001746
Edited by Ibrahim Yitmen and Amjad Almusaed

Contributors
Abin George, Ahmed Al Jarwan, Ali Elrashidi, Amjad Almusaed, Andrisha Beharry-Ramraj, Basma El Zein, Ghassan Jabbour, Hala Nassereddine, Ibrahim Yitmen, Makram Bou Hatoum, Mohanad Dahlan, Motshidisi Masilo, Nompumelelo Mbhele, Sheng Wang, Shizi Ma, Zhitao Ma



First published in London, United Kingdom, 2024 by IntechOpen
IntechOpen is the global imprint of INTECHOPEN LIMITED, registered in England and Wales, registration number: 11086078, 167-169 Great Portland Street, London, W1W 5PF, United Kingdom

British Library Cataloguing-in-Publication Data
A catalogue record for this book is available from the British Library

Additional hard and PDF copies can be obtained from orders@intechopen.com

Industry 4.0 Transformation Towards Industry 5.0 Paradigm - Challenges, Opportunities and Practices
Edited by Ibrahim Yitmen and Amjad Almusaed
p. cm.

This title is part of the Artificial Intelligence Book Series, Volume 27
Topic: Applied Intelligence
Series Editor: Andries Engelbrecht
Topic Editor: Carlos M. Travieso-Gonzalez

Print ISBN 978-0-85466-095-7
Online ISBN 978-0-85466-094-0
eBook (PDF) ISBN 978-0-85466-096-4
ISSN 2633-1403

For EU product safety concerns:
IN TECH d.o.o., Prolaz Marije Krucifikse Kozulić 3, 51000 Rijeka, Croatia,
info@intechopen.com or visit our website at intechopen.com.

IntechOpen Book Series

# Artificial Intelligence

Volume 27

## Aims and Scope of the Series

Artificial Intelligence (AI) is a rapidly developing multidisciplinary research area that aims to solve increasingly complex problems. In today's highly integrated world, AI promises to become a robust and powerful means for obtaining solutions to previously unsolvable problems. This Series is intended for researchers and students alike interested in this fascinating field and its many applications.

# Meet the Series Editor

Andries Engelbrecht received the Masters and Ph.D. degrees in Computer Science from the University of Stellenbosch, South Africa, in 1994 and 1999 respectively. He is currently appointed as the Voigt Chair in Data Science in the Department of Industrial Engineering, with a joint appointment as Professor in the Computer Science Division, Stellenbosch University. Prior to his appointment at Stellenbosch University, he has been at the University of Pretoria, Department of Computer Science (1998-2018), where he was appointed as South Africa Research Chair in Artifical Intelligence (2007-2018), the head of the Department of Computer Science (2008-2017), and Director of the Institute for Big Data and Data Science (2017-2018). In addition to a number of research articles, he has written two books, Computational Intelligence: An Introduction and Fundamentals of Computational Swarm Intelligence.

# Meet the Volume Editors

Professor Ibrahim Yitmen, a distinguished scholar in architectural technology, obtained his Ph.D. from Istanbul Technical University, Turkey. Since February 2018, he has been a professor at Jönköping University, Sweden, in the Management of Construction Production Department. His research integrates cutting-edge technologies in the built environment, focusing on Digital Twin-based Smart Built Environments, Augmented Reality/Mixed Reality in Cognitive Buildings, and integrating Digital Twins with Deep Learning for advanced planning and construction. Dr. Yitmen is also deeply involved in exploring the application of blockchain technology in construction supply chains and the development of Cyber-Physical Systems in the context of Construction 4.0. Dr. Yitmen has made notable contributions to academic literature, serving as the editor of influential books such as *BIM-enabled Cognitive Computing for Smart Built Environment: Potential, Requirements, and Implementation* and *Cognitive Digital Twins for Smart Lifecycle Management of Built Environment and Infrastructure: Challenges, Opportunities and Practices*. His editorial expertise was further recognized through his role as a guest editor for *Applied Sciences*, specifically for the Special Issue on "Cognitive Buildings." Currently, Dr. Yitmen is leading several significant research projects in Sweden, funded by organizations like Smart Built Environment, Vinnova, and Jönköpings Läns Byggmästareförening. These projects underscore his commitment to advancing the integration of smart technologies in construction and built environment sectors, positioning him as a critical figure in sustainable and intelligent architecture.

Professor Amjad Almusaed, Ph.D., a distinguished scholar in architecture focusing on environmental design, obtained his doctoral degree from Ion Mincu University, Romania. He further honed his sustainable and bioclimatic housing expertise with a postdoctoral research stint in 2004 at the School of Architecture, Aarhus University, Denmark. Prof. Almusaed's research primarily orbits around the ecological facets of architectural design and urban planning, contributing significantly to these fields. His academic journey is replete with extensive research endeavors, encompassing in-depth technical surveys and empirical studies. As a prominent figure in international architectural academia, Prof. Almusaed actively engages with various global architectural organizations, contributing profoundly to sustainable design and urban planning discourse. His editorial roles in numerous academic publications highlight his stature in the scholarly community. Prof. Almusaed's literary output is voluminous and impactful, with more than 198 scholarly journal publications to his credit. These include articles, research papers, books, and chapters published in multiple languages. This extensive work underscores his relentless pursuit of advancing global knowledge in sustainable architecture and environmental design. His contributions are pivotal in shaping contemporary understanding and practices in these critical areas of study, solidifying his position as an eminent figure in environmental and sustainable architectural academia.

# Contents

# Preface

The transition from Industry 4.0 to Industry 5.0 marks a pivotal shift in the manufacturing landscape, emphasizing human-robot collaboration as a cornerstone of the new paradigm. Industry 5.0 seeks to integrate human intelligence and creativity with the capabilities of robots to optimize performance and efficiency. This symbiotic relationship between humans and machines holds the potential to revolutionize production processes, making them more adaptive, resilient, and sustainable. Industry 5.0 technologies like collaborative robots and Human Digital Twins foster safe and efficient collaboration, aligning technological advancements with human needs for harmonious work environments and tailored processes.

As industries navigate the digital transformation, Industry 4.0 affects the tourism sector, grappling with challenges like the digital gap and workforce adaptability post-COVID-19. With Industry 5.0 on the horizon, emphasis is placed on human-centric approaches and the need for updated educational practices, industry strategies, and governmental policies to navigate the transition to a digital tourism era.

Construction firms are actively transforming their traditional practices in response to the technological advancements of Industry 4.0, known as Construction 4.0 in the sector. However, understanding the organizational impacts of technology adoption remains a challenge. To address this, the Technology-Organization-Environment (TOE) framework is applied, identifying decision-making factors for Construction 4.0 adoption to evolve in the digital era.

The transportation sector is also undergoing significant transformation with the advent of Transportation 5.0. This paradigm shift involves moving from traditional Cyber-Physical Transportation Systems to Cyber-Physical-Social Transportation Systems, which prioritize ethical, responsible, and sustainable transportation solutions. It leverages advanced technologies to improve efficiency, safety, and accessibility while considering the social impact of transportation systems.

Nano and Society 5.0 represent another dimension of the human-centric revolution, where nanotechnology is harnessed to improve the quality of life for individuals and society as a whole and address global challenges including water purification and resource conservation. Nanotechnology enables personalized health care, sustainable energy solutions, and inclusive education in science, technology, engineering, and mathematics (STEM) disciplines, contributing to the advancement of Society 5.0's goals.

Industry 4.0, driven by digital technologies, has reshaped the landscape of entrepreneurship, particularly in the digital realm, prompting a reevaluation of strategies amidst confusion. Digital entrepreneurship thrives as technology spearheads this evolution, presenting both challenges and opportunities. Exploring the interplay between Industry 4.0, digital entrepreneurship, and the pandemic's impact, insights are gleaned to navigate the evolving entrepreneurial landscape amid the pandemic and technological advancements.

In the realm of education, sustainable and resilient practices are essential for preparing students for the Industry 5.0 paradigm. Online Distance e-Learning (ODeL) practices leverage digitalization to support authentic knowledge creation and foster interactive learning environments. These practices emphasize multidimensional thinking, critical analysis, and industry-relevant skills, ensuring that students are equipped to thrive in the digital age.

The transition to Industry 5.0 represents a holistic transformation across various industries, driven by the integration of human intelligence, advanced technologies, and sustainable practices. By embracing innovation and leveraging digitalization, organizations can adapt to the evolving landscape and pave the way for a more inclusive, resilient, and human-centric future.

This book is an essential guide to successfully navigating the technical breakthroughs of Industry 4.0 and transitioning to the more human-centric approach of Industry 5.0. The objective is to provide readers with the information they require to successfully navigate this new industrial change and foster a future in which technological breakthroughs are dispersed relatively and benefit all aspects of society. This comprehensive handbook illustrates the route forward for enterprises seeking efficiency, creativity, and sustainability by linking automation's technological narratives with Industry 5.0's human-centric methods. For industry professionals, policymakers, and academic researchers, this book explores how human ingenuity and modern technology alter the industrial environment. It enables readers to meet the difficulties and seize the possibilities of these transformational times with detailed analysis, case studies, and expert insights.

**Ibrahim Yitmen and Amjad Almusaed**
Department of Construction Engineering and Lighting Science,
Jönköping University,
Jönköping, Sweden

Section 1

# Evolution and Challenges of Industry 4.0 and 5.0

**Chapter 1**

# Synopsis of Industry 5.0 Paradigm for Human-Robot Collaboration

*Ibrahim Yitmen and Amjad Almusaed*

## Abstract

This chapter explores the synopsis of the Industry 5.0 paradigm, focusing on Human-robot collaboration, encompassing critical elements from following the progression of evolution from Industry 4.0 to Industry 5.0 to the implementation of cutting-edge technologies and human-centric approaches within this framework. Industry 5.0 paradigm shift builds upon the foundation laid by Industry 4.0, with a renewed focus on integrating human intelligence and creativity with the capabilities of robots. The Operator of Industry 5.0 embodies the idea of skilled human operators working alongside automated systems to optimize performance and efficiency. Industry 5.0 technologies encompass collaborative robots (cobots) and advancements in robot learning, enabling safe and efficient collaboration between humans and machines and facilitating dynamic partnerships in shared workspaces. Human-centric approaches within Industry 5.0 technologies ensure that technological advancements align with human needs and preferences, fostering a work environment where humans and robots collaborate harmoniously. The concept of the Human Digital Twin offers a compelling instrument for identifying and optimizing human behavior within the context of Industry 5.0, enabling organizations to tailor processes and workflows to individual capabilities and preferences.

**Keywords:** industry 4.0, industry 5.0, human-robot collaboration, operator 5.0, society 5.0, human digital twin

## 1. Introduction

Industry 5.0 (5IR) has been developed as the heir to Industry 4.0 (4IR), considering ecological and societal aspects [1]. The compliance of production techniques and their impact on the ecosystem are also important focal points within the 5IR paradigm [2–4]. According to the European Commission (EC) [1], 5IR signifies an expected evolution from 4IR, primarily emphasizing the driving forces behind European resilient, human-centric, and sustainable production. In opposition to the technology-centered method of 4IR, 5IR identifies a strong prominence on the worth of novel technologies while underscoring the significance of resilience, sustainability, and human-centricity in systems for generating value [5]. Scholars like Kusiak [6, 7] and Xu et al. [8] support the idea of resiliency in production, emphasizing the value-added perspective of 5IR. As per the EC [9], 5IR aims to create more inclusive workplaces, strengthen supply networks, and adopt ecologically responsive developed practices. Choi et al. [10] delve into the theme of "sustainable social well-being" concerning human-robot interactions (HRI) during the era of 5IR.

Zizic et al. [5] analyze the fundamental principles of 4IR and 5IR, emphasizing the pivotal roles of people, organizations, and technology in enabling their performance within a theoretical and practical framework. Ivanov [4], from a perspective of operations and supply chain management, presents a framework for 5IR. This framework considers feasible models for chain of supply, reconfigurable chains of supply, and human-centric environments, providing insights into societal, network, and plant-level considerations.

Within the process transformation and supply chain management framework, the principles and expertise associated with 5IR gain clarity when examined through the dimensions of resilience, sustainability, and human-centric approaches. Leng et al. [11] delineate three pivotal aspects of 5IR, which include prioritizing human needs and comfort, emphasizing environmental sustainability, and ensuring resilience in the face of potential adversities. Furthermore, Maddikunta et al. [12] present nuanced definitions and insights concerning 5IR, derived from reflections of experts and academics from various sectors. They further elaborate on potential applications and methodologies that could advance the adoption of 5IR. Despite the increasing focus on the technological aspects of the 5IR paradigm, a profound comprehension of this emergent concept remains imperative across management, organization, and technology [4, 5, 11, 12].

Nahavandi [13] emphasizes the fundamental difference between the two industries, highlighting the shift from mere robots to "cobots" in 5IR—robots collaborating with human operators. This viewpoint is echoed by Adel [14], defining 5IR as a paradigm shift rooted in human-machine collaboration. Correspondingly, Akundi et al. [15] note that 5IR's primary trend is establishing human-robot workplaces and creating more innovative societies. Numerous researchers have explored human-robot collaboration (HRC) in the context of 5IR [16–19].

This chapter lays out the synopsis of the 5IR Paradigm for HRC. First, the path from 4IR to 5IR is presented and followed by 5IR and its Operator. Second, 5IR knowledge and human-centric approaches within 5IR technologies are introduced. Finally, HRC, communication strategies in HRC, collaborative robots, and robot learning are depicted.

## 2. Following the progression from industry 4.0 to industry 5.0

The concept of 5IR was recently endorsed by the Directorate General for Research and Development (DGRD) of the EC, considering it not merely a sequential extension or alternative to 4IR but a forward-thinking extension that supplements the existing paradigm [20]. However, the 5IR theory outlined in several EC DGRD publications (e.g., [1, 20, 21]) places less emphasis on technological aspects and emphasizes the sustainability factor of the idea. Publications like Ref. [21] emphasize waste reduction, the circular economy, and decarbonization as fundamental characteristics of 5IR, although Breque et al. [20] criticize 4IR for fostering technological monopolies and neglecting current societal sustainability challenges.

The EC suggests that 5IR represents a vital progression from 4IR due to critical reasons [21]:

- 4IR does not align with the objectives of Europe 2030, as the existing digital economy fosters a winner-takes-all structure, resulting in significant wealth gaps and technological monopolies.

- 5IR is not solely a technological advancement; instead, it offers a broader perspective on 4IR, infusing a regenerative essence and orientation to the technical evolution of industrialized fabrication, emphasizing the interconnected welfare of society, the world, and wealth.

The key variations concerning 4IR and 5IR in progressive production are shown in **Figure 1**.

As the evolution of 4IR continues, the emergence of 4IR has already begun to exert a significant influence on the production sector and is swiftly gaining attention in scholarly discourse [13]. The precise definition of 5IR still needs to be discovered, attributable to its recent introduction [15]. The conceptualization of 5IR arises from criticisms that 4IR overly emphasizes digitalization and AI-based technologies, neglecting the foundational tenets of social equity and sustainability [8]. This critique is supported by Maddikunta et al. [12], who argue that 5IR re-incorporates human labor into the manufacturing process, fostering the creation of higher-skilled employment opportunities. This paradigmatic shift seeks to move beyond the constrained HRI characteristic of 4IR, encouraging more cooperative, adaptable, and customized interactions within the context of 5IR [23].

Additionally, Muller [1] suggests that 5IR involves concepts and technologies like bioinspired technologies, energy efficiency, digital twins (DT), cybersecurity, and artificial intelligence (AI). However, the last three ideas are integral to 4IR and need to be distinctly characterized in 5IR. The industrial progression from 4IR-5IR is illustrated in **Figure 2**.

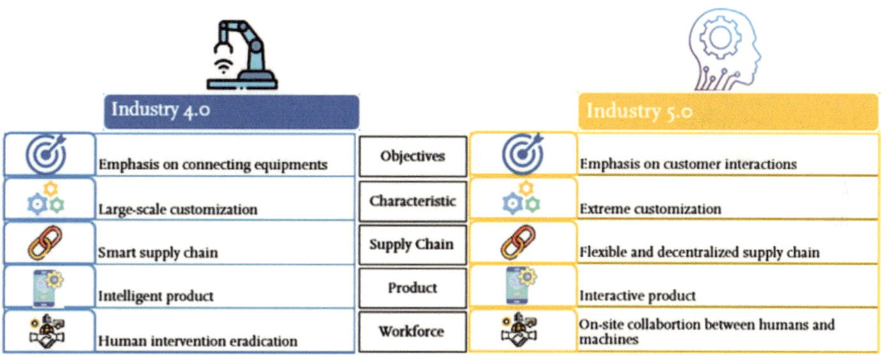


**Figure 1.**
*Key variations concerning 4IR and 5IR in progressive production. (Adapted from: Xian et al. [22]).*

**Figure 2.**
*Industrial progression from 4IR-5IR. (Adapted from: Adel [14]).*

### 2.1 Industry 5.0

5IR prioritizes sustainability, emphasizing human-driven initiatives rooted in industrial production, encapsulated by the 6R's policy: recognize, reconsider, realize, reduce, reuse, and recycle [24]. This framework aims to curb waste while enabling the creation of bespoke, high-quality products [12]. However, there needs to be more contention surrounding how 5IR's strategy aligns with sustainable development [25]. Contrarily, it revolves around reintegrating humans into factories and fostering collaborative work with machines to enhance production efficiency by leveraging human cognitive abilities like creativity and knowledge in tandem with intelligent systems' workflows [11–13]. Professionals in industries, IT experts, and researchers are urged to emphasize human factors in implementing 5IR's new technological systems [11, 12].

From a technological standpoint, 5IR marks the "Social Smart Industry era," intertwining social business networks with individuals for seamless communication. It is characterized by cyber-physical production systems (CPPS) synergizing with the human aspect [11, 12, 26]. Moreover, 5IR is human-centric, emphasizing collaborative work between humans and technologies like collaborative robots. Machines manage tasks that require significant labor or repetition, while humans supervise activities involving personalization and critical thought [12]. The alternative perspective describes 5IR as an innovation shaping the future of global governance, focusing on secure production outputs by segregating automation systems [12].

This concept repositions human agency within global industrial contexts, endeavoring to empower individuals through advanced technologies. The foundational premise is to integrate human centrality with systemic resilience and sustainability by facilitating the harmonization of machines and humans within industrial environments [11]. Nevertheless, the principles and theoretical frameworks of 5IR remain fluid, evolving, and comprehensive, grounded in these core tenets. The primary objective is to emphasize the welfare of workers in manufacturing processes, striving for a balance between human-machine collaboration while fostering resilience and sustainable development across environmental, economic, and social realms. **Table 1** provides a comparative analysis of previous studies that significantly contributed to understanding 5IR.

### 2.2 Operator of industry 5.0

The advent of 4IR brought forth computerized and competent manufacturing approaches yet somewhat sidelined the welfare of workers. In this context, 4IR appears to overlook the human element. Conversely, in 5IR, the operator performs a strategic function in leveraging technology to enhance the quality of the work environment. This concept revolves around placing humans at the core of production processes, with technology supporting and empowering them. This fosters a harmonious interaction between individuals and machines, allowing human involvement to cooperate, merge, and effectively interact with emerging digital technologies [32].

With the advent of 5IR, the concept of Operator 5.0 has emerged, representing the next evolution of Operator 4.0, distinguished by enhanced resilience as encapsulated in the model of the Resilient Operator 5.0 [33]. Operator 5.0 may be categorized based on its objectives: One dimension involves a self-resilient operator who has evolved to mitigate inherent weaknesses and confront emerging challenges. At the same time, another focuses on system resilience, underscoring robust human-machine interactions [12]. Understanding the complexities of future industrial production

| Reference | Study type | Conception of 5IR | Key results and impacts |
|---|---|---|---|
| Özdemir and Hekim [28] | Conceptual | 5IR evolves gradually, expanding upon the concept of 4IR. | 5IR employs digital advancements such as big data and IoT to make knowledge accessible and guide society toward sustainable environmental advancement. |
| Nahavandi [13] | Conceptual | 5IR represents an evolutionary advancement toward a harmonious relationship between humans and machines. | 5IR endeavors to tackle the human-centered facet of sustainability, wherein collaborative robots work alongside operators rather than engaging in competition. |
| Longo et al. [26] | Empirical | 5IR signifies a fresh transformation where CPPS merges with human operators to materialize CPPS, and human agents collaborate to establish the concept of symbiotic factories. | One of the crucial elements of 5IR is the focus on technology engineering that prioritizes values and ethics. |
| Xu et al. [8] | Conceptual | 5IR is an evolving theory that supplements 4IR by fostering innovation to advance ecological and social principles. | Virtualization technologies and integration between humans and machines are essential components of 4IR. Attaining the sustainability objectives envisioned by 5IR could pose significant challenges. |
| Ivanov [4] | Conceptual | 5IR is a complex occurrence that utilizes technological advancements, organizational strategies, and management approaches to advance sustainability. | 5IR encompasses businesses, supply chains, and communities, prioritizing resilience in value creation, human-centricity, and societal requirements. |
| Ghobakhloo et al. [27] | Empirical | 5IR is complementary to 4IR, leveraging the collaboration between society and industry to advance sustainability. | 5IR has the potential to foster sustainable progress through a multifaceted mechanism that includes various sustainability functions like integrating value networks. |
| Huang et al. [29] | Conceptual | 5IR is an innovative framework that utilizes flexible and compliant technological advancements to drive industrial expansion while prioritizing socio-environmental conservation. | 5IR and Society 5.0 intersect, with both aiming for similar sustainability goals. Human-CPS, employment, virtualization, and the integration of humans and machines present opportunities and challenges for 5IR. |
| Leng et al. [11] | Conceptual | 5IR is a vigorous and developing framework that strives for collaborative and stakeholder-oriented industrial progress. | 5IR intersects with the concepts of 4IR, Society 5.0, and Operator 5.0. It embodies a comprehensive approach encompassing multiple industries and business sectors. |
| Maddikunta et al. [12] | Conceptual | 5IR evolves by harnessing the innovative results of the collaboration between humans and machines. | 5IR is primarily propelled by technology. A key objective of 5IR is achieving widespread customization. This study also delves into the foundational technologies of 5IR. |
| Sharma et al. [30] | Empirical | 5IR signifies a groundbreaking and transformative innovation that redefines the manufacturing landscape, catalyzing a shift from a linear economic model to a circular economy. | The transformation of 5IR may encounter various technical facilitators and obstacles, including expenses, interoperability issues within systems, and the dissemination of inaccurate information. |

| Reference | Study type | Conception of 5IR | Key results and impacts |
|---|---|---|---|
| Sindhwani et al. [31] | Empirical | 5IR builds upon the foundations of 4IR, emphasizing collaboration between humans and robots, digital innovations, and regulatory measures to foster a digital bioeconomy that advances sustainability. | 5IR depends on various technical facilitators, including bionics, virtual reality, digital twinning, and the internet of things (IoT). |

**Table 1.**
*Comparison of studies contributing to the conceptualization of 5IR. (Adapted from: Ghobakhloo et al. [27]).*

systems, characterized by significant volatility, requires intricate and multifaceted decision-making capabilities from workers. Consequently, future operators must have human-centric technology and comprehensive training to control production and manufacturing systems [34]. It is essential to support employees of diverse experiences and backgrounds, with particular attention to the sustainability of the human workforce, including aging workers engaged in high-intensity tasks [34, 35].

### 2.3 Industry 5.0 technologies

The shift toward 5IR necessitates a socio-technical evolution, redefining the role of operators as the focal point of manufacturing and production systems. This evolution hinges on sophisticated strategies and approaches supported by progressive ICT [36]. 5IR principles can be applied across various aspects, spanning CPPS, data interoperability, and utilizing AI-based systems, 5G and 6G networks, augmented reality (AR), and collaborative robots to accomplish clever production methods [18, 37–45].

Introducing robotics into production systems boosts productivity, enhances workers' well-being, and improves workplace health and safety [35, 36]. Collaborative robots working alongside humans capitalize on individual and technological capabilities, overcoming limitations in executing cumbersome, repetitive, and potentially hazardous tasks, enhancing workplace conditions, process repeatability, and reliability [46]. These robots assist in reducing low-value-added operations while enabling workers to focus on more advanced tasks requiring sensitivity, mental agility, adaptation, customization, and critical thinking [23, 36].

HRI necessitates continuous assessment of human factors to analyze and evaluate working conditions during these interactions [23]. A unique aspect of robotics is the advancement of DTs, high-fidelity, simulated representations that communicate in real time [42, 47]. These systems and simulation models optimize production and conduct safety tests [48]. DTs also promise to mitigate educational disparities by facilitating remote learning and training opportunities [49], potentially integrating into educational systems [48]. Interactive productive systems with robots further create learning environments [50].

However, 5IR raises concerns regarding safety and ethical issues in HRI [41, 51]. More stringent safety standards demand resilient safety approaches, guaranteeing increased dependability and adaptability in production through dynamic approaches from mutually human and robotic viewpoints [51]. Ethical concerns regarding the utilization of autonomous smart methods necessitate their prompt incorporation into the design phase of novel digital manufacturing methods [41, 52].

Amidst these developments, companies and industries should prioritize human-centered production processes by deploying consistent tools that enhance working environments and workers' comfort [53]. Retaining and leveraging organizational memories and operators' past experiences are vital for reusing successful practices [54]. To adopt the principles and advantages of 5IR, organizations must utilize 4IR digital technologies, such as CPS, big data, AI, DT, and collaborative robots [40]. The EC has outlined six directives for 5IR technologies, highlighting personalized HRI, advanced bio-inspired technologies, simulation and DT, data transmission, storage and analysis, AI, and technologies for environmental sustainability [40]. The architecture of 5IR advanced manufacturing is depicted in **Figure 3**.

5IR has changed its focus from distinct technologies to a systemic approach, prioritizing societal well-being beyond growth and employment and placing worker welfare at the heart of production [8]. Nahavandi [13] envisions 5IR as a phase where humans rely on cobots as collaborators, enhancing efficiency, productivity, and cost savings while minimizing waste. The International Federation of Robotics (IFR) emphasizes that cobots are created to support human workers by handling strenuous and repetitive tasks. Other researchers echo similar views on enhancing ergonomics, productivity, safety, and affordability [55]. This shift aims to create more diverse job profiles, granting workers autonomy in task planning and decision-making and fostering effective human-cyber-physical systems [56].

Ensuring the well-being of workers in collaborative human-robot systems is crucial. Safety measures following ISO standards specific to industrial, personal, and collaborative robots are paramount. Control systems and collision detection mechanisms are pivotal in safe collaboration [57, 58]. Research focuses on AI applications controlling safety and ergonomic performance [59–62].

Stress, workload, and trust are factors impacting operators' performance in HRC [63]. Robots' physical attributes and autonomous actions can cause mental stress and increased cognitive workload [64]. Trust plays a pivotal role; a lack of it can diminish an operator's performance. Robot design elements can influence trust levels, emphasizing the importance of effective HRI.

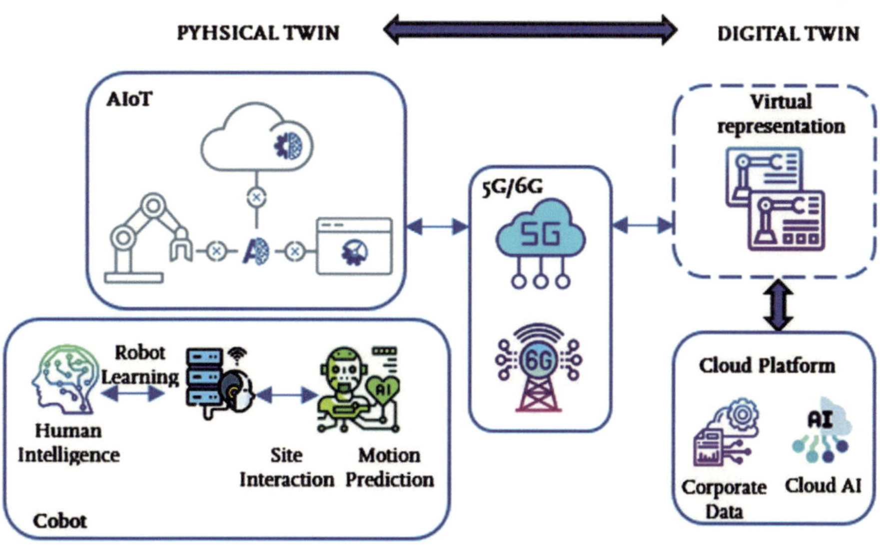


**Figure 3.**
*Architecture of 5IR advanced manufacturing. (Adapted from: Xian et al. [22]).*

### 2.4 Human-centric approaches within industry 5.0 technologies

The concept of human-centered manufacturing approaches is a fresh and contentious area that warrants clarity and thorough discussion. Nonetheless, this idea draws from ongoing research on human welfare, encompassing areas like Ergonomics, Operator 4.0, and HRC [65]. The trajectory of industrial production and manufacturing is steering toward 5IR, backed by the involvement of collaborative robots [66], AI, and cognitive computing technologies [14]. The integration of HRI serves as a technical catalyst for transitioning from digital system-oriented production to operator-centered production, fostering a digital production ecosystem that equally values human and robotic traits [67]. Effective interaction between humans and robots should optimize available resources for the benefit of production systems [67]. Implementing these cooperative methods also reduces demanding and monotonous tasks that might pose probable health and safety risks to workers, negating the necessity for investing in costly and intricate digital equipment [46]. AR stands as a tool to amplify the cognitive capabilities of humans and robots by seamlessly integrating humans into real-time and dynamic production systems [51]. Furthermore, assessing the effect of HRI proves challenging due to classical evaluation tools focusing solely on dynamic and static aspects, often overlooking crucial facts. Hence, current studies explore alternative assessment methods employing computerized and sensory systems for an additional comprehensive, innovative, and dynamic analysis [23].

A comprehensive overhaul of engineering education is imperative to foster sustainability and resilience across social, environmental, and economic dimensions within industries and firms. This reform aims to prepare future engineers with sophisticated technological skills, proficiency in data management, and a profound understanding of complex systems. The goal is to cultivate industries that are more resilient, sustainable, and attuned to human needs in the era of 5IR [68]. The future workforce must be able to discern and understand various production systems, enabling them to make informed choices among different operational models: those relying solely on human effort, those driven by technological capabilities, or those integrating both approaches. Consequently, engineering education should emphasize human-robot interaction (HRI), particularly focusing on the diverse methods of interaction and cooperation with emerging CPS [68]. Human-assisted learning strategies should also be implemented to manage and regulate automated additive manufacturing systems and error detection mechanisms within manufacturing processes [69, 70].

## 3. Human-robot collaboration

Advances in technology envision robots collaborating with humans in daily life. HRC involves a human and a robot working cognitively and physically together toward a common goal. This collaboration is pivotal in manufacturing, facilitating surveillance, prognostics, health management systems, and bolstering safety and sustainability in manufacturing processes [71, 72].

HRC aids in making critical decisions. Machines can assist in collecting information, evaluating uncertainty, and sharing crucial information with human decision-makers, potentially reducing cognitive loads. Furthermore, human decision-makers can argue their opinions with machine assistance, minimizing emotional influences [73].

As machines become more sophisticated, the relationship between humans and automation is transitioning from a "master-servant" dynamic to a "master-collaborator" one. This shift necessitates different approaches to system design, HRC, interfaces, and additional requirements for machines [74].

Current technological advancements are fostering physical interaction between humans and machines. This phase of HRI, mainly through the haptic channel, is termed HRC [75].

This development has led to the emergence of cobots, collaborative robots designed for human collaboration. These robots know human presence, prioritize safety, understand human goals and expectations, and learn tasks similar to humans [76, 77].

In human-centered production, advanced cognitive science and personalized AI suggest that empathic machines can sense human reactions, requirements, and partialities, providing situational assistance alongside cooperation [78].

Such circumstances may lead to reciprocal monitoring between humans and empathic machines, with the machine's health measured quantitatively based on workload, task fluctuations, and more. This approach marks a new chapter in the human-machine relationship—human-machine empathy. Intimate interactions concerning humans and machines may foster continuous human-machine co-evolution, paving the way for new relationships centered on mutual enhancement rather than competition, shaping a better future for both machines and humans [79].

### 3.1 Communication strategies in human-robot collaboration

HRC has become a focal point in interdisciplinary research, concentrating on the cooperative efforts between humans and robots to achieve shared objectives [80]. HRC involves hypothetical and applied investigations into the investigation, plan, and assessment of robotic systems engaging with humans [81–83]. Interaction between humans and robots, a pivotal aspect of optimal HRC, has been extensively explored by researchers [63, 84, 85].

As a foundational step in HRC, communication methods can be categorized into tacit and specific forms. Gustavsson et al. outlined sophisticated interaction techniques, such as AR for spatial interaction, text-to-speech (TTS) technologies for verbal information, automatic speech recognition (ASR) for dictating tasks, and gestures for transmitting commands [84, 86–88]. Additionally, haptic feedback, virtual reality (VR), and audible sound systems were suggested to bridge communication barriers between construction workers and robots [81, 89–92].

Berg et al. suggested enhancing communication through gestures and eye-tracking technologies, omitting speech recognition due to noisy environments and VR use limitations [63]. Explicit communication techniques primarily transmit specific information (e.g., distance, contact force), while biosensor-based methods have been explored to capture implicit signals (e.g., physiological data) [93, 94].

Numerous theoretical frameworks have been suggested to influence and enhance HRC, including Weiss et al.'s multi-level HRC framework, which integrates usability, social acceptance, user experience, and societal impact (USUS) factors [95]. Aaltonen et al., Johannsmeier, and Haddadin also presented theoretical frameworks focusing on refining collaboration levels between humans and robots [96, 97]. While these frameworks provide taxonomies for collaboration, they emphasize overall collaboration levels and lack detailed solutions for physical HRC.

### 3.2 Human digital twin (HDT) in the context of industry 5.0

HDTs are envisioned as digital replicas of individuals, crafted to complement human abilities, boost efficiency, unleash potential, and prioritize well-being within intelligent production systems [98, 99]. As a crucial technology within the framework of 5IR, HDTs forge explicit links concerning humans and technologies to amplify their capabilities, fostering seamless cooperation in advanced intelligent production environments. By leveraging real-time sensing, analysis, and automated feedback, HDTs reshape the dynamics of human-system integration, improving system design and execution while advocating for the sustainable advancement of personalized human skills. Integrating humans' innate senses and cognitive capabilities into intelligent production systems through HDTs facilitates the conception of intricate and innovative industrial processes, ultimately enriching the manufacturing sector and cultivating more profound respect for future workers [100].

The evolution of HDT involves several stages, namely human digitalization awareness, enablement, involvement, and integration [101–103]. Human participation in the system spans various roles, from a passive spectator forced into the system to an active member providing information, an intelligent agent with complex responsibilities, and a program coordinator leading the system. The evolution of human digital depiction illustrates the interaction between physical and cyber systems, progressing from initial phases characterized by basic digital representations to more sophisticated 2D and 3D visualizations [104, 105].

Human factor indicators encompass human operators' physical, psychological, and cognitive features. Physical guides include postures, workload, and efficiency, while psychological indicators encompass mental fatigue, concentration, and more. Cognitive indicators capture factors influencing human-system interaction, such as reasoning, memory, and motivation abilities. More detailed descriptions correlate with increased levels of indicators related to human factors.

Collaborating instruments, including tools and software, facilitate communication among humans, physical systems, and cyber systems. Human-machine interfaces have developed from early devices with controls and indicators to sophisticated visualizations on touch panels, motion capture devices, and X-reality interfaces that integrate virtual and physical worlds [106, 107].

HDT can contribute to innovation in industrial processes through human-centric design principles, focusing on creating technologies that enhance the well-being, satisfaction, and safety of workers. Davila-Gonzalez et al. [108] introduced a conceptual framework designed to enhance worker safety and well-being in industrial environments, such as oil and gas construction plants, by leveraging HDT cutting-edge technologies and advanced AI techniques. Wang et al. [109] presented a conceptual framework and system architecture of HDT from an Industry 5.0 perspective. Representative HDT applications in different lifecycle phases are presented including product design, production, optimization, and maintenance. As an example for production phase, an HDT system operator safety and worker management were proposed by Kim et al. [110] as illustrated in **Figure 4**. Mobile devices and motion capture equipment gather real-time location coordinates and musculoskeletal data to implement digital human modeling in virtual environments. This collected data is also utilized for analysis, including localization and posture detection for assessing worker safety *via* rule-based reasoning. Additionally, skeleton data processing aids in fatigue analysis using rapid upper limb assessment and standardizing work time.

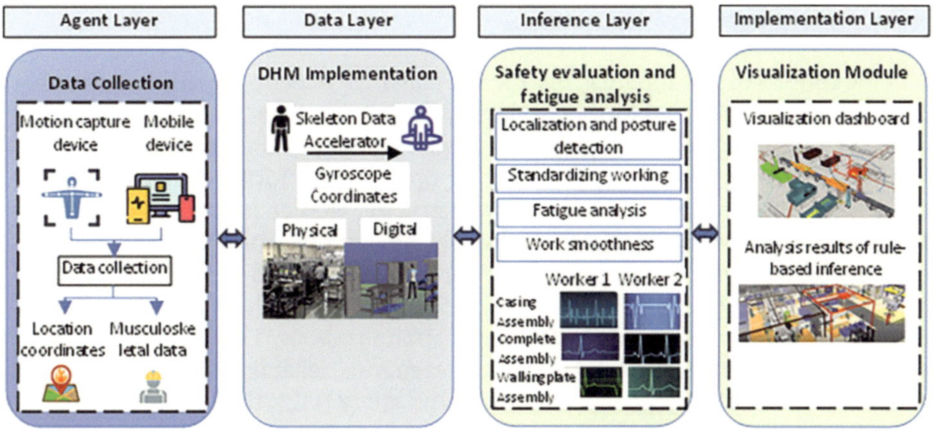


**Figure 4.**
*An HDT system for operator safety and work management. (Adapted from: Kim et al. [110]).*

The resulting outputs, such as accident safety levels and fatigue-related work performance, assist shop floor workers in timely posture adjustments. This system enables safety managers to monitor shop floor workers and prevent potential accidents, while also supporting process managers in ensuring productivity and safety, particularly concerning musculoskeletal injuries.

### 3.3 Collaborative robots (cobots)

Despite robots being utilized in industries for decades, 4IR has introduced highly connected robots capable of autonomous operation, playing an active role in various factories. In contrast, the 5IR generation anticipates a shift toward collaborative robots, or "cobots," devised to operate with humans under their guidance. Enabled by advancements in digital technologies like AI, machine learning, and traditional robotics, cobots can sense and adapt to their surroundings, learning in real time. This adaptability renders them highly flexible, ideal for manufacturing small batch sizes, and meeting the demands of personalized products, a crucial aspect of future manufacturing. Unlike their predecessors confined within fenced environments, cobots are released to coexist, cooperate, and collaborate (3Cs) with human counterparts. These lightweight, precise, and easily programmable cobots can assist humans by handling physically demanding, hazardous, or repetitive tasks [111].

To guarantee human safety and build trust in robots, the industry has implemented regulations for CoBots by establishing safety standards for HRC. These standards govern the safe behavior of both practitioners and CoBots, providing direction for developing smart production systems. Notably, ISO 10218, categorized as a Type C technical standard, outlines safety design guidelines and obligations for protective measures in industrial robots. It details fundamental hazards associated with robotics and stipulates measures to eliminate or effectively mitigate them. Complementing ISO 10218 and ISO/TS 15066 introduces additional safety requirements for collaborative industrial robot systems and their work environments. Beyond safety standards, various technical solutions have been developed for preventive measures, focusing on collision detection, robot motion planning, and assessing risks associated with collaborative robots.

### 3.4 Robot learning

In the context of 4IR robotics, instructions involve collecting many images and posing data acquisition and programming challenges. However, 5IR introduces a paradigm shift where robots acquire motion skills through demonstrations, facilitating more flexible and precise human-robot cooperation [22]. Demonstrations can be conducted by either a robot or a human instructor. Human instructors offer the advantage of showcasing intricate and task-specific motions more easily than robot instructors. Consequently, the prevalent approach in advanced production is robot learning through human demonstrations. In 5IR, introducing humans into industrial manufacturing involves more intricate application scenarios. Therefore, cobots must exhibit flexibility and adaptability to various scenarios, leading to extensive research on transfer learning between different tasks. In a study [112], the robot's acquired skills are generalized and applied to diverse tasks, enabling rapid adaptation to new learning tasks. This approach demonstrates that leveraging prior knowledge through knowledge transfer allows for higher expected returns with reduced exploration in the learning process.

## 4. Conclusions

The transition from 4IR to 5IR signifies a profound evolution in the dynamics of human-robot interactions, setting the stage for unprecedented collaboration and synergy. 5IR represents a paradigmatic shift toward human-centric methodologies within technological advancements, underscoring the necessity of integrating human intelligence and creativity with robotic capabilities.

In 5IR, operators exemplify skilled practitioners working with automated systems to enhance performance and efficiency. 5IR technologies are characterized by a synthesis of advanced innovations, including collaborative robots (cobots), robot learning, and communication strategies designed explicitly for HRC.

Within the framework of 5IR, human-centric approaches are prioritized to uphold the well-being and enhance the capabilities of human workers, ensuring that technological progress augments rather than supplants their roles. HRC emerges as a fundamental element of 5IR, fostering dynamic and productive partnerships where humans and robots strive collectively toward shared objectives.

Effective HRC communication strategies facilitate smooth interaction and coordination between humans and robots. Additionally, the HDT concept is vital for identifying and optimizing human actions within the 5IR context.

Collaborative robots, or cobots, illustrate the potential within 5IR to enable safe and effective cooperation between humans and machines in shared work environments. Concurrently, robot learning is advancing, allowing robots to adapt and learn from human interactions, thereby enhancing their effectiveness in dynamic settings.

The comprehensive vision of 5IR for HRC encapsulates a transformative agenda where humans and robots coalesce seamlessly, utilizing their strengths to drive innovation, efficiency, and prosperity in the digital era. As we embrace 5IR's potential, we are propelled toward a future where human creativity and technological sophistication merge, redefining the prospects for both industry and society.

## Author details

Ibrahim Yitmen* and Amjad Almusaed
Department of Construction Engineering and Lighting Science, Jönköping University, Jönköping, Sweden

*Address all correspondence to: ibrahim.yitmen@ju.se

## References


[1] Müller J. Enabling Technologies for Industry 5.0—Results of a Workshop with Europe's Technology Leaders. Luxembourg: Publications Office of the European Union; 2020

[2] Demir KA, Döven G, Sezen B. Industry 5.0 and human-robot co-working. Procedia Computer Science. 2019;**158**:688-695

[3] Iftikhar HM, Iftikhar L. Post COVID-19 industrial revolution 5.0. The dawn of cobot, chipbot, and curbot. Pakistan Journal of Surgery and Medicine. 2020;**1**:122-126

[4] Ivanov D. The industry 5.0 framework: Viability-based integration of the resilience, sustainability, and human-centricity perspectives. International Journal of Production Research. 2023;**61**:1683-1695

[5] Zizic MC, Mladineo M, Gjeldum N, Celent L. From industry 4.0 towards industry 5.0: A review and analysis of paradigm shift for the people, organization and technology. Energies. 2022;**15**:5221

[6] Kusiak A. Open manufacturing: A design-for-resilience approach. International Journal of Production Research. 2020;**58**:4647-4658

[7] Kusiak A. From digital to universal manufacturing. International Journal of Production Research. 2022;**60**:349-360

[8] Xu X, Lu Y, Vogel-Heuser B, Wang L. Industry 4.0 and industry 5.0—inception, conception, and perception. Journal of Manufacturing Systems. 2021;**61**:530-535

[9] EC 2021. Industry 5.0: Towards More Sustainable, Human-Centric, and Resilient European Industry. 2021. Available from: https://op.europa.eu/en/publication-detail/-/publication/468a892a-5097-11eb-b59f-01aa75ed71a1/ [Accessed: April 15, 2023].

[10] Choi TM, Kumar S, Yue X, Chan HL. Disruptive technologies and operations management in the industry 4.0 era and beyond. Production and Operations Management. 2022;**31**:9-31

[11] Leng J, Sha W, Wang B, Zheng P, Zhuang C, Liu Q, et al. Industry 5.0: Prospect and retrospect. Journal of Manufacturing Systems. 2022;**65**:279-295

[12] Maddikunta PKR, Pham QV, Prabadevi B, Deepa N, Dev K, Gadekallu TR, et al. Industry 5.0: A survey on enabling technologies and potential applications. Journal of Industrial Information Integration. 2022;**26**:100257

[13] Nahavandi S. Industry 5.0-a human-centric solution. Sustainability. 2019;**11**:4371

[14] Adel A. Future of industry 5.0 in society: Human-centric solutions, challenges and prospective research areas. Journal of Cloud Computing. 2022;**11**:40

[15] Akundi A, Euresti D, Luna S, Ankobiah W, Lopes A, Edinbarough I. State of industry 5.0—analysis and identification of current research trends. Applied System Innovation. 2022;**5**:27

[16] Jabrane K, Bousmah M. A new approach for training cobots from small amount of data in industry 5.0. International Journal of Advanced Computer Science and Applications. 2021;**12**:634-646

[17] Prassida GF, Asfari U. A conceptual model for accepting collaborative robots in industry 5.0. Procedia Computer Science. 2021;**197**:61-67

[18] Kaasinen E, Anttila A-H, Heikkilä P, Laarni J, Koskinen H, Väätänen A. Smooth and resilient human–machine teamwork as an industry 5.0 design challenge. Sustainability. 2022;**14**:2773

[19] Pizoń J, Cioch M, Kanski L, García ES. Cobots implementation in the era of industry 5.0 using modern business and management solutions. Advances in Science and Technology. Research Journal. 2022;**16**:166-178

[20] Breque M, de Nul L, Petridis A. Industry 5.0: Towards a Sustainable, Human-Centric, and Resilient European Industry. Luxembourg: European Commission, Directorate-General for Research and Innovation; 2021. Available from: https://op.europa.eu/en/publication-detail/-/publication/468a892a-5097-11eb-b59f-01aa75ed71a1/ [Accessed: March 8, 2023]

[21] Renda A, Schwaag Serger S, Tataj D, Morlet A, Isaksson D, Martins F, et al. Industry 5.0: A Transformative Vision for Europe. Luxembourg: European Commission, Directorate General for Research and Innovation; 2022. Available from: https://op.europa.eu/en/publication-detail/-/publication/38a2fa08-728e-11ec-9136-01aa75ed71a1/language-en [Accessed: March 8, 2023]

[22] Xian W, Yu K, Han F, Fang L, He D, Han QL. Advanced manufacturing in industry 5.0: A survey of key enabling technologies and future trends. IEEE Transactions on Industrial Informatics. 2023;**20**(2):1055-1068

[23] Coronado E, Kiyokawa T, Ricardez GAG, Ramirez-Alpizar IG, Venture G, Yamanobe N. Evaluating quality in human-robot interaction: A systematic search and classification of performance and human-centered factors, measures and metrics towards an industry 5.0. Journal of Manufacturing Systems. 2022;**63**:392-410

[24] Alves J, Lima TM, Gaspar PD. Is industry 5.0 a human-centred approach? A systematic review. Processes. 2023;**11**(1):193

[25] Ghobakhloo M, Iranmanesh M, Mubarak MF, Mubarak M, Rejeb A, Nilashi M. Identifying industry 5.0 contributions to sustainable development: A strategy roadmap for delivering sustainability values. Sustainable Production and Consumption. 2022;**33**:716-737

[26] Longo F, Padovano A, Umbrello S. Value-oriented and ethical technology engineering in industry 5.0: A human-centric perspective for the design of the factory of the future. Applied Sciences. 2020;**10**:4182

[27] Ghobakhloo M, Iranmanesh M, Morales ME, Nilashi M, Amran A. Actions and approaches for enabling industry 5.0-driven sustainable industrial transformation: A strategy roadmap. Corporate Social Responsibility and Environmental Management. 2023;**30**(3):1473-1494

[28] Özdemir V, Hekim N. Birth of industry 5.0: Making sense ofbig data with artificial intelligence, "the internet of things "and next-generation technology policy. OMICS A: Journal of Integrative Biology. 2018;**22**(1):65-76

[29] Huang S, Wang B, Li X, Zheng P, Mourtzis D, Wang L. Industry 5.0 and society 5.0—comparison, complementation and coevolution. Journal of Manufacturing Systems. 2022;**64**:424-428

[30] Sharma M, Sehrawat R, Luthra S, Daim T, Bakry D. Moving towards industry 5.0 in the pharmaceutical manufacturing sector: Challenges and solutions for Germany. IEEE Transactions on Engineering Management. 2022:1-18

[31] Sindhwani R, Afridi S, Kumar A, Banaitis A, Luthra S, Singh PL. Can industry 5.0 revolutionize the wave of resilience and social value creation? A multi-criteria framework to analyze enablers. Technology in Society. 2022;**68**:101887

[32] Wan PK, Leirmo TL. Human-centric zero-defect manufacturing: State-of-the-art review, perspectives, and challenges. Computers in Industry. 2023;**144**:103792

[33] Romero D, Stahre J. Towards the resilient operator 5.0: The future of work in smart resilient manufacturing systems. Procedia CIRP. 2021;**104**:1089-1094

[34] Brauner P, Ziefle M. Beyond playful learning—serious games for the human-centric digital transformation of production and a design process model. Technology in Society. 2022;**71**:102140

[35] Battini D, Berti N, Finco S, Zennaro I, Das A. Towards industry 5.0: A multi-objective job rotation model for an inclusive workforce. International Journal of Production Economics. 2022;**250**:108619

[36] Prassida GF, Asfari U. A conceptual model for the acceptance of collaborative robots in industry 5.0. Procedia Computer Science. 2022;**197**:61-67

[37] Bitsch G. Conceptions of man in human-centric cyber-physical production systems. Procedia CIRP. 2022;**107**:1439-1443

[38] Wang B, Zheng P, Yin Y, Shih A, Wang L. Toward human-centric smart manufacturing: A human-cyber-physical systems (HCPS) perspective. Journal of Manufacturing Systems. 2022;**63**:471-490

[39] Khan AA, Abonyi J. Information sharing in supply chains—interoperability in an era of circular economy. Cleaner Logistics and Supply Chain. 2022;**5**:100074

[40] Maier M, Ebrahimzadeh A, Beniiche A, Rostami S. The art of 6G (TAO 6G): How to wire society 5.0 [invited]. Journal of Optical Communications and Networking. 2021;**14**:A101-A112

[41] Fraga-Lamas P, Varela-Barbeito J, Fernandez-Carames TM. Next generation auto-identification and traceability technologies for industry 5.0: A methodology and practical use case for the shipbuilding industry. IEEE Access. 2021;**9**:140700-140730

[42] Turner CJ, Garn W. Next generation DES simulation: A research agenda for human centric manufacturing systems. Journal of Industrial Information Integration. 2022;**28**:100354

[43] Kolaei AZ, Hedayati E, Khanzadi M, Amiri GG. Challenges and opportunities of augmented reality during the construction phase. Automation in Construction. 2022;**143**:104586

[44] Doyle-Kent M, Kopacek P. Adoption of collaborative robotics in industry 5.0. An Irish industry case study. IFAC-Papers OnLine. 2021;**54**:413-418

[45] Mourtzis D, Angelopoulos J, Papadokostakis M, Panopoulos N. Design for 3D printing of a robotic arm tool changer under the framework of industry 5.0. Procedia CIRP. 2022;**115**:178-183

[46] Colla V, Matino R, Schröder A, Schivalocchi M, Romaniello L.

Human-centered robotic development in the steel shop: Improving health, safety and digital skills at the workplace. Metals. 2021;**11**:647

[47] Montini E, Cutrona V, Bonomi N, Landolfi G, Bettoni A, Rocco P, et al. An IIoT platform for human-aware factory digital twins. Procedia CIRP. 2022;**107**:661-667

[48] Eriksson K, Alsaleh A, Behzad Far S, Stjern D. Applying digital twin technology in higher education: An automation line case study. Advances in Transdisciplinary Engineering. 2022;**21**:461-472

[49] Kaarlela T, Arnarson H, Pitkäaho T, Shu B, Solvang B, Pieskä S. Common educational teleoperation platform for robotics utilizing digital twins. Machines. 2022;**10**:577

[50] Pozo E, Patel N, Schrödel F. Collaborative robotic environment for educational training in industry 5.0 using an open lab approach. IFAC-Papers OnLine. 2022;**55**:314-319

[51] Li C, Zheng P, Yin Y, Pang YM, Huo S. An AR-assisted deep reinforcement learning-based approach towards mutual-cognitive safe human-robot interaction. Robotics and Computer-Integrated Manufacturing. 2023;**80**:102471

[52] Ciobanu AC, Meșniță G. AI Ethics for industry 5.0—From principles to practice. In: Proceedings of the Workshop of I-ESA'22, Valencia, Spain, 23-24 March 2022. Aachen: RWTH Aachen University; 2022. CEUR-WS.org

[53] Khamaisi RK, Brunzini A, Grandi F, Peruzzini M, Pellicciari M. UX assessment strategy to identify potential stressful conditions for workers. Robotics and Computer-Integrated Manufacturing. 2022;**78**:102403

[54] Melendez S, Sima X, Coudert T, Geneste L, de Valroger A. An experience feedback process for learning from collaboration experiences. Computers in Industry. 2022;**141**:103693

[55] IFR. A positioning paper by the international federation of robotics. In: The Impact of Robots on Productivity, Employment and Jobs. Frankfurt: IFR; 2017

[56] De Simone V, Di Pasquale V, Giubileo V, Miranda S. Human-robot collaboration: An analysis of worker's performance. Procedia Computer Science. 2022;**200**:1540-1549

[57] IFR, 2018. A positioning paper by the international federation of robotics. In: Robots and the Workplace of the Future. Frankfurt: IFR; 2018

[58] Gualtieri L, Rauch E, Vidoni R. Emerging research fields in safety and ergonomics in industrial collaborative robotics: A systematic literature review. Robotics and Computer-Integrated Manufacturing. 2021;**67**:101998

[59] Proia S, Carli R, Cavone G, Dotoli M. Control techniques for safe, ergonomic, and efficient human-robot collaboration in the digital industry: A survey. IEEE Transactions on Automation Science and Engineering. 2021;**19**:1798-1819

[60] Ibrahim A, Alexander R, Shahid M, Sanghar U, Dsouza R, Souza D. Control systems in robotics: A review. International Journal of Engineering and Science Invention. 2016;**5**:2278-7461

[61] Jantsch A, Dutt ND, Rahmani AM. Self-awareness in systems on chip—A survey. IEEE Design and Test of Computers. 2017;**34**:8-26

[62] Han L, Xu W, Li B, Kang P. Collision detection and coordinated

compliance control for a dual-arm robot without force/torque sensing based on momentum observer. IEEE/ ASME Transactions on Mechatronics. 2019;**24**:2261-2272

[63] Berg J, Lottermoser A, Richter C, Reinhart G. Human-robot-interaction for mobile industrial robot teams. Procedia CIRP. 2019;**79**:614-619

[64] Xiao J, Dou S, Zhao W, Liu H. Sensorless human–robot collaborative assembly considering load and friction compensation. IEEE Robotics and Automation Letters. 2021;**6**:5945-5952

[65] Lu Y, Zheng H, Chand S, Xia W, Liu Z, Xu X, et al. Outlook on human-centric manufacturing towards industry 5.0. Journal of Manufacturing Systems. 2022;**62**:612-627

[66] Doyle Kent M, Kopacek P. Do we need synchronization of the human and robotics to make industry 5.0 a success story? In: ISPR 2020: Digital Conversion on the Way to Industry 4.0; Lecture Notes in Mechanical Engineering. Cham, Switzerland: Springer; 2020. pp. 302-311

[67] Nourmohammadi A, Fathi M, Ng AH. Balancing and scheduling assembly lines with human-robot collaboration tasks. Computers and Operations Research. 2021;**140**:105674

[68] Broo DG, Kaynak O, Sait SM. Rethinking engineering education at the age of industry 5.0. Journal of Industrial Information Integration. 2021;**25**:100311

[69] Li Y, Mu H, Polden J, Li H, Wang L, Xia C, et al. Towards intelligent monitoring system in wire arc additive manufacturing: A surface anomaly detector on a small dataset. International Journal of Advanced Manufacturing Technology. 2022;**120**:5225-5242

[70] Xia C, Pan Z, Li Y, Chen J, Li H. Vision-based melt pool monitoring for wire-arc additive manufacturing using deep learning method. International Journal of Advanced Manufacturing Technology. 2022;**120**:551-562

[71] Wang T, Li J, Kong Z, Liu X, Snoussi H, Lv H. Digital twin improved via visual question answering for vision-language interactive mode in human–machine collaboration. Journal of Manufacturing Systems. 2021;**58**:261-269

[72] Simmler M, Frischknecht R. A taxonomy of human–machine collaboration: Capturing automation and technical autonomy. AI & Society. 2021;**36**:239-250

[73] Xiong W, Fan H, Ma L, Wang C. Challenges of human—machine collaboration in risky decision-making. Frontiers of Engineering Management. 2022;**9**:89-103

[74] Trujillo AC, Gregory IM, Ackerman KA. Evolving relationship between humans and machines. IFAC-Papers OnLine. 2019;**51**:366-371

[75] Inga J, Ruess M, Robens JH, Nelius T, Kille S, Dahlinger P, et al. Human-machine symbiosis: A multivariate perspective for physically coupled human-machine systems. International Journal of Human-Computer Studies. 2023;**170**:102926

[76] Simões AC, Pinto A, Santos J, Pinheiro S, Romero D. Designing human-robot collaboration (HRC) workspaces in industrial settings: A systemic literature review. Journal of Manufacturing Systems. 2022;**62**:28-43

[77] Pizoń J, Gola A, Świć A. The role and meaning of the digital twin Technology in the Process of implementing intelligent collaborative robots. In: Lecture Notes in Mechanical

Engineering. Cham, Switzerland: Springer; 2022. pp. 39-49

[78] Pizoń J, Gola A. Human–machine relationship—perspective and future roadmap for industry 5.0 solutions. Machines. 2023;**11**(2):203

[79] Santosuosso A. About coevolution of humans and intelligent machines: Preliminary notes. BioLaw Journal - Rivista di BioDiritto. 2021;**1**:445-454

[80] Villani V, Pini F, Leali F, Secchi C. Survey on human–robot collaboration in industrial settings: Safety, intuitive interfaces and applications. Mechatronics. 2018;**55**(March):248-266

[81] Czarnowski J, Dąbrowski A, Maciaś M, Główka J, Wrona J. Technology gaps in human-machine interfaces for autonomous construction robots. Automation in Construction. 2018;**94**(June):179-190

[82] Herath DC, Jochum E, Vlachos E. An experimental study of embodied interaction and human perception of social presence for interactive robots in public settings. IEEE Transactions on Cognitive and Developmental Systems. 2018;**10**(4):1096-1105

[83] Hinwood D, Ireland J, Jochum EA, Herath D. A proposed wizard of OZ architecture for a human-robot collaborative drawing task. In: International Conference on Social Robotics, 11357 LNAI. Cham: Springer International Publishing; 2018. pp. 35-44

[84] Gustavsson P, Holm M, Syberfeldt A, Wang L. Human-robot collaboration – towards new metrics for selection of communication technologies. Procedia CIRP. 2018;**72**:123-128

[85] Kim D, Goyal A, Newell A, Lee S, Deng J, Kamat VR. Semantic relation detection between construction entities to support safe human-robot collaboration in construction. Computing in Civil Engineering. 2019;**2019**:265-272

[86] Habibnezhad M, Shayesteh S, Liu Y, Fardhosseini MS, Jebelli H. The architecture of an intelligent digital twin for a cyber-physical route-finding system in smart cities. In: The 8th international conference on construction engineering and project management, Hong Kong SAR. 7-8 Dec 2020. pp. 510-519

[87] Liu Y, Jebelli H. Worker-aware robotic motion planner in construction for improved psychological well-being during worker-robot interaction. Construction Research Congress. 2022;**2022**:205-214

[88] Seagers J, Liu Y, Jebelli H. Smart robotic system to fight the spread of COVID-19 at construction sites. Construction Research Congress. 2022;**2022**:452-461

[89] Shayesteh S, Jebelli H. Feasibility of virtual avatar simulator for human-robot collaboration training in construction. In: Computing in Civil Engineering. 2021. Reston, VA: ASCE; 2021. pp. 1417-1424

[90] Shayesteh S, Jebelli H. Investigating the impact of construction robots autonomy level on workers' cognitive load. In: Canadian Society of Civil Engineering Annual Conference. Singapore: Springer Nature Singapore; 2021. pp. 255-267

[91] Shayesteh S, Jebelli H. Enhanced situational awareness in worker-robot interaction in construction: Assessing the role of visual cues. Construction Research Congress. 2022;**2022**:422-430

[92] Shayesteh S, Jebelli H. Toward human-in-the-loop construction robotics: Understanding workers'

response through trust measurement during human-robot collaboration. Construction Research Congress. 2022;**2022**:631-639

[93] Peternel L, Tsagarakis N, Caldwell D, Ajoudani A. Adaptation of robot physical behaviour to human fatigue in human-robot co-manipulation. In: IEEE-RAS 16th International Conference on Humanoid Robots. Cancun, Mexico: IEEE; 2016. pp. 489-494

[94] Schaaff K, Schultz T. Towards an EEG-based emotion recognizer for humanoid robots. In: Proceedings -18th IEEE International Workshop on Robot and Human Interactive Communication. Vol. 2. Toyama, Japan: IEEE; Sep 27-Oct 2009. pp. 792-796

[95] Weiss A, Bernhaupt R, Tscheligi M. The USUS evaluation framework for user centered HRI. In: Proceedings of the Symposium on New Frontiers in Human-Robot Interaction. Vol. 2. Benjamins Publishing Company; 2011. pp. 89-110

[96] Aaltonen I, Salmi T, Marstio I. Refining levels of collaboration to support the design and evaluation of human-robot interaction in the manufacturing industry. Procedia CIRP. 2018;**72**:93-98

[97] Johannsmeier L, Haddadin S. A hierarchical human-robot interaction-planning framework for task allocation in collaborative industrial assembly processes. IEEE Robotics and Automation Letters. 2017;**2**(1):41-48

[98] Zhou J, Zhou Y, Wang B, Zang J. Human-cyber-physical systems (HCPSs) in the context of new-generation intelligent manufacturing. Engineering. 2019;**5**(4):624-636

[99] Wang B, Zhou H, Yang G, Li X, Yang H. Human digital twin (HDT) driven human-cyber-physical systems: Key technologies and applications. Chinese Journal of Mechanical Engineering. 2022;**35**:11

[100] Li X, Nassehi A, Wang B, Hu SJ, Epureanu BI. Human-centric adaptive manufacturing with human-system coevolution. CIRP Annals - Manufacturing Technology. 2023;**72**:393-396

[101] Zheng P, Li S, Fan J, Li C, Wang L. A collaborative intelligence-based approach for handling human-robot collaboration uncertainties. CIRP Annals - Manufacturing Technology. 2023;**72**(1):1-4

[102] Budziszewski P, Grabowski A, Milanowicz M, Jankowski J, Dzwiarek M. Designing a workplace for workers with motion disability with computer simulation and virtual reality techniques. International Journal on Disability and Human Development. 2011;**10**(4):355-358

[103] Perez MJ, Meza SM, Bravo FA, Trentesaux D, Jimenez JF. Evolution of the human digital representation in manufacturing production systems. International Workshop on Service Orientation in Holonic and Multi-Agent Manufacturing. 2021;**2021**:201-211

[104] Ahmed S, Irshad L, Gawand MS, Demirel HO. Integrating human factors early in the design process using digital human modelling and surrogate modelling. Journal of Engineering Design. 2021;**32**:165-186

[105] Baskaran S et al. Digital human and robot simulation in automotive assembly using siemens process simulate: A feasibility study. Procedia Manufacturing. 2019;**34**:986-994

[106] Papcun P, Kajati E, Koziorek J. Human machine interface in concept of

industry 4.0. In: 2018 World Symposium on Digital Intelligence for Systems and Machines. Košice, Slovakia: IEEE; 23-25 Aug 2018. pp. 289-296

[107] Andronas D, Apostolopoulos G, Fourtakas N, Makris S. Multi-modal interfaces for natural human-robot interaction. Procedia Manufacturing. 2021;**54**:197-202

[108] Davila-Gonzalez S, Martin S. Human digital twin in industry 5.0: A holistic approach to worker safety and well-being through advanced AI and emotional analytics. Sensors. 2024;**24**:655

[109] Wang B, Zhou H, Li X, Yang G, Zheng P, Song C, et al. Human digital twin in the context of industry 5.0. Robotics and Computer-Integrated Manufacturing. 2024;**85**:102626

[110] Kim GY et al. Human digital twin system for operator safety and workmanagment. In: IFIP International Conference on Advances in Production Management Systems. Cham: Springer; 2022. pp. 529-536

[111] Raja Santhi A, Muthuswamy P. Industry 5.0 or industry 4.0 S? Introduction to industry 4.0 and a peek into the prospective industry 5.0 technologies. International Journal on Interactive Design and Manufacturing (IJIDeM). 2023;**17**(2):947-979

[112] Deng Z, Guan H, Huang R, Liang H, Zhang L, Zhang J. "Combining model-based Q-learning with structural knowledge transfer for robot skill learning." IEEE Transactions on Cognitive and Developmental Systems. 2019;**11**(1):26-35

Chapter 2

# Navigating the Digital Transformation: Unveiling Industry 4.0 Challenges and Preparing for Industry 5.0

*Abin George*


## Abstract

This chapter delves into the intricate relationship between Industry 4.0 and the Indian tourism workforce, with a specific focus on faculty and student perceptions. Tourism is an important economic contributor in India, and this study explores how Industry 4.0, characterized by digital, physical, and biological convergence, impacts a sector recovering from the profound disruption caused by COVID-19. The challenges faced by the Indian tourism industry in adopting Industry 4.0 are elucidated, including the digital divide, workforce adaptability, job displacement concerns, and the need for updated education and training. Human-centric approaches are becoming increasingly important as the industry prepares for Industry 5.0, focusing on critical thinking, emotional intelligence, and sustainability. The Indian tourism sector's journey towards a digital future is explored in the study, highlighting both the promises and challenges encountered along the way. A mixed-method research approach was used in the research combining in-depth interviews, surveys, and real-time case studies to glean nuanced insights. The recommendations include further examination of specific skills, teaching methodologies, and business challenges associated with Industry 4.0. This research informs educational practices, industry strategies, and governmental policies, offering a roadmap for a successful transition to the digital tourism era.


**Keywords:** Industry 4.0, Industry 5.0, tourism workforce, digital transformation, human-centric approach

## 1. Introduction

Industry 4.0 is the fourth industrial revolution, characterized by the convergence of digital, physical, and biological technologies. It is having a significant impact on all industries, including tourism. In India, the tourism industry is a major contributor to the economy, accounting for around 9.2% of GDP and 39.5 million jobs in 2019 and the industry is expected to grow rapidly in the coming years, with the number of foreign tourist arrivals projected to reach 30.5 million by 2025 [1]. The adoption of Industry 4.0 technologies is still in its early stages in India, but it is picking up pace. The tourism sector in India was severely impacted by the COVID-19 pandemic. According to [2], the number of foreign tourist arrivals in India fell by 74.9%, from 27.41 million in 2019 to 6.33 million in 2020. The number of domestic tourist visits fell by 58.3% in 2020, from 1.85 billion in 2019 to 774 million in 2020. Even though in 2021, the number of foreign tourist arrivals in India increased by 25.2%, to 7.94 million. The domestic tourism sector also recovered in 2021. The number of domestic tourist visits increased by 33.7%, to 1.03 billion.

Imagine weaving through bustling Indian bazaars with a hyper-personalized AR guide whispering historical secrets in your ear. Or picture scaling the Himalayas with VR, conquering the peaks from any corner of the globe. These fantastical experiences, once dreams, are now on the horizon as the Indian tourism industry undergoes a seismic shift driven by Industry 4.0. This technological revolution, infused with automation, data analytics, and hyper-connectivity, promises to reshape every facet of travel, from destination marketing to guest interactions. Yet, amidst this whirlwind of disruption, a crucial question lingers: how will the Indian tourism workforce adapt and thrive in this new digital landscape?

The COVID-19 pandemic has had a significant impact on the tourism workforce in India. Millions of tourism workers have lost their jobs or had their hours reduced. The pandemic has also made it difficult for tourism businesses to operate profitably and working with the government to develop policies and programs that support the transition to Industry 4.0. Azmi et al. [3] found that academicians in the field prefer traditional teaching methods and face challenges in adapting to Industry 4.0, such as limited internet accessibility. Shah et al. [4] highlighted the impact of COVID-19 on students' perceptions of career opportunities, with many expressing a preference for the industry despite concerns about job security and entry-level positions. Bilotta et al. [5] emphasized the need to incorporate Industry 4.0 technologies into tourism education, focusing on data acquisition, analysis, and communication systems. Dhiman [6] provided insight into employers' perceptions of employability skills, suggesting a need for enhanced human resource and dynamic business skills. Atef and Balushi [7] explores the perceptions of Omani tourism and hospitality students, revealing a lack of interest in the industry as a long-term career path. These studies [3–7] collectively underscore the need for a comprehensive examination of the impact of Industry 4.0 on the Indian tourism workforce, particularly in terms of skills development and career perceptions.

### 1.1 Challenges in adapting to Industry 4.0

The digital divide introduces [8] inequalities in technology access, particularly between rural and urban areas, hindering inclusivity and widening economic gaps. Workforce adaptability encounters resistance from established businesses and reluctance among older generations to embrace new skills, potentially impeding the pace of digital transformation. Concerns about Job Displacement and Reskilling arise due to the automation of repetitive tasks, necessitating effective programs to equip displaced workers with new skills. The lag in the education and training curriculum in tourism, not aligning with Industry 4.0 advancements, leaves graduates unprepared for critical skills such as data analytics and AI. Moreover, ethical and regulatory concerns emerge with increased data collection, posing challenges related to privacy, security, and potential bias in AI algorithms. The absence of clear regulations around emerging technologies further complicates the industry's adaptation.

### 1.2 Preparing for Industry 5.0 in tourism

As the tourism industry prepares for the imminent evolution into Industry 5.0 [9], a shift towards human-centric values becomes pivotal. This necessitates a renewed focus on critical thinking, creativity, and adaptability to navigate the ever-evolving technological landscape. Emphasizing emotional intelligence and ethics is crucial to cultivating empathy and responsible technology use, guarding against AI bias and ensuring inclusivity. Collaboration and co-creation take center stage, encouraging partnerships among industry, government, and academia to create a supportive ecosystem for adaptation and innovation. Examples of Industry 5.0 technologies for tourism education, such as human-centered AI, virtual reality with empathy training, gamification for sustainable tourism, and collaborative platforms for tourism planning, emerge as integral components to shape a future that seamlessly blends technological advancement with human-centric values, promising authentic and sustainable travel experiences for generations to come.

This study aims to achieve two primary objectives. Firstly, research seeks to identify the key skills and competencies that tourism students and professors perceive as essential for success in the Industry 4.0 era. Secondly, to assess the perspectives of faculty and students regarding the transition towards a human-centric approach of Industry 5.0 within the Indian tourism workforce. Understanding these perceptions is integral to shaping future workforce strategies and educational frameworks. To address these objectives, the study poses specific research questions: firstly, what skills and competencies are identified as critical for success in the Industry 4.0-driven tourism industry by students and professors, and secondly, how do tourism faculty and students perceive the transition towards the human-centric approach of Industry 5.0 within the Indian tourism workforce?

## 2. Literature review

The literature review provides insights into the new types of jobs and skills needed in the context of Industry 4.0. The review identifies the importance of skills such as adaptability, soft skills, software engineering, data analytics, and technical skills. It emphasizes the need for preparing the youth for future technology and the requirement to master a blend of skills. Eva and Květa [10] suggested the need for further research on the readiness of the education system to the changes faced by Industry 4.0, case studies of countries with the best fit of the education system and industry needs, and empirical research on the match between industry expectations and system readiness. Wang and Huang [11] identified intrinsic factors as the most influential in shaping students' perceptions of tourism careers. These studies collectively highlight the need for a balance between traditional and modern teaching methods, the importance of adapting to technological advancements, and the influence of personal factors on career perceptions.

The rapid advancement of technology and the emergence of Industry 4.0, characterized by the fusion of digital technology, data analytics, automation, and the Internet of Things (IoT), are transforming various industries, including the tourism sector [12, 13]. This transformation is impacting the skills and competencies required for success in the tourism workforce [14, 15]. To fully grasp the impact of Industry 4.0 on the Indian tourism workforce, it is crucial to explore the perceptions of both tourism students and professors regarding this transformative phenomenon. Research suggests that both groups possess a moderate to high level of familiarity with Industry 4.0, indicating an awareness of its potential to reshape the tourism industry [16, 17]. This familiarity is reflected in their positive perceptions of Industry 4.0's impact on the future of tourism, with a focus on its ability to enhance efficiency, personalization, and customer experience [15, 18].

### 2.1 Critical skills and competencies for Industry 4.0 tourism

Studies have identified a range of critical skills and competencies essential for success in the Industry 4.0-driven tourism industry. These include digital literacy, data analysis, social media marketing, adaptability, problem-solving, communication. Refs. [12, 14] define adaptability as the ability to adjust to new technologies and changing workplace requirement. The competence in problem-solving, entailing the capability to identify and effectively resolve issues, is expounded by [12, 15]. Digital literacy, defined as the proficiency in utilizing technology for both work and communication, is encapsulated by the insights presented by [14, 16]. Refs. [15, 16] articulate the importance of proficiency in social media marketing to promote tourism products and services. According to [15, 17] aptitude for data analysis encompasses the ability to collect, analyze, and interpret data to make informed decisions. It is important to be able to communicate effectively with colleagues, customers, and stakeholders.

### 2.2 Perceptions of Industry 4.0 and its impact on tourism

Research suggests that both tourism students and professors have a moderate to high level of familiarity with Industry 4.0 [16, 17]. They perceive Industry 4.0 to have a positive impact on the future of the tourism industry, with a focus on its potential to enhance efficiency, personalization, and customer experience [15, 18]. The impact of Industry 4.0 on the Indian tourism workforce is significant, requiring new skills and competencies for success. Tourism education and training institutions need to adapt their curricula to incorporate these essential skills and prepare students for the demands of the Industry 4.0-driven tourism industry.

## 3. Theoretical framework for examining the impact of Industry 4.0 on the Indian tourism workforce

The rapid advancement of Industry 4.0, characterized by the convergence of digital, physical, and biological technologies, is revolutionizing industries worldwide, including the tourism sector. This transformative shift presents both opportunities and challenges for the Indian tourism workforce, demanding a comprehensive understanding of its impact on skills, competencies, and education.

### 3.1 Impact of Industry 4.0 on the tourism workforce

Industry 4.0 is having a mixed impact on the tourism workforce in India. On the one hand, it is automating many routine tasks, which is leading to job losses in some areas. On the other hand, it is also creating new jobs in areas such as data analytics, software development, and digital marketing. In the enchanting tapestry of the tourism industry, the threads of technology weave both a spell of promise and a tale of stark divisions. According to [8], unequal access to technology across regions and demographics amplifies existing inequalities, restricting participation and career advancement for marginalized groups. The impact of Industry 4.0 on the tourism workforce is a complex and multifaceted issue [19, 20] and highlight the potential for positive and negative impacts, with the former emphasizing the need for training in smart device and software development, and the latter discussing the effects on touristic businesses' financials and the tourism economy. Refs. [21, 22] both underscore the importance of innovation and the integration of technology in the tourism sector, with the former focusing on the relationship between tourism innovation and business competitiveness, and the latter emphasizing the potential for technologies like AI, IOT, and robotics to transform travel and tourism.

Automation poses a significant threat to jobs involving repetitive tasks like booking, check-in, and housekeeping [23]. Research suggests 85 million jobs globally could be lost by 2025, with tourism facing potential disruption [8]. Effective reskilling and upskilling programs are essential to equip workers with new skills in data analysis, AI, and digital marketing. Unequal access to technology exacerbates existing inequalities, limiting career advancements for marginalized groups [24]. New roles emerge in data management, AI development, and digital marketing, offering exciting career paths for skilled professionals [25]. Industry 4.0 fosters innovation and entrepreneurship, creating a dynamic job market. Technology can be harnessed to promote sustainable practices like resource optimization and waste reduction [26]. This contributes to a more resilient and environmentally conscious tourism industry, aligning with Industry 5.0's focus on sustainability. These studies collectively suggest that while Industry 4.0 presents significant opportunities for the tourism workforce, it also requires careful management and adaptation to ensure its benefits are maximized.

### 3.2 Changing skills and competencies for the tourism industry

Industry 4.0 is changing the skills and competencies that are required for tourism workers. The rapid advancements of Industry 4.0, fueled by automation, data analytics, and hyper-connectivity, are significantly impacting the tourism workforce landscape in 2023. In the past, tourism workers needed to have strong interpersonal skills and knowledge of the local area. In the future, they will also need to have strong digital skills and be able to use technology to personalize the customer experience. The digital transformation in the Indian tourism industry has led to a shift in consumer behavior, with a focus on experiences rather than products. However, there is still a gap in the development of these skills, particularly in the areas of digital capability and communication [27].

The adoption of Industry 4.0 technologies is driving a paradigm shift in the skills and competencies required for success in the tourism industry. Traditional tourism roles are evolving, demanding a new set of capabilities to navigate the digital landscape and harness the potential of emerging technologies. This has created a need for digital skills and competencies in the industry, which are being addressed in tourism education through cooperative-experiential learning [28]. The use of digital technology in teaching and learning is seen as a way to address this gap, with a focus on both students and faculty members [29]. In the Indian context, the attitude of customers towards online travel services is influenced by the service and trust attributes of travel websites [30]. Effective reskilling and upskilling programs are crucial to equip displaced workers with new skills [24]. Navigating the constantly evolving technological landscape demands the ability to learn new skills quickly, solve problems creatively, and adapt to changing scenarios [25]. Empathy, cultural sensitivity, and responsible use of technology are crucial to ensure inclusivity, avoid AI bias, and foster ethical tourism practices [26]. It's a symphony of human values, playing harmoniously with the digital notes of progress.

### 3.3 Assessing faculty and student perceptions

To effectively address the impact of Industry 4.0 on the Indian tourism workforce, understanding the perceptions and preparedness of faculty and students is crucial. This involves assessing their awareness of Industry 4.0 concepts, their perceptions of its impact on the tourism industry, and their level of preparedness to integrate these technologies into their teaching and learning practices. Students are more likely to pursue careers in tourism if they perceive it as offering good job opportunities, growth potential, and attractive salaries. Positive perceptions of the tourism industry, including its contribution to economic development, cultural exchange, and environmental sustainability, can attract students to the field [31]. This refined presentation of the theoretical framework provides a comprehensive and scholarly basis for examining the impact of Industry 4.0 on the Indian tourism workforce. It highlights the transformative nature of Industry 4.0 in the tourism sector, the changing skills and competencies required for success, and the critical role of tourism education and training in preparing the workforce for the future.

## 4. Research methodology

This study utilizes a mixed-method approach drawing inspiration from established research methodologies to ensure a nuanced exploration of the impact of Industry 4.0 on the Indian tourism workforce. It includes in-depth interviews with faculty members and surveys with tourism students, complemented by real-time case studies of companies actively adopting Industry 4.0 technologies in the Indian tourism industry and also case studies from the previous research. The study employs a combination of quantitative and qualitative data collection methods.

In alignment with [32, 33], this study conducted in-depth interviews with esteemed faculty members and surveyed 110 tourism students to garner diverse perspectives on Industry 4.0. Hair et al. [34] conducted quantitative research by collecting data involved surveying 110 tourism students to evaluate students' perceptions and attitudes towards Industry 4.0 technologies. The interviews, inspired by Bryman's qualitative research approach [35], aimed at delving into the personal experiences and insights of 40 experienced tourism professors regarding the integration of Industry 4.0 in tourism education. To augment the qualitative and quantitative findings, real-time case studies of companies actively adopting Industry 4.0 technologies in the Indian tourism industry were undertaken. Additionally, insights from previous research enriched the study's historical context. Interview transcripts underwent a rigorous thematic analysis using NVivo software [36], enabling the identification of key themes and patterns in the faculty's insights. The coded data was exported to Excel for further visualization and exploration of relationships between identified themes and survey findings. Quantitative data, collected through a survey of 110 tourism students, underwent analysis using SPSS software. This involved coding the interview transcripts to identify recurring themes and patterns. The coded data was exported to Excel for further data processing and visualization, following the principles outlined by [37]. This meticulous combination of qualitative and quantitative methods ensures a holistic understanding of the challenges, opportunities, and practices associated with Industry 4.0 in the Indian tourism sector.

**Figure 1** illustrates a comprehensive and integrated research approach employed to investigate the multifaceted impact of Industry 4.0 on the Indian tourism workforce. The combination of mixed-methods, including in-depth interviews, surveys, and real-time case studies, provides a nuanced understanding of faculty and student perspectives, as well as practical insights from industry implementations, contributing to a holistic exploration of the evolving landscape within the Indian tourism industry.

### 4.1 Case studies

Case study 1: reskilling and upskilling the tourism workforce in Goa, India.

This case study [38] highlights the proactive approach taken by the Goa Tourism Development Corporation (GTDC) to address the challenges and opportunities posed by Industry 4.0. By implementing initiatives to enhance the awareness and adoption

**Figure 1.**
*Research approach for examining the impact of Industry 4.0 on the Indian tourism workforce.*

of Industry 4.0 technologies among tourism businesses and employees, the GTDC has demonstrated a commitment to upskilling and reskilling the local workforce to meet the demands of the digital tourism era. The GTDC's efforts have resulted in the development of new training programs specifically tailored to the skill needs of the digital tourism industry. This case study serves as an example of how government organizations can play a crucial role in facilitating the transition of the tourism workforce towards Industry 4.0 readiness. By proactively addressing the skill gaps and providing the necessary training and support, the GTDC is ensuring that the Goa tourism sector remains competitive and adaptable in the face of technological advancements.

Case study 2: the impact of Industry 4.0 on employment patterns in the Indian tourism sector.

This study [39] delves into the transformative impact of Industry 4.0 on the employment patterns within the Indian tourism sector. The study emphasizes the growing demand for skilled labor in the tourism sector, particularly in areas such as data analysis, digital marketing, and technology support. These emerging skill requirements necessitate a shift in focus towards upskilling and reskilling the existing workforce to ensure their adaptability to the changing demands of the industry. By identifying the emerging skill requirements and developing targeted training programs, policymakers and industry stakeholders can play a crucial role in minimizing job displacement and fostering a skilled and adaptable workforce for the digital tourism area.

Case study 3: the role of education and training in preparing the Indian tourism workforce for Industry 4.0.

This study [40] emphasizes the critical role of education and training in preparing the Indian tourism workforce for the demands of Industry 4.0. It highlights the need for a greater emphasis on integrating digital skills and competencies into tourism education and training programs. The study proposes a collaborative approach between industry and academia to ensure that the curriculum and training programs align with the evolving skill requirements of the digital tourism industry. This case study underscores the importance of aligning education and training with the realities of the digital tourism industry. By incorporating industry insights and fostering practical learning experiences, educational institutions can prepare graduates with the knowledge, skills, and adaptability necessary to thrive in the Industry 4.0-driven tourism landscape.

Case study 4: embracing Industry 4.0 for sustainable tourism in Kerala, India.

Kerala, a renowned tourist destination in India, is embracing Industry 4.0 technologies to promote sustainable tourism practices and enhance the overall visitor experience [41]. The state government and tourism industry stakeholders are collaborating to implement innovative solutions that optimize resource utilization, reduce environmental impact, and promote responsible tourism. Implementation of Smart Tourism Infrastructure: Kerala is deploying smart tourism infrastructure, including IoT sensors and AI-powered systems, to monitor and manage resource consumption, such as energy and water usage. This real-time data analysis enables the state to optimize resource allocation, reduce waste, and promote more sustainable tourism practices.

AI-driven waste management solutions: to address waste management challenges in tourist hotspots, Kerala is implementing AI-powered waste collection and recycling systems. These systems utilize sensors and algorithms to identify waste bins that require emptying and optimize collection routes, reducing the environmental impact of tourism activities.

Personalized eco-friendly recommendations: Kerala is leveraging AI to provide personalized eco-friendly recommendations to tourists, encouraging them to adopt sustainable practices during their stay. This personalized approach promotes responsible tourism and raises awareness of environmental conservation efforts.

Case study 5: Empowering tourism micro-entrepreneurs through Industry 4.0 in Himachal Pradesh, India.

In Himachal Pradesh, India, Industry 4.0 technologies are being harnessed to empower tourism micro-entrepreneurs, enhancing their digital literacy, connectivity, and access to market opportunities [42]. This initiative aims to bridge the digital divide and enable micro-entrepreneurs to participate effectively in the digital tourism economy.

Digital literacy and skills training: Himachal Pradesh government and industry partners are providing digital literacy and skills training to tourism micro-entrepreneurs, equipping them with the knowledge and skills to utilize digital tools and platforms effectively. This training covers areas such as online marketing, social media management, and e-commerce.

Digital marketplace platforms: Online marketplaces and e-commerce platforms are being developed to provide tourism micro-entrepreneurs with a wider reach and access to potential customers. These platforms enable them to showcase their products and services, connect with tourists, and expand their customer base.

Financial inclusion and payment solutions: Digital payment solutions and financial inclusion initiatives are being implemented to facilitate cashless transactions and enhance the financial well-being of tourism micro-entrepreneurs. This promotes financial inclusion and empowers them to manage their finances more effectively.

#### *4.1.1 Real-time case studies*

Case study 1: Airbnb India's embrace of Industry 4.0.

Airbnb India is a prime example of how Industry 4.0 is transforming the tourism industry in India. Airbnb India has emerged as a leading hospitality provider in the country, revolutionizing the tourism industry through its innovative adoption of Industry 4.0 technologies [43]. The company's data-driven approach has enabled it to personalize guest experiences, predict demand with greater accuracy, and optimize pricing strategies, contributing to its rapid growth and market dominance.

Personalized guest experiences: Airbnb India leverages data analytics to gain deep insights into customer preferences and behaviors. By analyzing booking patterns, past reviews, and user profiles, the company can tailor recommendations and curate listings that align with individual interests. This personalized approach enhances guest satisfaction and encourages repeat bookings.

Demand forecasting and pricing optimization: Airbnb India utilizes sophisticated algorithms to predict demand fluctuations and optimize pricing across its vast network of accommodations. This data-driven strategy ensures that the company can maximize revenue while maintaining competitive pricing and attracting guests during peak seasons.

Case study 2: Taj Hotels' implementation of smart hospitality.

Taj Hotels is a leading luxury hotel chain in India that has been at the forefront of adopting Industry 4.0 technologies [44]. The company has implemented smart hospitality solutions that use sensors, artificial intelligence, and machine learning to improve guest experiences, optimize resource utilization, and enhance operational efficiency.

Sensor-based guest experience enhancement: Taj Hotels has deployed sensors throughout its properties to gather real-time data on guest behavior and preferences. This data is analyzed to identify potential issues, anticipate guest needs, and provide personalized services, leading to enhanced guest satisfaction and loyalty.

AI-powered resource optimization: the hotel chain has implemented AI-powered systems to optimize resource utilization, such as energy consumption, water usage, and staff scheduling. These systems analyze usage patterns and predict future demand, enabling Taj Hotels to operate more efficiently and sustainably.

Machine learning-driven operational excellence: Taj Hotels leverages machine learning algorithms to analyze vast amounts of operational data, identifying areas for improvement and streamlining processes. This data-driven approach has led to reduced costs, improved service delivery, and enhanced operational efficiency.

Case study 3. Yatra.com's use of artificial intelligence for travel recommendations.

Yatra.com, a leading online travel agency in India, has harnessed the power of artificial intelligence to provide personalized travel recommendations to its customers [45]. The company's AI-powered recommendation engine has transformed the travel booking experience, catering to individual preferences and enhancing customer satisfaction.

AI-powered recommendation engine: Yatra.com's AI-powered recommendation engine analyzes customer data, including past travel history, search patterns, and demographic information, to predict travel preferences and suggest relevant travel options. This personalized approach ensures that customers receive tailored recommendations that align with their interests and needs.

Real-time travel recommendations: the recommendation engine operates in real-time, continuously updating suggestions as new information becomes available, such as changes in search patterns, seasonal trends, and dynamic pricing. This real-time adaptability ensures that customers receive the most relevant and up-to-date recommendations.

Case study 4: OYO Rooms' leveraging of AI for hotel management.

OYO Rooms, a leading hotel aggregator in India, has adopted AI to optimize its hotel operations, enhancing efficiency and improving guest experiences [46]. The company's AI-powered system analyzes data from its vast network of hotels to identify areas for improvement and make data-driven recommendations.

AI-powered pricing optimization: OYO Rooms utilizes AI algorithms to analyze demand patterns, competitor pricing, and guest preferences to optimize pricing across its hotels. This data-driven approach ensures that the company can maximize revenue while maintaining competitive pricing and attracting guests.

AI-driven housekeeping and maintenance: OYO Rooms employs AI to analyze housekeeping and maintenance data, identifying potential issues and scheduling tasks proactively. This predictive approach helps prevent problems from arising, ensuring that guests enjoy clean, well-maintained accommodations.

Case study 5: MakeMyTrip's use of chatbots for customer support.

MakeMyTrip, a prominent online travel agency in India, has deployed chatbots to provide 24/7 customer support, enhancing the travel booking experience and resolving customer inquiries efficiently [47].

AI-Powered chatbots for customer interaction: MakeMyTrip's chatbots are equipped with natural language processing capabilities, enabling them to understand customer queries, provide relevant information, and resolve issues promptly. This automated approach allows the company to handle a high volume of customer interactions effectively.

Chatbots for personalized assistance: the chatbots can personalize interactions based on customer data and booking history, providing tailored assistance and recommendations. This personalized approach enhances customer satisfaction and encourages repeat bookings.

These case studies illustrate the transformative impact of Industry 4.0 on the Indian tourism industry, showcasing how companies are leveraging data analytics, artificial intelligence, and machine learning to personalize experiences, optimize operations.

### 4.2 Description of data collection and analysis

#### *4.2.1 Quantitative data collection*

A structured survey was conducted with 110 tourism and hospitality students from across India aimed at evaluating how they perceive Industry 4.0's impact on their career prospects. Students were specifically asked about their views regarding skill development needs arising from Industry 4.0 and their expectations for tourism's future trajectory. The data was analyzed using descriptive statistics, including frequency distributions, means, and standard deviations to evaluate their perceptions of Industry 4.0's impact on their career prospects and the future of the tourism industry.

Five real-time case studies were conducted to gain a deeper understanding of the implementation and impact of Industry 4.0 in the tourism industry. These case studies involved in-depth interviews with key stakeholders, observations of Industry 4.0 technologies in use, and document analysis of organizational strategies and initiatives. Five case studies from previous research were reviewed to gain insights from similar contexts and broaden the scope of analysis. These case studies provided valuable perspectives on the challenges and opportunities of Industry 4.0 adoption in different tourism settings.

#### *4.2.2 Qualitative data collection*

Semi-structured interviews were conducted with forty faculty members hailing from members from prominent tourism institutions in India were interviewed through semi-structured interviews. The interviews were specifically designed to gather insights into the faculty's perceptions of the impact of Industry 4.0 on tourism education and training. The focus areas included the assessment of skill requirements and the examination of employment patterns within the tourism sector. The qualitative data from the professor interviews was analyzed using thematic analysis to identify recurring themes and patterns in their perceptions and expectations.

#### *4.2.3 Descriptive statistical analysis*

Descriptive statistical analysis was employed to summarize the quantitative data collected from the student survey. Measures of central tendency, dispersion, and frequency distributions were used to describe the students' perceptions, expectations, and preparedness levels.

#### *4.2.4 Thematic analysis*

For qualitative data analysis, the data collected from the real-time case studies and the case studies from previous research were analyzed using thematic analysis.

This method involved identifying recurring themes, patterns, and variations in the data to gain a deeper understanding of the implementation, challenges, and impact of Industry 4.0 in the tourism industry.

*4.2.5 Cross-case analysis*

Cross-case analysis was conducted to compare and contrast the findings from the real-time case studies and the case studies from previous research. This process allowed for the identification of common themes and patterns across different contexts and the development of generalizations about the implementation and impact of Industry 4.0 in the tourism industry.

## 5. Data analysis and results

In this section, the findings of mixed-method research approach are presented. Utilizing a combination of in-depth interviews with 40 faculty members and a survey of 110 tourism students, complemented by real-time case studies and insights from previous research, our study provides a comprehensive analysis of the evolving landscape within the Indian tourism industry. The data collection methods, including qualitative thematic analysis and descriptive statistical analysis, offer a nuanced understanding of faculty and student perspectives, as well as real-world implementations of Industry 4.0 technologies in the tourism sector.

**Figure 2** not only showcases a systematic and holistic research methodology applied to explore the diverse implications of Industry 4.0 on the Indian tourism workforce but also incorporates a model of framework summarizing the findings. This integration of mixed-methods, spanning in-depth interviews, surveys, and

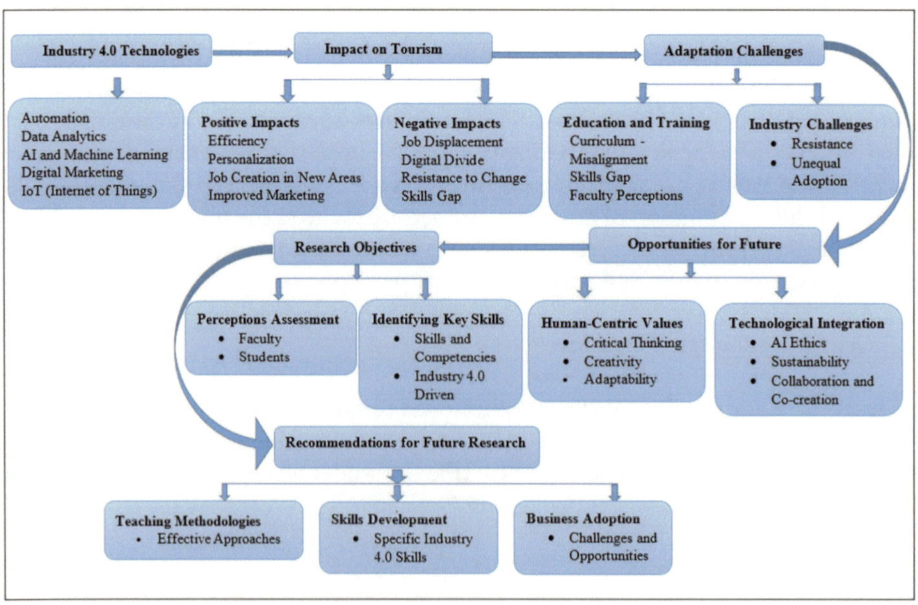


**Figure 2.**
*A framework summarizing the findings.*

real-time case studies, facilitates a nuanced comprehension of faculty and student perspectives, accompanied by valuable practical insights from industry implementations, thereby enriching the comprehensive exploration of the dynamic changes within the Indian tourism industry.

**Table 1** reveal key themes and patterns in faculty perceptions of Industry 4.0 (I4.0) and its impact on the tourism industry. There is a unanimous belief among faculty that I4.0 is significantly transforming the tourism sector, prompting the necessity for an adaptation in teaching methods to effectively prepare students for the evolving landscape. The analysis indicates that faculty and student perceptions of I4.0 align in the shared understanding that students must cultivate digital fluency, data analytics skills, and adaptability to emerging technologies. The identified theme emphasizes the skills deemed crucial for the I4.0-driven tourism workforce by faculty, emphasizing students' ability to leverage technology for enhancing guest experiences, optimizing operations, and making informed, data-driven decisions. These themes collectively emphasize the urgency for educational adaptation, collaboration with industry partners, and a focus on skill development to effectively prepare students for the dynamic challenges presented by Industry 4.0 in the tourism industry.

The students in the sample are relatively young as per **Table 2**, descriptive statistical analysis of survey data, with an average age of 22 years. The majority of them are male (3 out of 5) and in their second year of study (2 out of 5). The majority of the students have a moderate level of familiarity with Industry 4.0 (2 out of 5). They also have a positive perception of the impact of Industry 4.0, with the majority believing that it will have a positive impact on the tourism industry (2 out of 5). The students

| Theme | Description | Excerpts from transcripts |
|---|---|---|
| Impact of I4.0 on tourism | Faculty believe that I4.0 is transforming the tourism industry and that faculty need to adapt their teaching methods to prepare students for the future. | I4.0 is bringing about a paradigm shift in the tourism industry, and we need to ensure that our students are equipped with the skills they need to succeed and also faculty need to adapt their teaching methods to prepare students for the future. I4.0 is revolutionizing the way we do business in the tourism industry, and we need to prepare our students for this new reality. |
| Faculty and student perceptions of I4.0 | Faculty believe that students need to develop digital fluency, data analytics skills, and adaptability to new technologies. Traditional tourism curriculum is no longer adequate and that more hands-on learning and industry collaboration are needed. | Students need to develop digital fluency, data analytics skills, and adaptability to new technologies. The demand for skilled labor in the tourism sector is increasing, and we need to focus on developing students' digital literacy and problem-solving abilities. We need to work closely with industry partners to ensure that our curriculum is up-to-date and relevant to the needs of the workforce. |
| Skills required for the I4.0 tourism workforce | Faculty stress the need for students to use technology effectively in enhancing guest experiences, optimizing operations, and making data-driven decisions, emphasizing hands-on exposure to Industry 4.0 technologies. | Students need to be able to use technology to enhance guest experiences, optimize operations, and make data-driven decisions. We need to provide students with opportunities to learn about and experiment with I4.0 technologies in a real-world setting. |

**Table 1.**
*Themes and patterns in faculty perceptions of Industry 4.0 and its impact on the tourism industry.*

| Variable | Description | Frequency distribution | Mean | Std. dev. | Min | Max |
|---|---|---|---|---|---|---|
| *Section 1: demographic information* | | | | | | |
| Age | Student age | | 22.00 | 1.58 | 20.00 | 24.00 |
| Gender | Student gender | | 3.00 | 1.58 | 1.00 | 5.00 |
| Academic level | Student academic level | | 2.00 | 1.58 | 1.00 | 3.00 |
| *section 2: industry 4.0 awareness and perceptions* | | | | | | |
| Industry 4.0 familiarity | Familiarity with Industry 4.0 | Low: 1 | Moderate: 2 | High: 2 | Moderate | — |
| Industry 4.0 Impact | Perception of Industry 4.0 impact | Neutral: 1 | Positive: 2 | Very positive: 2 | Positive | — |
| *Section 3: skill development needs* | | | | | | |
| Digital literacy | Importance of digital literacy | Not important: 0 | Somewhat important: 0 | Moderately important: 1 | Very important: 3 | Extremely important: 1 |
| Data analysis | Importance of data analysis | Not important: 0 | Somewhat important: 0 | Moderately important: 1 | Very important: 2 | Extremely important: 2 |
| Social media marketing | Importance of social media marketing | Not important: 0 | Somewhat important: 1 | Moderately important: 2 | Very important: 1 | Extremely important: 1 |
| Adaptability | Importance of adaptability | Not important: 0 | Somewhat important: 0 | Moderately important: 0 | Very important: 3 | Extremely important: 2 |
| Problem solving | Importance of problem-solving | Not important: 0 | Somewhat important: 0 | Moderately important: 0 | Very important: 1 | Extremely important: 4 |
| Communication | Importance of communication | Not important: 0 | Somewhat important: 0 | Moderately important: 0 | Very important: 1 | Extremely important: 4 |
| *Section 4: career prospects and expectations* | | | | | | |
| Industry 4.0 job opportunities | Confidence in Industry 4.0 job creation | Somewhat confident: 1 | Moderately confident: 2 | Very confident: 1 | Extremely confident: 1 | Moderate |
| Industry 4.0 preparedness | Preparedness for Industry 4.0 demands | Somewhat prepared: 1 | Moderately prepared: 2 | Very prepared: 1 | Extremely prepared: 1 | Moderately prepared |

**Table 2.**
*Descriptive statistical analysis of survey data.*

believe that a number of skills are important for success in the Industry 4.0 era. The most important skills are problem-solving, communication, and adaptability (4 out of 5 students believe that these skills are extremely important). Digital literacy and data analysis are also seen as important, with the majority of students believing that they are extremely important or very important (3 out of 5 students for digital literacy and 2 out of 5 students for data analysis). Social media marketing is seen as less important, with the majority of students believing that it is moderately important or very important (2 out of 5 students). The students are moderately confident in the creation of Industry 4.0 jobs (2 out of 5 students are moderately confident or very confident). They are also moderately prepared for the demands of Industry 4.0 (2 out of 5 students are moderately prepared or very prepared).

Industry 4.0 is bringing significant changes to the Indian tourism industry, requiring new skills and competencies for its workforce. This transformation is leading to both automation and the creation of new jobs in the digital tourism sector. Educational institutions and training providers need to adapt their curriculums to prepare students for these evolving skill demands. Government policies and initiatives play a crucial role in supporting the development of a digital tourism infrastructure and facilitating the adoption of Industry 4.0 technologies by businesses. Empowering tourism micro-entrepreneurs through access to digital tools and training is essential to ensure their participation in the digital economy. The cross analysis of the case studies as per **Table 3**, highlight the need for a concerted effort from stakeholders in the Indian tourism industry to address the challenges and opportunities presented

| Case study | Key findings | Recommendations |
|---|---|---|
| *Case study 1*: reskilling and upskilling the tourism workforce in Goa, India | The Goa Tourism Development Corporation (GTDC) has taken a proactive approach to address the challenges and opportunities posed by Industry 4.0. | Develop comprehensive training programs to upskill and reskill tourism professionals in digital skills such as data analytics, artificial intelligence, and social media marketing. |
| *Case study 2*: the impact of Industry 4.0 on employment patterns in the Indian Tourism Sector | Industry 4.0 is leading to both automation and the creation of new jobs in the digital tourism realm. | Collaborate between industry and academia to ensure that educational programs align with the evolving skill requirements of the digital tourism industry. |
| *Case study 3*: the role of education and training in preparing the Indian tourism workforce for Industry 4.0 | Educational institutions and training providers need to integrate digital skills and competencies into their curriculum. | Foster a culture of digital literacy and entrepreneurship among tourism professionals to encourage innovation and adoption of Industry 4.0 technologies. |
| *Case study 4*: embracing Industry 4.0 for sustainable tourism in Kerala, India | Kerala is using Industry 4.0 technologies to promote sustainable tourism practices. | Implement government policies that support the development of a digital tourism infrastructure and promote the adoption of Industry 4.0 technologies by tourism businesses. |
| *Case study 5*: empowering tourism micro-entrepreneurs through Industry 4.0 in Himachal Pradesh, India | Himachal Pradesh is using Industry 4.0 technologies to empower tourism micro-entrepreneurs. | Provide financial assistance and support to tourism micro-entrepreneurs to enable them to access digital tools, platforms, and training opportunities. |

**Table 3.**
*Cross-case analysis of the provided case studies.*

by Industry 4.0. By proactively investing in reskilling and upskilling the workforce, adapting educational programs, and creating a supportive policy environment, India can ensure the long-term success of its tourism industry in the digital age.

## 6. Discussion

The findings resonate with a positive perspective held by tourism students towards I4.0, envisioning its favorable impact on the industry. Students identified critical skills, including problem-solving, communication, adaptability, digital literacy, and data analysis, as essential for success in the I4.0 era. The digital divide, underscored in UNWTO's findings [8], emphasizes how unequal access to technology amplifies existing inequalities. Workforce adaptability challenges align with Azmi et al.'s insights [3], emphasizing the need for adaptability among tourism academicians. Concerns about job displacement and the call for effective reskilling programs align with Shah et al.'s study [4], highlighting the impact of COVID-19 on the need for reskilling in the tourism sector. The study's findings regarding the lag in education and training curriculum correspond with Bowen and Morosan's recommendations [12] to align education with Industry 4.0 advancements.

Faculty members unanimously agreed on the transformative impact of I4.0 on the tourism industry. Their emphasis on adapting teaching methods underscores the dynamic nature of the digital landscape and the need for educational institutions to be agile in response. Faculty highlighted the pivotal role of technology in enhancing guest experiences, optimizing operations, and fostering data-driven decision-making. Recognizing the need for a curriculum overhaul and the infusion of hands-on learning experiences, faculty members advocate for a holistic approach to address the evolving skill set required in the digital age. Ethical concerns, particularly related to data collection, align with the broader ethical considerations raised by UNWTO [8]. Preparing for Industry 5.0 in tourism, as outlined in this study, aligns with global priorities [9], emphasizing human-centric values, emotional intelligence, ethics, sustainability, resilience, and collaboration. The identified critical skills align with Guttentag's insights [14], emphasizing the importance of skills like digital literacy, data analysis, and communication in the tourism workforce. The transition to a human-centric approach aligns with the overarching shift emphasized by the World Tourism Organization [9]. Real-time case studies align with existing literature [5, 13], emphasizing the need for upskilling, the impact on employment patterns, and the role of education and training in Industry 4.0 adaptation. This alignment underscores the consistency and relevance of the study's findings with existing literature, reinforcing broader trends and challenges in the context of Industry 4.0 in the tourism industry.

The strengths of this study lie in the meticulous mixed-method approach, integrating in-depth interviews, surveys, and real-time case studies. This robust methodology enhances the credibility of the findings by triangulating data from diverse sources, contributing to a comprehensive understanding of the subject matter. The study's strength also lies in its relevance to the real-world application, evident in the integration of case studies from the Indian tourism industry. While the discussion delves into the transformative impact of I4.0 on the tourism industry, the study indicates the dual nature of I4.0, acknowledging both automation-induced job losses and the creation of new opportunities. However, expanding on specific instances or case studies illustrating how I4.0 technologies have reshaped operational processes, customer experiences, and business models within the tourism sector would provide a richer and more vivid portrayal. A deeper exploration of how technologies like artificial intelligence, data analytics, and automation have been harnessed by tourism businesses in India could amplify the discussion on transformation, illustrating the tangible effects of I4.0 on various facets of the industry. The study indicates the transformative impact of I4.0 on the Indian tourism industry. Exploring how the observed challenges and opportunities align with or diverge from trends in the global tourism landscape would enhance the study's broader relevance. Additionally, a comparison with findings from studies conducted in other countries or regions facing similar digital transformations could provide a cross-cultural perspective. Such comparative analysis would contribute to a more comprehensive understanding of the universal and context-specific aspects of I4.0 challenges in the tourism sector.

The study is limited to the Indian context, which may limit the generalizability of the findings to other cultural and economic contexts. The sample size of faculty interviews and student surveys could also be considered a limitation, impacting the representativeness of the study. Additionally, the temporal aspect, given the rapidly evolving nature of I4.0 technologies, should be acknowledged.

The research on the impact of Industry 4.0 on the Indian tourism workforce recommends several avenues for future exploration. First, a detailed investigation into the specific skills required for success in Industry 4.0 within various tourism roles is suggested. Second, there is a call to examine the effectiveness of different teaching methodologies in preparing students for the demands of Industry 4.0. Third, researchers are encouraged to delve into the challenges and opportunities faced by tourism businesses in adopting Industry 4.0 technologies. Additionally, an analysis of the employment landscape, an evaluation of government policies, and comparative studies across different regions are proposed. Ethical implications of Industry 4.0 and the role of emerging technologies in shaping the tourism industry's future are also highlighted as areas deserving further research attention. Conducting comparative studies across different countries or regions is recommended to identify best practices and challenges in adapting to Industry 4.0 within the tourism industry. This research approach can offer valuable insights into global variations and successful strategies, providing a comprehensive understanding of the diverse impacts and adaptations related to Industry 4.0 in the tourism sector.

## 7. Conclusion

As the tourism industry in India stands at the cusp of the fourth industrial revolution, the profound impacts of Industry 4.0 are unmistakable. The synthesis of insights from faculty interviews, student surveys, and real-time case studies provides a comprehensive understanding of the dynamic interplay between technology and the tourism industry in India. Faculty members unanimously agree on the transformative impact of I4.0 on the tourism industry. Adaptive teaching methods are deemed necessary to prepare students for the demands of the digital tourism era. Faculty emphasizes the use of technology for enhancing guest experiences, optimizing operations, and making data-driven decisions. The importance of developing digital fluency, data analytics skills, and adaptability among tourism students is underscored. The study acknowledged the need to update the traditional tourism curriculum and incorporate more hands-on learning experiences. These perceptions align with the growing demand for digital skills in the tourism industry. Tourism students express a positive view of I4.0, anticipating a positive impact on the tourism industry. Identified critical skills for success include problem-solving, communication, adaptability, digital literacy, and data analysis. Emphasized the transformative impact of I4.0 on employment patterns in the Indian tourism sector.

The imminent shift towards Industry 5.0 demands a recalibration of values in the tourism sector. Prioritizing human-centric values, the industry must emphasize critical thinking, creativity, and adaptability. Emotional intelligence and ethical considerations take precedence to foster empathy and responsible technology use, addressing concerns related to AI bias and ensuring inclusivity. Sustainability and resilience become imperative, woven into the fabric of tourism practices. Collaboration and co-creation emerge as central tenets, advocating for partnerships among industry, government, and academia to create an ecosystem conducive to adaptation and innovation. Industry 5.0 technologies, such as human-centered AI, virtual reality with empathy training, gamification for sustainable tourism, and collaborative platforms, are envisioned as integral components shaping a future that seamlessly integrates technological advancement with human-centric values. These insights provide valuable guidance for tourism educators and policymakers in preparing the workforce for the demands of the digital tourism area. In conclusion, this chapter contributes a holistic examination of the digital transformation journey in the Indian tourism industry, navigating the challenges of Industry 4.0 and preparing for the human-centric paradigm of Industry 5.0.

## Author details

Abin George
CSIR-NAL, Bangalore, India

*Address all correspondence to: abin@nal.res.in

## References

[1] World Travel & Tourism Council (WTTC). Economic Impact Reports – India 2023. 2023. Available from: https://www.wttc.org/research/economic-impact-reports/india-2023

[2] Ministry of Tourism, Government of India. Annual Report 2022-2023. 2022. Available from: https://tourism.gov.in/sites/default/files/2023-02/MOT%20Annual%20Report_2022-23_English.pdf

[3] Azmi A, Ahmad NC, Kayat K, Abdullah D, Zubir HA. Industry 4.0: Teaching Preferences, Perceptions, and Challenges among Tourism and Hospitality Academicians. International Journal of Academic Research in Business and Social Sciences. 2018;**8**(15):350-365. Available from: https://hrmars.com/papers_submit-ted/5111/Industry_4_0_Teaching_Preferences,_Perceptions,_and_Challenges_among_Tourism_and_Hospitality_Academicians.pdf

[4] Shah C, Chowdhury A, Gupta V. Impact of COVID-19 on tourism and hospitality students' perceptions of career opportunities and future prospects in India. Journal of Teaching in Travel & Tourism. 2021;**21**:359-379

[5] Bilotta E, Bertacchini F, Gabriele L, Giglio S, Pantano PS, Romita T. Industry 4.0 technologies in tourism education: Nurturing students to think with technology. Journal of Hospitality Leisure Sport & Tourism Education. 2020;**29**:100275. DOI: 10.1016/j.jhlste.2020.100275

[6] Dhiman MC. Employers' perceptions about tourism management employability skills. Anatolia. 2012;**23**:359-372

[7] Atef TM, Balushi MA. Omani tourism and hospitality students' employment intentions and job preferences: Ramifications on Omanization plans. Quality Assurance in Education. 2017;**25**:440-461

[8] UNWTO. Digital Divide in Tourism: Towards a More Inclusive and Sustainable Industry. 2023. Available from: https://link.springer.com/content/pdf/10.1007/978-3-030-05324-6_109-1.pdf

[9] World Tourism Organization. Rethinking Tourism: Priorities for a New World. 2023. Available from: https://www.unwto.org/events/world-tourism-day-2023

[10] Eva K, Květa O. Industry 4.0 and preparedness of the workforce: A bibliometric analysis. In: 21st International Joint Conference Central and Eastern Europe in the Changing Business Environment: Proceedings. 2021. p. 139. DOI: 10.18267/pr.2021.krn.4816.12

[11] Wang S, Huang X. College students' perceptions of tourism careers in China: Implications for the industry and education providers. Journal of Human Resources in Hospitality & Tourism. 2014;**13**:211-233

[12] Bowen J, Morosan C. Beware hospitality industry: The robots are coming. Worldwide Hospitality and Tourism Themes. 2015;**10**(6):726-733. DOI: 10.1108/WHATT-07-2018-0045

[13] Ivanov D, Pavlov D, Sokolov B. Digital technologies and the tourism industry. In: Handbook of Tourism and Hospitality Research. Cham: Springer; 2019. pp. 1263-1278

[14] Guttentag D. Skills and competencies for the future tourism workforce: An

international perspective. Journal of Hospitality and Tourism Education. 2016;**27**(2):1-18

[15] Sigala M, Stavrakis K, Panagiotis GC. Industry 4.0 in tourism: An overview. In: Tourism and Hospitality in the Age of Industry 4.0. Cham: Springer; 2020. pp. 1-20

[16] Ahmad S, Zafar Z. Perceptions of Industry 4.0 and its impact on tourism education: A comparative study of faculty and students in India. Journal of Hospitality Management and Tourism. 2020;**11**(2):199-214

[17] Park J, Kim H, Kim W, Kim S. Industry 4.0 and tourism workforce development: A literature review. Journal of Hospitality and Tourism Education. 2020;**35**(2):1-15

[18] Buhalis D, Amaranggani S. A review of augmented and virtual reality applications in tourism. International Journal of Tourism Research. 2019;**21**(2):171-198

[19] Abdurakhmanova GK, Astanakulov OT, Goyipnazarov SB, Irmatova AB. Tourism 4.0: Opportunities for applying Industry 4.0 technologies in tourism. In: Proceedings of the 6th International Conference on Future Networks & Distributed Systems. 2022. pp. 33-38. DOI: 10.1145/3584202.3584208

[20] Mil B, Dirican C. Industry 4.0 technologies and its effects on tourism economics. Journal of Multidisciplinary Academic Tourism. 2018;**3**(1):1-9

[21] Ramos CMQ, Brito IS. The effects of industry 4.0 in tourism and hospitality and future trends in Portugal. In: Hassan A, Sharma A. editors. The Emerald Handbook of ICT in Tourism and Hospitality. 2020. pp. 367-378. DOI:10.1108/978-1-83982-688-720201023

[22] Mazilescu V. Tourism and Travel can effectively benefit from technologies associated with Industry 4.0. In: International Conference "Risk in Contemporary Economy," XXth Edition, Galati, Romania, "Dunarea de Jos" University of Galati, Romania – Faculty of Economics and Business Administration. 2019. pp. 53. Available from: https://web.archive.org/web/20200507035203id_/http://www.rce.feaa.ugal.ro/images/stories/RCE2019/Mazilescu.pdf

[23] World Economic Forum. Global Future Council on Sustainable Tourism. 2023. Available from: https://www.weforum.org/communities/gfc-on-sustainable-tourism/

[24] UNWTO. Reskilling and Upskilling the Tourism Workforce for the Digital Age. 2022. Available from: https://intranet.eulacfoundation.org/en/system/files/9258d999-en.pdf

[25] World Future Council. Creativity for a Sustainable Future: A Guide for Tourism Businesses. 2022. Available from: https://www.weforum.org/communities/gfc-on-sustainable-tourism/

[26] UNWTO. Building a Human-Centric Future of Tourism: Ethical Considerations in Tourism Development. 2023. Available from: https://www.unwto.org/un-tourism-news-tourism-moving-tourism-forward-into-2023

[27] Pratiwi R, Hartono S, Nurdiana E, Dasmadi D. Digital Capability and Communication Skill for Empowering Self-Efficacy in Tourism Industry. In: Proceedings of the 1st International Conference on Accounting, Management and Entrepreneurship (ICAMER 2019). Atlantis Press. 2019. pp. 126-129. DOI: 10.2991/aebmr.k.200305.032

[28] Morellato M. Digital competence in tourism education: Cooperative-experiential learning. Journal of Teaching in Travel & Tourism. 2014;**14**:184-209

[29] Balula A, Moreira G, Moreira A, Kastenholz E, Eusébio C, Breda Z. Digital Transformation in Tourism Education. Tourism in Southern and Eastern Europe. 2019;**5**:61-72. DOI: 10.20867/tosee.05.45

[30] Khare A, Khare A. Blending information technology in indian travel and tourism sector. Services Marketing Quarterly. 2011;**32**:302-317

[31] Rosyidi MI. Undergraduate students'perceptions and attitudes towards a career in tourism industry: The case of Indonesia. Jurnal Manajemen dan Kewirausahaan. 2021;**23**(1):40-51

[32] Creswell JW. Designing Mixed-Methods Research. 6th ed. Sage Publications Ltd.; 2017. Available from: https://cumming.ucalgary.ca/sites/default/files/teams/82/communications/Creswell%202003%20-%20Research%20Design%20-%20Qualitative%2C%20Quantita-tive%20and%20Mixed%20Methods.pdf

[33] Morse JM. Mixed Method Design: Principles and Procedures. 1st ed. New York: Routledge; 2009. DOI: 10.4324/9781315424538

[34] Hair JF, Black WC, Babin BJ, Anderson RE. Multivariate Data Analysis. 7th ed. Cengage Learning; 2019. Available from: https://www.drnishikantjha.com/papersCollection/Multivari-ate%20Data%20Analysis.pdf

[35] Bryman A. Social Research Methods (Fifth Edition). Oxford University Press; 2016. Available from: https://www.google.co.in/books/edition/Social_Research_Methods/N2zQCgAAQBAJ?hl=en&gbpv=1&dq=inauthor:%22Alan+Bryman%22&printsec=frontcover

[36] Braun V, Clarke V. Successful Qualitative Research: A Practical Guide for Beginners. 3rd ed. SAGE Publications Ltd.; 2022. Available from: https://www.researchgate.net/publication/256089360_Success-ful_Qualitative_Research_A_Practical_Guide_for_Beginners

[37] Yin RK. Case Study Research and Applications: Design and Methods. 6th ed. SAGE Publications Ltd.; 2023. Available from: https://us.sagepub.com/en-us/nam/case-study-research-and-applications/book250150

[38] Goa Tourism Development Corporation. Goa Tourism Development Corporation Annual Report 2021-2022. 2022. Available from: https://goa-tourism.com/

[39] Dutta S, Majumdar A. The impact of industry 4.0 on employment patterns in the Indian tourism sector. Journal of Tourism and Hospitality Management. 2022;**30**(1):24-38

[40] Sharma S, Kaur J. The role of education and training in preparing the Indian tourism workforce for industry 4.0. Journal of Tourism Management Education. 2022;**9**(1):1-12

[41] Kerala Tourism Development Corporation. Sustainable Tourism Initiatives in Kerala. 2022. Available from: https://www.keralatourism.org/responsible-tourism/

[42] Government of Himachal Pradesh. Economic Survey 2022-23. 2023. Available from: https://himachalservices.nic.in/economics/pdf/economic_survey_2022-23.pdf

[43] Ramaswamy S, Murthy SR. The impact of industry 4.0 on the Indian tourism industry: A case study of Airbnb

India. Journal of Hospitality and Tourism Management. 2023;**45**:1-10

[44] Gupta S, Singh S. The role of smart hospitality technologies in enhancing guest experience: A case study of Taj Hotels. International Journal of Hospitality Management. 2023;**119**:105062

[45] Aggarwal S, Singh R. Leveraging artificial intelligence for personalized travel recommendations: A case study of Yatra.com. International Journal of Tourism and Hospitality Management. 2023;**46**:1-14

[46] Rai N, Sinha A. The impact of AI on hotel revenue management: A study of OYO rooms. International Journal of Business Management and Economics. 2021;**12**(3):1-12

[47] Tripathi A, Sharma V. Chatbots: Transforming customer service in the travel industry - A case study of MakeMyTrip. Journal of Marketing and Communication. 2021;**9**(3):1-10

Section 2

# Industry-Specific Technological Advances

Chapter 3

# Determining Decision-Making Factors for Technology Adoption in the Construction Industry

*Makram Bou Hatoum and Hala Nassereddine*


## Abstract

Construction organizations have been undergoing major efforts as the industry acknowledges the need to improve and change its traditional business-as-usual model. Inspired by the wave of technological advancement brought forward by the fourth industrial revolution (i.e., Industry 4.0 or its construction counterpart known as Construction 4.0), the need to investigate and successfully exploit technologies has never been more critical for construction researchers and practitioners. One research topic that remains limited pertains to the organizational aspect of successful technology adoption and the impact on the business environment in which the organization operates. To address the gap, the study utilizes the Technology-Organization-Environment (TOE) framework and synthesizes the existing research corpus to develop a comprehensive list of 23 decision-making factors for construction organizations to evaluate when adopting technologies. The study also offers an overview of existing research on the adoption of Construction 4.0 technologies, proposes 97 potential measures to evaluate the factors, and provides a discussion of the research trends. Accordingly, findings from this study can lay the foundation for decision-making processes and frameworks as technology adoption research grows and change efforts expand across the construction industry.


**Keywords:** Construction 4.0, construction management, decision making, digitalization, innovation, organizational change

## 1. Introduction

The construction industry holds significant global importance, contributing substantially to the world's economy. Projections indicate that by 2030, the industry is anticipated to contribute approximately 15% to the global GDP, with an 85% predicted increase in the volume of construction output reaching US$ 15.5 trillion worldwide [1, 2]. Despite its strong economic impact, the construction industry faces major problems that are affecting its performance. Notably, construction projects are highly likely to face cost and schedule overruns [3], design delays [4], safety problems [5], material and equipment issues [4, 6], and litigation [7]. Additionally, the industry faces resistance to change [8], repels younger workers [9, 10], lacks standardization [11], suffers from a high turnover rate [12], and has ineffective knowledge management systems [5]. Considering these challenges and the anticipated growth of the construction industry, the traditional business-as-usual model falls short of the industry's expectations and is no longer sustainable [13, 14], especially as the industry's annual productivity is capped at a staggeringly low growth of 1% annually versus a 2.8% total economic growth [15].

To address the challenges plaguing the construction industry, practitioners and researchers have prioritized the initiation of digitization and industrialization initiatives and explored the use of various technologies across the project lifecycle [16, 17]. Specifically over the past decade, the industry has made substantial investments in significant technological advancements and trends that have been introduced or

| Aspect | Findings | References |
|---|---|---|
| Definition | Construction 4.0 is defined as the "digitization and industrialization of the construction industry" that (1) enables real-time vertical integration, horizontal integration, and end-to-end engineering, (2) advances construction processes through mechanization and automation, and (3) bridges the gap between the physical and cyber environments across the entire lifecycle of all types of assets. | [25–27] |
| Design principles | The design principles of Construction 4.0 include:<br>• Interconnection and interoperability through effective coordination, collaboration, and communication (human-human, human-machine, and machine-machine).<br>• Decentralization notably at the level of decision-making both internally (i.e., within the organizations' cross-functional teams) and externally (among project players and supply chain players).<br>• Transparency through open, clear, and readily available information for relevant parties that require access to it.<br>• Technical assistance through embracing technologies that enhance processes, empower people, and boost project performance. | [28, 29] |
| Transformations | The transformations of Construction 4.0 include:<br>• Product transformation or transforming the physical asset that results from a construction project.<br>• Delivery transformation or transforming the delivery of the project from conceptualization through decommissioning and/or demolition.<br>• Digital transformation through enhancing the physical-cyber interaction.<br>• Mindset Transformation through focusing on people and encompassing "scientific thinking". | [30] |
| Technologies | Construction 4.0 embraces, enables, and introduces a set of technological tools and technology concepts to the industry such as additive manufacturing, artificial intelligence, augmented and virtual reality, autonomous vehicles, blockchain, big data, cloud computing, cybersecurity, digital twins, drones, internet of things, geographic information systems, laser scanning, precast, prefabrication, modularization, robotics, and sensors. | [21, 27, 31–36] |

**Table 1.**
*Construction 4.0 fundamental aspects.*

pushed by the fourth industrial revolution, also known as Industry 4.0 [18]. Recent events have also pushed organizations to accelerate technology adoption, such as the surge in infrastructure investments, the demand for transparency within the supply chain, the rise in legislation to combat climate change, the arrival of Generation Z into the workforce, and the unexpected and unplanned outbreak of the COVID-19 pandemic that compelled organizations to conduct business in contactless environments and ensure the continuity of their operations [19, 20].

The rise in technology adoption led to "Construction 4.0", a term coined to represent the mapping of Industry 4.0 into the construction industry [21]. The term was conceptualized in 2016 as part of a roadmap to digitize the construction industry of Europe and unleash the potential of automation, digital data, digital access, and connectivity across the construction supply chain players [22, 23]. Since then, research on Construction 4.0 has expanded to further understand the concept and its effect on the industry [24]. **Table 1** summarizes the fundamental aspects of Construction 4.0 as pertained in the construction body of knowledge.

### 1.1 Point of departure and motivation

The adoption of cutting-edge technology across industries can have a significant contribution to the industrial restructuring and economic transformation of the countries in which they operate, as well as increase the profits of organizations within these industries [37]. Organizational success can also largely depend on the organization's ability to foster new technologies, especially that embracing the fourth industrial revolution's technologies and achieving its components have shown great promise in enabling project success such as budget and schedule compliance, customer satisfaction, strategic accomplishments, and functionality or value achievements [38]. Thus, by embracing Construction 4.0 and effectively adopting its technologies, the construction industry can unlock a multitude of applications that bring benefits to all stakeholders involved in construction projects [18, 39]. This will also allow construction organizations to prepare for the fifth industrial revolution—i.e. Industry 5.0, which is beginning to unfold across various sectors [24].

However, the unique nature of the construction industry, particularly the high level of fragmentation, can make it challenging to adopt Construction 4.0 technologies and exploit their full potential [5]. It has been well documented that the construction industry suffers from vertical fragmentation with the various trade specialties, horizontal fragmentation with the dominance of small and medium-sized firms facing intense competition, and longitudinal fragmentation with the high turnover of clients and suppliers between one project and another [40, 41]. In such a fragmented context, even cutting-edge technologies developed for the construction industry can face potential failure, as technology providers and adopters must overcome numerous barriers including regulatory, commercial, cultural, organizational, and even psychological barriers [41, 42].

With the multi-faced and complex problems facing the industry, construction organizations must base technology adoption decisions on a sufficient volume of reliable and high-quality information [43]. Relying on such information can limit uncertainty, decrease the likelihood and severity of risks, and increase decision-makers confidence by better understanding consequences [43, 44]. This is especially important for technology adoption decisions, as the implementation of technologies comes with risks and challenges that may not only overshadow the success of the implementation but also extinguish the value of the technologies being adopted [45].

Thus, before adoption, decision-makers should evaluate the extent to which technologies of interest are a good fit with the organization's business from various aspects.

Although previous studies have investigated technology adoption, the focus has mostly targeted the adoption from an individual level and how users can implement and exploit the potential of the technology [46, 47]. This creates a need to comprehensively understand and examine the decision-making factors that may influence the successful adoption of technologies from the perspective of the organization and the business environment in which it operates [13, 48, 49]. The holistic evaluation of such decision-making factors can allow organizations to justify financial investments [50], ensure that the technology can deliver the desired benefits over time [51], evaluate the impact of the technology on stakeholders and partners [52], assess the technology's compliance with regulations and standards [53], gain more flexibility and efficiency when applying technologies to projects [54], and look "beyond the cognitive selling points of a technology" [55].

## 2. Objective and scope

### 2.1 Research objective

To address the gap, this chapter aims to develop a comprehensive list of decision-making factors for construction organizations to evaluate when adopting technologies. The chapter offers an overview of existing research on the adoption of Construction 4.0 technologies, extracts the decision-making factors, proposes potential measures for every factor, and provides a discussion of the research trends derived from the literature review. It is important to note that the scope of the chapter focuses on determining the decision-making factors rather than conducting a comparative analysis, assigning weights, quantifying, or evaluating the relative importance of every factor. The value of this comprehensive approach is two-fold, as it centralizes available information for industry practitioners and decision-makers while providing scholars with solid groundwork to expand on the decision-making research area. This comprehensive approach also serves to minimize redundancies and duplication of efforts within the dynamic field of technology adoption, especially as technologies continue to evolve and more studies are expected to emerge.

### 2.2 Selection of theoretical underpinning

To examine the concept of innovation adoption in organizations, research from different industries utilized several theories such as the Technology Adoption Model (TAM) [56], the theory of planning behavior (TPB) [57], the unified theory of acceptance and use of technology (UTAUT) [58], diffusion of innovation (DOI) [59], theory of reasoned action (TRA) [60], and technology-organization-environment (TOE) [61]. Theories of TAM, TBP, UTAUT, and TRA focus more on the individual level of analysis and the user perspective [62], making them unsuitable for the objective of this chapter. DOI and TOE investigate technology at the organizational level, but TOE is advantageous in studying adoption, use, and value creation as it accounts for the organization as well as the environment [63]. The TOE theory also has many strengths:

- TOE has a robust theoretical basis and solid empirical evidence as it was used in various technology adoption investigations across all industries [64];

- TOE has guided scholars in identifying the drivers of technology adoption from a corporate perspective, and the flexible nature of its factor makes the evaluation suitable for companies of all sizes and their intended use of the technology [65, 66];

- The extensive assessment of the external and internal capabilities of the technology as well as the internal and external factors that can affect the company makes TOE valuable in supporting sound decisions, predicting the success of adoption, and providing a comprehensive understanding of the adoption process [67, 68];

- The TOE aspects can be constantly extended to ensure the relevancy of the theory to timely business contexts [65];

- The TOE aspects present both opportunities and limitations for adoption, demonstrating broad applicability across several technological, industrial, and cultural contexts [69];

- TOE has proved its broad applicability across several technological industrial and cultural contexts [62, 69];

- TOE is the only framework that united both human and non-human factors by incorporating technology, organization, and environmental perspectives, and the literature offers strong empirical validation of the TOE framework [64, 70].

Thus, TOE was chosen as the underpinning theory for this study. In summary, the "Technological" aspect is concerned with technologies that are relevant to the organization including technologies available in the market as well as those being utilized by the organization [62]. The technology decision-making factors mostly stem from the DOI theory, and they allow the organization to assess new technologies and evaluate the added value and benefits that they can bring to the existing business [71]. The "Organizational" aspect refers to the inherent characteristics and resources of the organization [72]. The organizational decision-making factors allow the organization to "assess inwardly" and evaluate its strengths and weaknesses regarding the technologies of interest [71]. The "Environmental" aspect illustrates the arena or the setting in which the organization conducts its business [73]. The environmental decision-making factors provide the organization with a lens into the organization's business ecosystem and understand the opportunities as well as challenges in the external environment surrounding the business [71].

## 3. Methodology

A systematic literature review (SLR) was conducted to identify the TOE decision-making factors that influence the adoption of Construction 4.0 technologies in the construction industry. SLR is a common and effective technique for investigating existing research and extracting knowledge on a targeted topic [74, 75]. The technique has extensively been used in construction management research, particularly for developing decision-making methods [76–78] and determining decision-making factors [54, 79, 80].

Since the outcome of SLR is dependent on the selected sample of studies, it is important to use "an objective and reproducible search system" [81, 82]. As such, this study utilized the Web of Science (WOS) database to extract the related studies as its one of the most comprehensive databases for systematic reviews, meta-analysis, and bibliometric analysis [83, 84], and contains access to unique journal titles, particularly in the fields of natural sciences and engineering [85]. A query-based search was performed to search the title, abstracts, and keywords of WOS publications using the keywords shown in **Figure 1**.

The review process for extracting the decision-making factors and possible measures is illustrated in **Figure 2**. Studies that passed the title/abstract scan were reviewed for two aspects: (1) to determine if they were construction-related (i.e., the literature, surveys, case studies, and/or interviews were from the construction industry), and (2) if the technology was unique and relevant to Construction 4.0. This resulted in 22 publications from which the TOE decision-making factors were extracted. As for studies that had TOE decision-making factors and measures

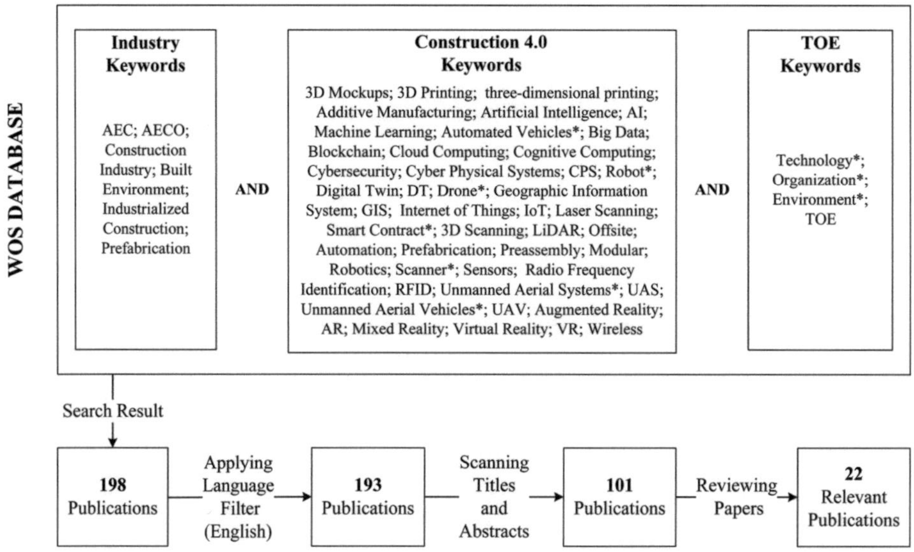


**Figure 1.**
*The WOS query-based search (* indicates an asterisk used for search purposes).*

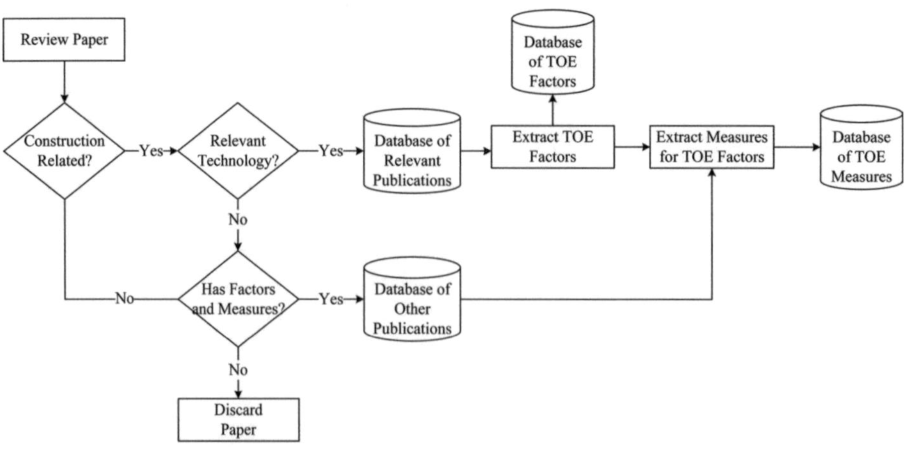


**Figure 2.**
*The review process for publications.*

| Database | Publications |
|---|---|
| Relevant publications | Aghimien et al. [86]; Attencia and Mattos [87]; Badi et al. [88]; Besklubova et al. [89]; Cai et al. [90]; Chaurasia and Verma [91]; Dashti and Viljevac-Vasquez [92]; Gan et al. [93]; Jadhav [94]; Katebi et al. [95]; Li et al. [96]; Lu and Deng [97]; Mabad et al. [64]; Muylle [98]; Na et al. [99]; Pan and Pan [100, 101]; Ram et al. [71]; Umar [102]; Viljakainen [66]; Wang et al. [103]; Wu et al. [104]; Yuan et al. [105] |
| Other publications (construction exclusive) | Chen et al. [106]; Jadhav [94]; Juan et al. [107]; Lee and Yu [108]; Li et al. [109]; Ma et al. [110]; Park et al. [111]; Tran et al. [112, 113] |
| Other publications (not construction exclusive) | Arnold et al. [114]; Bakici et al. [69]; Chandra and Kumar [115]; Gangwar et al. [63]; Ghaleb et al. [116]; Iranmanesh et al. [117]; Malak [118]; Tsai and Yeh [119]; Wong et al. [70]; Zhang et al. [120] |

**Table 2.**
*Publications in the above databases.*

but were not construction-related or did not analyze a relevant technology, they were added to a database that was scanned to only extract suggested measures that can be used to evaluate the factors. The database resulted in 19 publications. All publications used are presented in **Table 2**.

The following is a description of the review process illustrated in **Figure 2**. The study conducted by Pan and Pan [100] for instance used TOE to investigate the use of robotics in the Chinese construction industry. Since the paper covers a Construction 4.0 technology and relates to the construction industry, it was added to "relevant publications". On the other hand, the study conducted by Ma et al. [110] utilized TOE to investigate social media use in the Chinese construction industry. Since this study was construction related but did not investigate a construction 4.0 technology, it was added to "other publications" (construction related). Similarly, Bakici et al. [69] and Iranmanesh et al. [117] investigated big data adoption in France and Malaysia respectively, but both studies surveyed experts from inside and outside the construction industry. Thus, both studies were added to "other publications" (not construction related). This database of "other publications" was used to support the development of measures for the various TOE factors. Since TOE construction-related research is scarce, a review of the measures utilized in other studies provided additional resources to formulate construction-related measures to evaluate the TOE factors under study.

To further understand and detect research trends among the decision-making factors, three heatmaps were created to visualize the distribution of the factors by type of investigation (i.e., whether the factor was mentioned directly or indirectly), by technology (i.e., the technology that the publication targeted), and by year (i.e., the year of publication). The frequency of occurrence of the factors across the three distributions serves as the database for the heatmaps, as utilizing frequency is another commonly used approach to offer knowledge and detect trends in SLR-based construction management studies [18, 121, 122].

## 4. Results and analysis

### 4.1 Review of relevant publications

Based on the SLR and as depicted in **Figure 3**, Blockchain was the most investigated technology with 4 studies, followed by robotics, 3D printing, precast, and

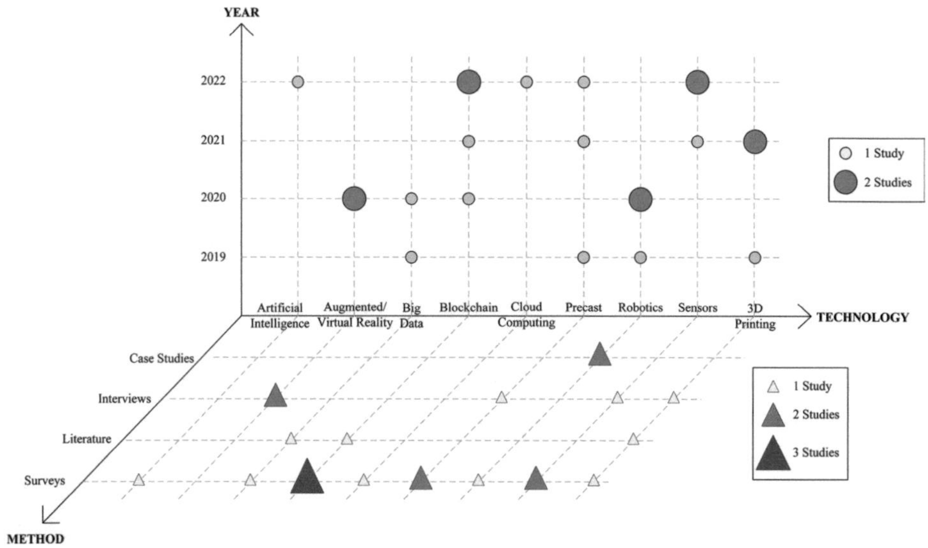


**Figure 3.**
*Profile of the 22 relevant publications.*

sensors with 3 studies each, then Big Data and Augmented/Virtual Reality with 2 studies each, and finally artificial intelligence and cloud computing with 1 study each. The earliest publication on TOE with Construction 4.0 technologies was in 2019 where four studies utilized TOE to evaluate the adoption of Robotics, 3D printing, big data, and precast.

### *4.1.1 Artificial intelligence*

The study by Na et al. [99] focused on the adoption and acceptance of AI-based technology in South Korean construction firms using a TOE-TAM model. Structural equation modeling (SEM) applied to survey data from 241 respondents showed that technological factors such as suitability, compatibility, and relative advantage had a positive influence on the adoption of AI-based technologies and the ease of use within the organization. However, environmental factors like social influence and competition did have any effect, which the study attributed to organizations' "conservatism" as they slowly adopt and test the technology. As for organizational factors like culture and structure, they had a positive impact on end-users' ease of use, but a negative one on the perceived usefulness of AI-based technology.

### *4.1.2 Augmented/virtual reality*

Two studies investigated the adoption of augmented reality (AR) and virtual reality (VR). Dashti and Viljevac-Vasquez [92] interviewed 13 construction professionals in Sweden and concluded that the lack of knowledge about the benefits, a limited number of vendors, insufficient knowledge about the interactions of AR/VR with other technologies, a lack of management expertise, financial constraints, high-risk investments, a lack of encouragement from owners, and the terms of contracts are significant TOE factors affecting adoption. Viljakainen [66] also conducted interviews with professionals in Finland using a "Who, What, Where, How many, How much" approach. Results showed that technological factors such as limited features and capability and compatibility concerns can restrict AR usage, organizational factors such as strategic long-term planning, leadership support, commitment, and resources are critical for the success of AR, and environmental factors in terms of environment, competition, reputation, and striving for innovation can help promote AR. The study further highlighted that a "forced trigger" event like the COVID-19 pandemic can push reluctant companies to adopt AR in their operations [66].

#### *4.1.3 Big data*

Two studies were conducted to understand the factors affecting the adoption of Big Data in the construction industry. Ram et al. [71] synthesized existing literature to develop a conceptual TOE model that is positively associated with Big Data adoption in the industry. The model highlighted the importance of integrating Big Data with existing organization technologies like BIM and the relative advantage of utilizing Big Data in reaping gains including cost savings, speed, efficiencies, and informed decision-making. A second study by Chaurasia and Verma [91] gathered data from 365 Indian AEC firms and proposed a TOE-PSVAM model to understand the factors affecting Big Data adoption in construction firms as well as service firms. The results showed that firm size was significant for construction firms, readiness and top management support were significant for service firms, while data quality, complexity, and competitive pressure were significant for both construction and service firms [91].

#### *4.1.4 Blockchain*

Two studies utilized TOE to investigate the adoption of Blockchain among Chinese construction organizations. Using a TOE-TAM based study, the empirical results conducted by Wang et al. [103] on 256 survey responses showed that relative advantage, compatibility, competitive pressure, technological maturity, organizational readiness, and policy can impact the adoption of Blockchain in China. Competitive pressure had the greatest positive impact on adoption while organization readiness had a negative impact. The authors attributed the results to the fundamental changes and disruptions that Blockchain could bring to organizations and the traditional ways of conducting business [103]. Similar results were obtained by Li et al. [96] who developed a conceptual TOE model to analyze the determinants of Blockchain adoption in construction using partial least squares (PLM) SEM and fuzzy-set qualitative comparative analysis via data gathered from 244 respondents. Results added firm size and top management support to factors that can significantly influence blockchain adoption in China, and highlighted that further investigation is needed into complexity, trialability, and pressure from training partners [96]. In the UK, Badi et al. [88] identified and investigated TOE factors that influence the adoption of smart contracts through a survey on 104 professionals. Results of a regression model showed top management support as an organizational facilitator that significantly facilitates smart contracts, competitive pressure, and supply chain pressure as two environmental aspects that significantly facilitate smart contracts, and observability as a technology aspect that significantly limits smart contracts. The study also explained that the relative immaturity of smart contracts may have contributed to all technological aspects being non-significant, notably relative advantage for the lack of empirical benefits, and compatibility due to the nature of current construction project contracts [88]. The fourth Blockchain study conducted by Wu et al. [104] took a different approach as it utilized TOE to summarize challenges facing blockchain adoption. The study highlighted that success can depend on several factors such as scalability, security, compatibility, training, contractual collaborations, consensus on data sharing, and industry standards [104].

#### *4.1.5 Cloud computing*

Aghimien et al. [86] aimed to identify the determinants for using cloud computing and predict its usage in South African construction organizations. Data from 154 experts were analyzed using SEM and regression models, revealing six significant factors including three technology factors related to cost-effectiveness, availability, and compatibility, and three environmental factors related to client demand, competitor pressure, and trust in vendors. However, no organizational factors were found significant due to the high awareness of the technology and most organizations being either early or laggard adopters in at least one aspect of the technology [86].

#### *4.1.6 Precast*

The adoption of prefabricated building technologies is influenced by various factors. Gan et al. [93] used fuzzy cognitive maps to identify critical factors through in-depth interviews with 39 experts representing six key stakeholder groups. Three factors in specific—cost, market demand, and policies and regulations—were perceived as critical by all stakeholders. The study also provided practical suggestions to promote prefabricated building technologies including establishing an information exchange platform, issuing mandatory policies and regulations by the government, and simulating the market demand [93]. Yuan et al. [105] adopted a TOE-TAM model via a survey of 234 professionals in China and found that relative advantage, corporate social responsibility, and market demand are significantly positively related to increasing the perceived usefulness of the technology, while regulatory support and trading partner support can decrease the complexity of using it. Results also showed that compatibility, organizational readiness, top management support, and competitive pressure did not impact the ease of use or perceived usefulness of the technology [105]. Katebi et al. [95] also used a TOE-TAM model to quantitatively investigate the factors influencing the adoption of precast concrete components (PCC) in Iran. They found that two environmental factors were critical: competitive pressure where the trend to adopt PCC will accelerate once companies see their competitors succeeding and reaping benefits and government provides support through effective policies, regulations, and incentives [95].

#### *4.1.7 Robotics*

Two studies conducted by Pan and Pan [100, 101] identified key factors affecting adoption such as relative advantage in terms of performance metrics like quality and productivity, top management support to strategize and invest, organizational readiness through financial resources and human talent, competitive pressure, and market demand. Their 2020 study further highlighted the importance of organizational factors such as top management support and readiness in the early stages of adoption. Meanwhile, technological and environmental factors such as compatibility and collaboration with trade partners, become more influential at later stages [100]. Another study by Cai et al. [90] provided 11 influential TOE factors for the successful implementation of construction automation and robotics, including interdisciplinary cooperation and continuous feedback, communication among internal teams and external stakeholders, and strategy development to expand the use of robots across the organization. The study also noted that the increase in market demand for robots can attract technology providers to further develop use cases and in turn motivate the industry to increase adoption rates [90].

#### *4.1.8 Wireless and sensing*

Three studies used TOE to investigate the adoption of Radio Frequency Identification (RFID), intelligence surveillance systems, and intelligent asset management systems. The first study by Mabad et al. [64] surveyed 297 Information Technology (IT) staff in Australian construction firms to evaluate factors affecting RFID investment decisions using SME. The study found that relative advantage, compatibility, cost, firm size, top management support, government regulations, external support, and anticipated benefits are significant factors affecting RFID adoption. The study further derived practical implications and guidelines designed to help construction organizations adopt RFID like evaluating the compatibility of the organization's IS infrastructure, promoting RFID and encouraging professionals to attend seminars, developing budgetary projections to address cost-effectiveness, procuring external consultancy for security concerns and facilitating trust, and identifying champions to lead and monitor RFID application and functionalities [64]. The second article by Lu and Deng [97] distributed questionnaires to 220 professionals in China to develop an acceptance model for intelligent surveillance systems in construction using TAM and TOE. The study found that the relevance of technology to job tasks, availability of training, availability of vendors and technical support, cost savings, government actions and incentives, technological support from vendors and IT, and privacy concerns are important factors affecting the acceptance of intelligent surveillance in the construction industry. Moreover, the study highlighted that such factors can help construction industry practitioners have a clearer understanding of the essential elements that affect the implementation of intelligent surveillance systems and guide organizations, governments, and technology developers to formulate strategies to promote the adoption of intelligent surveillance systems more effectively [97]. As for the third article, Attencia and Mattos [87] conducted interviews with 12 subject matter experts working on four construction projects within the energy infrastructure in Brazil to understand the factors affecting the adoption of intelligence asset management systems including tracking, monitoring, pointing, and positioning systems. Results revealed that technological factors with the strongest evidence include benefits for decision-making, risk analysis, and information management. Among the organizational factors, the strongest evidence pertained to attitudes towards innovation and creativity, organizational size, and the ability to implement and optimize technology, as well as integration into existing processes. Additionally, the most evident environmental factor was the support provided by technology providers during the asset management phase [87].

#### *4.1.9 3D printing*

The TOE factors influencing the adoption of 3D printing were evaluated using surveys, interviews, and literature reviews. The first study by Muylle [98] conducted in-depth interviews with 10 construction firms and labs in the Netherlands and Belgium, identifying 3D printing's ability to integrate within current projects, durability, flexibility, and efficiency as major technological factors, management support, and resource availability as organizational factors, and market trends and government regulations and subsidies as environmental factors influencing adoption. Another investigation by Besklubova et al. [89] surveyed 82 global researchers and scholars to identify the factors that affect the adoption of 3D printing in construction. SEM showed that the top significant factors were compatibility with existing processes, ability to print materials that integrate with projects, complexity in operating and maintaining printers, and the industry's need to simplify tasks and reduce transportation services and involved suppliers [89]. Moreover, Umar [102] conducted a systematic literature review of 137 articles published between 2000 and 2019 on 3D printing in construction, which highlighted technology-related factors such as compatibility and integration with CAD software and IT hardware, organizational factors such as readiness, management support, commitment, training, and IT infrastructure, and environmental factors such as competitive pressure, expectations from the market tendency, business partners, and government support. The study also highlighted the importance of financial resources to cover the costs related to machines, labor, and material [102].

## 4.2 Decision-making factors

A total of 23 decision-making factors were extracted from the 22 TOE-relevant studies. The factors are listed and defined in **Table 3**. Each factor is also presented with a list of potential measures compiled comprehensively from the publications shown in **Table 2**.

Moreover, the heatmaps showing the distribution of the factors are presented in **Figure 4**. The first heatmap to the left shows the distribution by type of investigation—i.e., whether the factor was investigated directly or indirectly in

| | Factor | Definition | Potential measures |
|---|---|---|---|
| Technology | Compatibility | The degree to which the technology is "consistent with the existing values, experiences, and needs of the company" [123]. | • Compatibility with culture<br>• Compatibility with mission and vision<br>• Compatibility with existing workflows<br>• Compatibility with existing capabilities |
| | Relative advantage | The degree that technology "is seen as better than the idea, program, or product it is replacing company" [123]. | • Better financial transactions and profit<br>• Better organizational networking advantage<br>• Better organizational performance<br>• Better organizational capabilities<br>• Better individual capabilities<br>• Better project performance<br>• Better data management and security |

| | Factor | Definition | Potential measures |
|---|---|---|---|
| | Complexity | The degree to which it "is perceived as relatively difficult to understand or use" [123]. | • Complexity of technology implementation including hardware and software<br>• Complexity of technology integration into existing workflows and capabilities<br>• Complexity of technology operation |
| | Industry standards | Set of policies, regulations, or best practices presenting a structured adoption and implementation plan for a technology [124]. | • Availability of in-house standards<br>• Access to external standards<br>• Feasibility of developing standards if needed |
| | Trialability | The extent to which the technology "can be tried on a small scale before adoption, or experimented with on a limited basis company" [123]. | • Scale of trialability<br>• Investment for piloting and/ or testing<br>• Level of risk and scalability<br>• Requirement for collaboration |
| | Observability | The extent to which the results of using the technology can provide tangible results that can be visible to other companies [123]. | • Technology market share<br>• Availability of a community of practice<br>• Frequency of updates or version releases<br>• Industry recommendations<br>• Tangible proven benefits |
| | Security and privacy | The measures and practices available to control access and protect information through authentication, authorization, accountability, data protection, disaster recovery, sharing, and the privacy of users [63]. | • Robust against threats<br>• Robust against risks<br>• Robust against vulnerability |
| Organization | Human resources | The demographic variables and capabilities of the people within the organization [119, 125]. | • Level of commitment<br>• Level of technical skills<br>• Level of digital literacy<br>• Percentage of turnover |
| | Financial resources | The monetary assets and capital available for investments and operations [126, 127]. | • Availability of funds to invest in hardware and software<br>• Availability of funds to invest and continuously support training<br>• Availability of funds for systems and infrastructure updates<br>• Availability of funds for maintenance and operation cost<br>• Availability of funds for required skills if needed |

| Factor | Definition | Potential measures |
|---|---|---|
| Change culture | The shared values, beliefs, norms, and behaviors that shape the organization's collective identity and guide the actions and interactions of its people [128]. | • Vision and policies for innovation and continuous improvement<br>• Focus on research, development, and technology watch<br>• Models for information sharing and funding<br>• Momentum for digitization and modernization |
| Top management support | Active endorsement, involvement, and commitment of leadership in change efforts [63, 98, 125]. | • Awareness and encouragement of technology<br>• Level of involvement and visibility into the process<br>• Willingness to allocate resources<br>• Availability of change management platforms |
| Information systems | The formal, sociotechnical, organizational system designed to collect, process, store, distribute, and interpret information in an organization [129]. | • Level of training readiness<br>• Level of hardware readiness<br>• Level of software readiness<br>• Level of integration readiness<br>• Level of workflow readiness<br>• Availability of data standards<br>• Availability of protocol for unexpected events (risks, failures, conflicts) |
| Scale of operations | The organization's characteristics like size, age (i.e. legacy or not), origin, location, and the number of customers and projects [115, 127, 130]. | • Scalability across the organization<br>• Applicability across organization<br>• Relevancy across organization |
| Nature of projects | The inherent characteristics and attributes of the projects that the organization works on [119]. | • Scalability across project characteristics (locations, size, types)<br>• Applicability across project complexities |
| Nature of workflows | The inherent characteristics and requirements of tasks that the organization will use the technology in [131]. | • Relevancy across project lifecycles or through project phases |
| Availability of training | The accessibility and provision of training opportunities to embed or enhance the required skills and knowledge [63, 132]. | • Availability of in-house training programs<br>• Access to external training programs<br>• Need and availability of third-party involvement if needed<br>• Frequency of training<br>• Modularity and delivery of training<br>• Requirements for training |

| | Factor | Definition | Potential measures |
|---|---|---|---|
| | Type of contracts | The type of contractual arrangements that the company utilizes with clients can enable or inhibit technology [133]. | • Applicability across project delivery systems<br>• Applicability across project contracts |
| Environment | Authorities and government influence | Role of governmental agencies and authorities in influencing the organization to adopt [91]. | • Availability of incentives<br>• Availability of subsidies<br>• Availability of tangible support<br>• Availability of intangible support<br>• Availability of mandate<br>• Comprehensiveness of regulations and legislation<br>• Extent of penalties |
| | Competitive pressure | The pressure resulting from the practices of competitors and the need to outperform competition and achieve superior performance in the marketplace [30]. | • Ability to improve performance<br>• Ability to grow in the market and expand in new ones<br>• Ability to customize services and offer new ones<br>• Ability to secure technology leads or early innovators<br>• Ability to grow customer base and clients<br>• Ability to recruit and retain talent<br>• Ability to enhance data-driven workflows |
| | Push from supply chain players, stakeholders, and trade partners | Pressure exerted by external players to push the organization to adopt [106, 127]. | • Extent of leverage gained from adoption<br>• Timing of investment<br>• Dependency of adoption on partners and supply chain<br>• Readiness of partners and supply chain |
| | Market demand | Capabilities to solve or assist the organization in addressing industry needs [13]. | • Ability to address legacy challenges<br>• Ability to react to current trends<br>• Ability to pull towards future visions |
| | Vendor access | Access to solution and technology providers and the services they provide [64, 134]. | • Requirement for customer support and vendor service<br>• Availability of customer support and vendor service<br>• Access to customer support and vendor service<br>• Type of customer support and vendor service |

| | Factor | Definition | Potential measures |
|---|---|---|---|
| | Social responsibility | Commitment to act ethically, contribute positively to society, and promote sustainable practices [19]. | • Incentive or requirement to reduce carbon footprint<br>• Incentive or requirement to lower emissions<br>• Incentive or requirement to adopt green practices<br>• Implementation of construction waste management<br>• Need to empower society |

**Table 3.**
*Decision-making factors and potential measures.*

| | | Total Investigations (n=22) | Direct Investigation | Indirect Invetsigation | Cloud Computing (n=1) | Artificial Intelligence (n=1) | Big Data (n=2) | Augmented/Virtual Reality (n=2) | Precast (n=3) | Wireless and Sensing (n=3) | Robotics (n=3) | 3D Printing (n=3) | Blockchain (n=4) | 2019 (n=4) | 2020 (n=6) | 2021 (n=5) | 2022 (n=7) |
|---|---|---|---|---|---|---|---|---|---|---|---|---|---|---|---|---|---|
| Technology | Compatibility | **18** | 17 | 1 | | 1 | 2 | 1 | 3 | 2 | 2 | 3 | 4 | 4 | 4 | 5 | 5 |
| | Relative Advantage | **17** | 15 | 2 | 1 | 1 | 1 | 1 | 2 | 3 | 2 | 3 | 3 | 3 | 3 | 4 | 7 |
| | Complexity | **14** | 13 | 1 | | 1 | 1 | 1 | 2 | 2 | 1 | 2 | 4 | 1 | 4 | 4 | 5 |
| | Industry Standards | **10** | 3 | 7 | 1 | | 2 | 1 | 1 | | 1 | 2 | 2 | 4 | 2 | 2 | 2 |
| | Triability | **8** | 7 | 1 | | | | 2 | | | 2 | 2 | 2 | 1 | 5 | 1 | 1 |
| | Observability | **8** | 3 | 5 | 1 | | | 2 | 1 | 1 | | | 3 | 1 | 3 | 2 | 2 |
| | Security and Privacy | **8** | 4 | 4 | 1 | | 1 | | | 2 | | | 4 | | 2 | 2 | 4 |
| Organization | Human Resources | **20** | 11 | 9 | 1 | 1 | 1 | 2 | 3 | 3 | 3 | 3 | 3 | 3 | 6 | 5 | 6 |
| | Financial Resources | **18** | 13 | 5 | 1 | 1 | | 2 | 3 | 3 | 2 | 3 | 3 | 2 | 4 | 5 | 7 |
| | Change Culture | **17** | 5 | 12 | 1 | | 1 | 2 | 3 | 2 | 3 | 3 | 2 | 3 | 5 | 5 | 4 |
| | Top Management Support | **17** | 13 | 4 | 1 | 1 | 1 | 1 | 1 | 3 | 3 | 2 | 4 | 2 | 5 | 4 | 6 |
| | Information Systems | **14** | 6 | 8 | 1 | 1 | 1 | 1 | | 3 | 2 | 2 | 3 | 1 | 5 | 3 | 5 |
| | Scale of Operations | **12** | 12 | | 1 | 1 | 1 | 2 | | 2 | 3 | 1 | 1 | 2 | 5 | 1 | 4 |
| | Nature of Projects | **9** | 2 | 7 | | 1 | 1 | 2 | 2 | | 1 | 1 | 1 | 2 | 3 | 2 | 2 |
| | Nature of Tasks | **8** | 3 | 5 | | 1 | 1 | 1 | 2 | 1 | 1 | 1 | | 2 | 2 | 1 | 3 |
| | Availability of Training | **7** | 2 | 5 | | | | 1 | 1 | 1 | 1 | 1 | 2 | | 2 | 3 | 2 |
| | Type of Contracts | **6** | 1 | 5 | | | 1 | 2 | 1 | | | | 2 | 2 | 3 | 1 | |
| Environment | Government Incentives | **19** | 18 | 1 | 1 | 1 | 1 | 1 | 3 | 3 | 2 | 3 | 4 | 3 | 4 | 5 | 7 |
| | Competitive Pressure | **18** | 16 | 2 | 1 | 1 | 1 | 2 | 2 | 1 | 3 | 3 | 4 | 2 | 6 | 4 | 6 |
| | Supply Chain/Stakeholders | **16** | 11 | 5 | 1 | 1 | 1 | 2 | 2 | 2 | 1 | 2 | 4 | 2 | 4 | 5 | 5 |
| | Market Demand | **15** | 11 | 4 | | 1 | 2 | 2 | 2 | 1 | 3 | 3 | 1 | 4 | 5 | 4 | 2 |
| | Vendors Access | **13** | 8 | 5 | 1 | 1 | 1 | 2 | 2 | 3 | 3 | | | 3 | 4 | 2 | 4 |
| | Social Responsibility | **7** | 2 | 5 | | | 1 | | 1 | | 1 | 3 | 1 | 2 | 1 | 3 | 1 |

**Figure 4.**
*Distribution of TOE decision-making factors ("n" represents the total number of papers for the investigated technology or year of publication).*

the reviewed publication. The darker the color, the higher the frequency of the investigation type for the factor. The second heatmap in the middle shows the distribution by technology. The darker the color, the higher the frequency of occurrence of the factor in the papers that targeted that technology. The third heatmap to the right shows the distribution by year of publication. The darker the color, the higher the frequency of occurrence of the factor in studies published in that year. The objective of the heatmaps is to illustrate the research trends discussed in the next section of the chapter.

## 5. Discussion

### 5.1 Technology decision-making factors

Starting with technology-related factors, *relative advantage* was the only technology factor that was investigated at least once for every technology, followed by *complexity* and *compatibility* which were investigated for every technology except cloud computing. The three factors were almost always investigated directly in research and maintained consistent or increased investigations between 2019 and 2022. In a traditional industry like construction, the domination of these three factors is expected because organizations are more likely to experiment with or adopt technologies that provide the maximum benefits and meet organizational needs with minimum complications and changes needed to the business model and organization infrastructures [135]. Similarly, technologies that can be highly reliable and functional with low maintenance requirements will be more attractive to organizations than complex ones that may become a burden on the business [136].

Two of the technology factors—*Trialability* and *Observability*—have a motivation component to them compared to the other factors which affect their investigation. *Trialability* was mostly investigated directly as it deals with a specific feature of the technology that allows users to pilot it or experiment with it on a limited scale, thus making it a dichotomous factor that is either available or not [137, 138]. *Observability* deals mostly with the technology's reputation across the industry which explains it's the nature of its indirect investigation, and it is only evident in research that relates to technologies that have been around long enough for the industry to develop a perception of them [137]. *Industry standards* is another factor that received attention but was mostly investigated indirectly. This reflects on one of the industry's major issues—i.e. lack of standardization and calls for a more direct investigation into the factor [11, 139].

While *security and privacy* was only investigated for four technologies, it can be noticed that the factor had a relative increase over time and was investigated in all Blockchain studies. This factor is expected to gain even more momentum as more industry research and legal discussions are being tailored towards confidentiality, integrity, fraud, theft, risks when accessing common platforms, data ownership and governance, and security breaches [140–142]. This also becomes especially important with technologies that create, store, and share sensitive and private information like Blockchain which encompasses digital ledgers and financial transactions [143].

### 5.2 Organization decision-making factors

As for organization-related factors, *human resources* and *top management support* were investigated at least once for every technology and maintained consistent or increased investigations between 2019 and 2022. *Financial resources* was also a heavily investigated factor across all technologies except Big Data and was investigated in every study published in 2021 and 2022. The domination of these three factors is no surprise as organizational determinants like budgets, high cost of implementation, preference for short-term profits over long-term ROIs, labor shortage, scarcity of skills and required talents, hesitancy to adopt, and need for management support and commitment remain major barriers facing technology adoption and slowing down the digital transformation of the fourth industrial revolution in construction [5, 144–146]. Moreover, organizations that strengthen human resources and financial investments can improve their technology's output capacity and technological achievements [37]. In addition to the three discussed factors, the trend for *information resources* has also been increasing. This trend is expected to continue and gain more momentum due to the vital role information systems play in the organization's response to internal and external changes [125]. Moreover, information systems enable the organization to effectively manage and utilize the information generated by the new technology and integrate it with the existing information from people, machinery, equipment, tools, materials, and projects [125, 147].

Another notable notice is *change culture* being a common factor that was extensively investigated. Several studies regarding innovation have highlighted the importance of organizational culture and the role it plays in successfully selecting and implementing technologies; such a culture should promote openness, adaptability, and receptiveness to change, foster a supportive and innovative environment, and create a culture that embraces change within the organization by incentivizing and supporting new technology efforts, building multidisciplinary teams, celebrating progress, and addressing resistance and concerns [148–150]. Innovation should also be fostered in the organization's core beliefs, behaviors, and practices such as active innovation champions, innovation training, technology watch, and knowledge management [150, 151].

While the focus on the *availability of training* has been low, it remains an important factor for the construction industry because of its low level of digitization and high tendency to resist change [13]. More investigations should target this since training can instruct employees, reduce anxiety and stress, provide motivation and a better understanding of benefits, reduce ambiguity, improve the perceived ease of use and usefulness, and open the door for improvements [63, 132]. As for *scale of operations*, *nature of projects*, *nature of workflows*, and *type of contracts*, these four factors are more customized to the construction industry's unique nature and business-as-usual ways. While the factors appear occasionally in research, the low investigation of *type of contracts* reflects on the continued domination of traditional project delivery methods in the construction industry and the rising need to adopt technology and digitize processes across all types of contracts used in the organizations' projects [152, 153].

### 5.3 Environment decision-making factors

Regarding environment-related factors, *authorities and government influence*, *competitive pressure*, and *push from external partners* were investigated at least once for every technology, almost always investigated directly, and maintained consistent or increased investigations between 2019 and 2022. The construction industry is generally considered to be competitive as firms compete over contracts and projects. As such, the pressure resulting from the practices of competitors and the need to gain competitive advantage can drive firms to change their business-as-usual mindset and innovate and adopt technologies that can "alter the rules of the competition and change the competitive playing field" [100, 106, 154]. At the same time, despite the competitive nature, most projects require collaborations between multiple firms with different areas of expertise, which in turn creates an incentive to adopt technology—pressure from owners, push from clients, incentives by consultants, pressure from trading partners across the supply chain, and project stakeholders adopting a certain technology can all push organizations to adopt [106, 127]. As for the government's roles, governmental agencies and authorities can affect the diffusion of technologies by passing rules, policies, and regulations, as well as providing incentives and opportunities to create a perception of the values associated with the technology [91, 106].

A drop in the investigation of *market demand* can also be witnessed—i.e., the factor that reflects the technologies' capabilities to solve or assist the industry in tackling major hurdles such as labor shortages, project overruns, and low productivity. In contrast, an increase is witnessed in the investigation of *vendor access*—i.e., the factor that reflects access to technology providers and the services that they offer. The trends of the two factors reflect the shift in the industry's perception regarding technology, where it is no longer "nice to have" but rather a "must" and a "necessity" for success [155]. Thus, while market demand can still accelerate technology adoption, it becomes less of a primary driver because the industry acknowledges the need for digitization [5, 156]. This also shifts the focus towards technology and solution providers who facilitate and expedite the adoption of technologies in organizations and provide them with licenses, partnering arrangements, software updates, and track records to prove the value of their technology [64, 134].

On another note, *social responsibility* was the only environment-related factor that was under-researched and mostly investigated indirectly. However, construction organizations and construction projects serve diverse communities and thus, may "either feel a voluntary obligation to a society based on social expectations, norms, and codes of conduct", or be "placed in situations where they cannot ignore the social community due to rising public pressures" and growing need for sustainable and green construction [127, 157]. Moreover, more research is providing evidence of digitalization's ability to enable better eco-friendly performance [158], by investigating how investment behavior is affected by an organization's social performance and responsibilities [159], and bringing organizations closer to their communities [19, 160]. As such, the *social responsibility* factor remains relevant and requires increased attention in research.

## 6. TOE factors and the path towards Construction 5.0

As industries switch from the technology-driven Industry 4.0 transformation to a value-driven Industry 5.0 transformation, organizations need to repurpose or readjust their journey to align with the core values of Industry 5.0 [161]. The three core values of Industry 5.0 include a *human-centric approach* that prioritizes humans and the use technology to support people, *sustainability* that respects planetary boundaries to meet today's needs without compromising those of future generations, and *resilience* achieved through the development of a higher degree of robustness [162]. These core values are interrelated with the concept of Society 5.0, which seeks to create a human-centric, knowledge-intensive, and data-driven society that seamlessly integrate the cyberspace with physical space while balancing economic development with resolving societal and environmental issues [162, 163]. Consequently, the shared challenges and opportunities of Industry 5.0 and Society 5.0 will manifest in different aspects, including human-cyber physical systems, human digital twin, greentelligent manufacturing, human-robot collaboration, as well as future jobs and future workers [164].

Thus, the technological, organizational, and environmental decision-making factors discussed in this chapter will remain pivotal for the construction industry as it transitions to Industry 5.0, or Construction 5.0. Decision-making in Construction 5.0

will aim to integrate human-centric, resilient, and sustainable approaches into existing industry processes including design, construction, delivery, and supply chain [165]. Accordingly, the 5.0 transformation will continue to be influenced by culture, leadership, collaboration, cooperation, workers expertise, technology infrastructure, as well the organizational context in terms of size, core business, and project types [16].

Moreover, the Industry 5.0 core values focus on the use of advanced technology to empower—rather than replace—people across industries [162]. As such, Construction 5.0 will emphasize the importance of human involvement and the value of human input by "prioritizing human needs and interests as the foundation of the construction process", and "ensuring that technological advancements align with human wellbeing and sustainability goals" [166]. A notable example is the proper use of the TOE factors discussed in this chapter to strengthen the adoption of robotics in the Construction 5.0 era and increase safety, efficiency, and quality resulting from the "intuitive interactions between robots and humans within the complex construction environments" [24].

## 7. Conclusion

This research aimed to develop and provide a comprehensive list of decision-making factors for technology adoption in the construction industry. The Technology-Organization-Environment (TOE) framework was utilized to perform a systematic literature review and examine the existing work on the adoption of Construction 4.0 technologies. A total of 22 TOE-relevant studies were retrieved from the Web of Science database to extract the decision-making factors, all published between 2019 and 2022. The reviewed papers used different quantitative and qualitative approaches to investigate the TOE factors affecting the adoption of nine Construction 4.0 technologies including artificial intelligence, augmented reality and virtual reality, big data, blockchain, cloud computing, precast, robotics, wireless and sensing technologies, and 3D printing.

The review of the studies resulted in a comprehensive list of 23 decision-making factors, alongside 97 potential measures for the factors extracted from the relevant publications and 19 other related studies. Of the 23 decision-making factors, seven were technology factors, 10 were organization factors, and six were environment factors. Compatibility, relative advantage, and complexity were the most evident technology factors which construction organizations considered when selecting a technology, as found in the literature synthesis. Additionally, trends depicted in the developed heatmaps showed that security and privacy was gaining more momentum. As for organization factors, human and financial resources were heavily investigated, and significant attention was given for change culture and top management support. It was also noticed that some factors were construction industry exclusive such as nature of projects and nature of workflows. Regarding environment factors, government incentives and competitive pressure were the most investigated factors, while social responsibility was the least investigated.

The study is twofold as of value for both researchers and practitioners. First, the comprehensive list of decision-making factors introduced in this chapter can be used to develop decision-making tools, methods, and/or frameworks regarding technology adoption in construction. Second, the revision provided in this chapter provides a centralized resource for decision-makers to pinpoint the existing work in understanding the existing work in the decision-making technology field. Third, the research trends discussed in this chapter can lay the foundation for future work and eliminate reduces as they highlight the factors that have been heavily investigated, the factors that are gaining momentum, and the factors that need more attention. The chapter also comes with certain limitations. The identified papers from the systematic literature review are English-only publications from one research database (i.e., Web of Science). Moreover, the scope of the chapter focused only on determining the decision-making factors without any attempts to evaluate, provide weights, compare, and quantify the factors, or quantitatively compare the impact of those factors on the decision-making process. This opens the door for further studies that can build on this work by conducting quantitative analysis that can evaluate the impact of the factors on the decision-making process in the construction industry.

## Author details

Makram Bou Hatoum[1*] and Hala Nassereddine[2]

1 Pyrovio, Ann Arbour, MI, USA

2 University of Kentucky, Lexington, KY, USA

*Address all correspondence to: bouhatoum@outlook.com

## References

[1] Bayraktaroğlu E, Genç H. Global Construction 2030: A Global Forecast for the Construction Industry to 2030. 2020. Available from: https://www.pwc.com.tr/en/hizmetlerimiz/altyapi-yatirimlari/yayinlar/pwc-global-construction-2030.html

[2] Soares R, Akhnoukh AK. Global construction 2030 market at top three nations. In: 10th International Conference on Construction in the 21st Century (CITC-10). Colombo, Sri-Lanka; 2018. pp. 134-142

[3] Kannimuthu M, Ekambaram P, Raphael B, Kuppuswamy A. Resource unconstrained and constrained project scheduling problems and practices in a multiproject environment. Advanced management in civil engineering projects. Advances in Civil Engineering. 2018:9579273

[4] Abbasi O, Noorzai E, Jafari KG, Golabchi M. Exploring the causes of delays in construction industry using a cause-and-effect diagram: Case study for Iran. Journal of Architectural Engineering. 2020;**26**(3):05020008

[5] Muñoz-La Rivera F, Mora-Serrano J, Valero I, Oñate E. Methodological-technological framework for Construction 4.0. Archives of Computational Methods in Engineering. 2021;**28**:689-711

[6] Bajjou MS, Chafi A. Exploring the critical waste factors affecting construction projects. Engineering, Construction and Architectural Management. 2022;**29**(6):2268-2299

[7] Jagannathan M, Delhi VSK. Litigation in construction contracts: Literature review. Journal of Legal Affairs and Dispute Resolution in Engineering and Construction. 2020;**12**(1):03119001

[8] Albalkhy W, Sweis R. Barriers to adopting lean construction in the construction industry: A literature review. International Journal of Lean Six Sigma. 2021;**12**(2):210-236

[9] Ramadan B, Nassereddine H, Taylor TRB, Goodrum P. Impact of technology use on workforce performance and information access in the construction industry. Frontiers in Built Environment. 2023;**9**:1079203. DOI: 10.3389/fbuil.2023.1079203

[10] Yap JBH, Goay PL, Woon YB, Skitmore M. Revisiting critical delay factors for construction: Analysing projects in Malaysia. Alexandria Engineering Journal. 2021;**60**(1):1717-1729

[11] Thunberg M, Rudberg M, Karrbom GT. Categorising on-site problems. Construction Innovation. 2017;**17**(1):90-111

[12] Ayodele OA, Chang-Richards A, González V. Factors affecting workforce turnover in the construction sector: A systematic review. Journal of Construction Engineering and Management. 2020;**146**(2):03119010

[13] Hatoum MB, Nassereddine H, Badurdeen F. Reengineering construction processes in the era of construction 4.0: A lean-based framework. In: Proc 29th Annual Conference of the International Group for Lean Construction (IGLC). Lima, Peru; 2021. pp. 403-412. Available from: http://www.iglc.net/papers/details/1854

[14] Oesterreich TD, Teuteberg F. Understanding the implications of

digitisation and automation in the context of Industry 4.0: A triangulation approach and elements of a research agenda for the construction industry. Computers in Industry. 2016;**83**:121-139

[15] Barbosa F, Woetzel J, Mischke J, Ribeirinho MJ, Sridhar M, Parsons M, et al. Reinventing Construction: A Route to Higher Productivity. McKinsey Global Institute; 2017. Available from: https://www.mckinsey.com/capabilities/operations/our-insights/reinventing-construction-through-a-productivity-revolution

[16] Costa S, Carvalho MS, Pimentel C, Duarte C. A systematic literature review and conceptual framework of construction industrialization. Journal of Construction Engineering and Management. 2023;**149**(2):03122013

[17] Nassereddine H, Bou Hatoum M, Musick S, Jazzar ME. Implications of digitization on a construction organization: A case study. In: Proceedings of the Creative Construction e-Conference 2022. Budapest, Hungary: Budapest University of Technology and Economics; 2022. pp. 71-79. Available from: http://hdl.handle.net/10890/31747

[18] Dou Y, Li T, Li L, Zhang Y, Li Z. Tracking the research on ten emerging digital technologies in the AECO industry. Journal of Construction Engineering and Management. 2023;**149**(3):03123003

[19] Hatoum MB, Nassereddine H, Musick S, El-Jazzar M. Investigation of PESTEL factors driving change in capital project organizations. Frontiers in Built Environment. 2023;**9**:1207564. DOI: 10.3389/fbuil.2023.1207564

[20] Chatterjee S, Chaudhuri R, Vrontis D, Giovando G. Digital workplace and organization performance: Moderating role of digital leadership capability. Journal of Innovation & Knowledge. 2023;**8**(1):100334

[21] Boton C, Rivest L, Ghnaya O, Chouchen M. What is at the root of Construction 4.0: A systematic review of the recent research effort. Archives of Computational Methods in Engineering. 2021;**28**:2331-2350. DOI: 10.1007/s11831-020-09457-7

[22] Forcael E, Ferrari I, Opazo-Vega A, Pulido-Arcas JA. Construction 4.0: A literature review. Sustainability. 2020;**12**(22):9755. Available from: https://www.mdpi.com/2071-1050/12/22/9755

[23] Schober KS, Hoff P, Nolling K. Digitization in the Construction Industry: Building Eruope's Road to "Construction 4.0.". Munich, Germany: Roland Berger GmbH; 2016. p. 16

[24] Marinelli M. From Industry 4.0 to Construction 5.0: Exploring the path towards human-robot collaboration in construction. Systems. 2023;**11**(3):152. Available from: https://www.mdpi.com/2079-8954/11/3/152

[25] Craveiro F, Duarte JP, Bartolo H, Bartolo PJ. Additive manufacturing as an enabling technology for digital construction: A perspective on construction 4.0. Automation in Construction. 2019;**103**:251-267

[26] El Jazzar M, Schranz C, Urban H, Nassereddine H. Integrating construction 4.0 technologies: A four-layer implementation plan. Frontiers in Built Environment. 2021;7:671408. DOI: 10.3389/fbuil.2021.671408

[27] Sawhney A, Riley M, Irizarry J, Pérez CT. A proposed framework for construction 4.0 based on a review

of literature. EPiC Series in Built Environment. 2020;**1**:301-309

[28] Hermann M, Pentek T, Otto B. Design principles for Industrie 4.0 scenarios. In: 2016 49th Hawaii International Conference on System Sciences (HICSS). Koloa, Hawaii; 2016. pp. 3928-3937

[29] Hossain MA, Nadeem A. Towards digitizing the construction industry: State of the art of construction 4.0. In: Proceedings of International Structural Engineering and Construction. Chicago, Illinois: ISEC Press; 2019. p. 13

[30] Hatoum MB, Nassereddine H. Proposing a house for lean construction 4.0. In: Lean Construction 40: Driving a Digital Revolution of Production Management in the AEC Industry. 1st ed. London, UK: Routledge; 2022. pp. 50-67. DOI: 10.1201/9781003150930-6

[31] Ammar A, Nassereddine H. Blueprint for construction 4.0 technologies: A bibliometric analysis. IOP Conference Series: Materials Science and Engineering. 2022;**1218**(1):012011

[32] Balasubramanian S, Shukla V, Islam N, Manghat S. Construction Industry 4.0 and sustainability: An enabling framework. IEEE Transactions on Engineering Management. 2021;**71**:1-19

[33] Dallasega P, Rauch E, Linder C. Industry 4.0 as an enabler of proximity for construction supply chains: A systematic literature review. Computers in Industry. 2018;**99**:205-225

[34] You Z, Feng L. Integration of Industry 4.0 related Technologies in Construction Industry: A framework of cyber-physical system. IEEE Access. 2020;**8**:122908-122922

[35] Statsenko L, Samaraweera A, Bakhshi J, Chileshe N. Construction 4.0 technologies and applications: A systematic literature review of trends and potential areas for development. Construction Innovation. 2023;**23**(5):961-993

[36] Sepasgozar SME, Khan AA, Smith K, Romero JG, Shen X, Shirowzhan S, et al. BIM and digital twin for developing convergence technologies as future of digital construction. Buildings. 2023;**13**(2):441. Available from: https://www.mdpi.com/2075-5309/13/2/441

[37] Tu W, Zhang L, Sun D, Mao W. Evaluating high-tech industries' technological innovation capability and spatial pattern evolution characteristics: Evidence from China. Journal of Innovation & Knowledge. 2023;**8**(1):100287

[38] Kanski L, Pizon J. The impact of selected components of industry 4.0 on project management. Journal of Innovation & Knowledge. 2023;**8**(1):100336

[39] Taherdoost H. A critical review of blockchain acceptance models—Blockchain technology adoption frameworks and applications. Computers. 2022;**11**(2):24. Available from: https://www.mdpi.com/2073-431X/11/2/24

[40] Hall DM, Whyte JK, Lessing J. Mirror-breaking strategies to enable digital manufacturing in Silicon Valley construction firms: A comparative case study. Construction Management and Economics. 2020;**38**(4):322-339

[41] Sacks R, Girolami M, Brilakis I. Building information modelling, artificial intelligence and construction tech. Developments in the Built Environment. 2020;**4**:100011

[42] Chowdhury T, Adafin J, Wilkinson S. Review of digital technologies to improve productivity of New Zealand construction industry. Journal of Information Technology in Construction (ITcon). 2019;**24**:569-587

[43] Dziadosz A, Aneta K. Review of selected methods of supporting decision-making process in the construction industry. Archives of Civil Engineering. 2016;**62**(1):111-126

[44] Kapliński O. Development and usefulness of planning techniques and decision-making foundations on the example of construction enterprises in Poland. Technology and Economic Development of Economy—Baltic Journal on Sustainability. 2008;**14**(4):492-502

[45] Taherdoost H. Importance of technology acceptance assessment for successful implementation and development of new technologies. Global Journal of Engineering Sciences. 2019;**1**(3)

[46] Ali O, Murray PA, Muhammed S, Dwivedi YK, Rashiti S. Evaluating organizational level IT innovation adoption factors among global firms. Journal of Innovation & Knowledge. 2022;**7**(3):100213

[47] Salahshour Rad M, Nilashi M, Mohamed DH. Information technology adoption: A review of the literature and classification. Universal Access in the Information Society. 2018;**17**(2):361-390

[48] Chiu CN, Yang CL. Competitive advantage and simultaneous mutual influences between information technology adoption and service innovation: Moderating effects of environmental factors. Structural Change and Economic Dynamics. 2019;**49**:192-205

[49] Peltier JW, Zhao Y, Schibrowsky JA. Technology adoption by small businesses: An exploratory study of the interrelationships of owner and environmental factors. International Small Business Journal. 2012;**30**(4):406-431

[50] Dekleva S. Justfying investments in IT. Journal of Information Technology Management. 2005;**16**(3):1-8

[51] Love PED, Matthews J. The 'how' of benefits management for digital technology: From engineering to asset management. Automation in Construction. 2019;**107**:102930

[52] Li Y, Wang Y, Wang L, Xie J. Investigating the effects of stakeholder collaboration strategies on risk prevention performance in a digital innovation ecosystem. Industrial Management & Data Systems. 2022;**122**(9):2045-2071

[53] Murphy J, Slater M, Holder J. Reviewed work: Environmental assessment—The regulation of decision making by HolderJane. Journal of Environmental Assessment Policy and Management. 2006;**8**(1):103-105

[54] Nabi MA, El-adaway IH. Modular construction: Determining decision-making factors and future research needs. Journal of Management in Engineering. 2020;**36**(6):04020085

[55] Straub ET. Understanding technology adoption: Theory and future directions for informal learning. Review of Educational Research. 2009;**79**(2):625-649

[56] Davis FD. Perceived usefulness, perceived ease of use, and user acceptance of information technology. MIS Quarterly. 1989;**13**(3):319-340

[57] Ajzen I. The theory of planned behavior. Organizational Behavior and Human Decision Processes. 1991;**50**(2):179-211

[58] Venkatesh V, Morris MG, Davis GB, Davis FD. User acceptance of information technology: Toward a unified view. MIS Quarterly. 2003;**27**(3):425-478

[59] Rogers EM. Diffusion of Innovations. 1st ed. New York, USA: The Free Press; 1962

[60] Ajzen I, Fishbein M. Understanding Attitudes and Predicting Social Behavior. Hoboken, New Jersey, USA: Prentice-Hall; 1980

[61] Tornatzky LG, Fleischer M. Processes of Technological Innovation. California, USA: Lexington Books; 1990

[62] Baker J. The technology–organization–environment framework. In: Dwivedi YK, Wade MR, Schneberger SL, editors. Information Systems Theory: Explaining and Predicting our Digital Society. New York, USA: Springer; 2012. pp. 231-245. (Integrated Series in Information Systems; vol. 1). DOI: 10.1007/978-1-4419-6108-2

[63] Gangwar H, Date H, Ramaswamy R. Understanding determinants of cloud computing adoption using an integrated TAM-TOE model. Journal of Enterprise Information Management. 2015;**28**(1):107-130

[64] Mabad T, Ali O, Ally M, Wamba SF, Chan KC. Making investment decisions on RFID technology: An evaluation of key adoption factors in construction firms. IEEE Access. 2021;**9**:36937-36954

[65] Fernando Y, Rozuar NHM, Mergeresa F. The blockchain-enabled technology and carbon performance: Insights from early adopters. Technology in Society. 2021;**64**:101507

[66] Viljakainen T. Adoption of Augmented Reality Solutions in Field Engineering and Maintenance –Drivers and Barriers for Organizations [PhD Thesis]. Helsinki, Finland: Arcada University of Applied Sciences; 2020

[67] Iftikhar W, Vistro DM, Mahmood Z. Blockchain technology adoption by Malaysian higher education institutes: A perspective of integrated tam model and toe framework. In: Proceedings of the 3rd International Conference on Integrated Intelligent Computing Communication & Security (ICIIC 2021). Bangalore, India: Atlantis Press; 2021. pp. 606-617. DOI: 10.2991/ahis.k.210913.077

[68] Molinillo S, Japutra A. Organizational adoption of digital information and technology: A theoretical review. The Bottom Line. 2017;**30**(01):33-46

[69] Bakici T, Nemeh A, Hazir Ö. Big data adoption in project management: Insights from French organizations. IEEE Transactions on Engineering Management. 2023;**70**(10):3358-3372

[70] Wong LW, Leong LY, Hew JJ, Tan GWH, Ooi KB. Time to seize the digital evolution: Adoption of blockchain in operations and supply chain management among Malaysian SMEs. International Journal of Information Management. 2020;**52**:101997

[71] Ram J, Afridi NK, Khan KA. Adoption of big data analytics in construction: Development of a conceptual model. Built Environment Project and Asset Management. 2019;**9**(4):564-579

[72] Schmitt G, Mladenow A, Strauss C, Schaffhauser-Linzatti M. Smart contracts

and internet of things: A qualitative content analysis using the technology-organization-environment framework to identify key-determinants. The 10th International Conference on Emerging Ubiquitous Systems and Pervasive Networks (EUSPN-2019) / The 9th International Conference on Current and Future Trends of Information and Communication Technologies in Healthcare (ICTH-2019)/Affiliated Workshops. 2019;**160**:189-196

[73] Zhu K, Kraemer KL, Dedrick J. Information technology payoff in E-business environments: An international perspective on value creation of E-business in the financial services industry. Journal of Management Information Systems. 2004;**21**(1):17-54

[74] Cobo MJ, López-Herrera AG, Herrera-Viedma E, Herrera F. Science mapping software tools: Review, analysis, and cooperative study among tools. Journal of the American Society for Information Science and Technology. 2011;**62**(7):1382-1402

[75] Munn Z, Stern C, Aromataris E, Lockwood C, Jordan Z. What kind of systematic review should I conduct? A proposed typology and guidance for systematic reviewers in the medical and health sciences. BMC Medical Research Methodology. 2018;**18**(1):5

[76] Radzi AR, Rahman RA, Doh SI. Decision making in highway construction: A systematic review and future directions. Journal of Engineering, Design and Technology. 2023;**21**(4):1083-1106. DOI: 10.1108/JEDT-06-2021-0306

[77] Wen Z, Liao H, Zavadskas EK, Antuchevičienė J. Applications of fuzzy multiple criteria decision making methods in civil engineering: A state-of-the-art survey. Journal of Civil Engineering and Management. 2021;**27**(6):358-371

[78] Zhu X, Meng X, Zhang M. Application of multiple criteria decision making methods in construction: A systematic literature review. Journal of Civil Engineering and Management. 2021;**27**(6):372-403

[79] Khalef R, El-adaway IH. Identifying design-build decision-making factors and providing future research guidelines: Social network and association rule analysis. Journal of Construction Engineering and Management. 2023;**149**(1):04022151

[80] Sharma K, Aswal C, Paul J. Factors affecting green purchase behavior: A systematic literature review. Business Strategy and the Environment. 2023;**32**(4):2078-2092

[81] Kugley S, Wade A, Thomas J, Mahood Q, Jørgensen AMK, Hammerstrøm K, et al. Searching for studies: A guide to information retrieval for Campbell systematic reviews. Campbell Systematic Reviews. 2017;**13**(1):1-73

[82] Naderi H, Shojaei A. Civil infrastructure digital twins: Multi-level knowledge map, research gaps, and future directions. IEEE Access. 2022;**10**:122022-122037

[83] Gusenbauer M, Haddaway NR. Which academic search systems are suitable for systematic reviews or meta-analyses? Evaluating retrieval qualities of Google Scholar, PubMed, and 26 other resources. Research Synthesis Methods. 2020;**11**(2):181-217

[84] Visser M, van Eck NJ, Waltman L. Large-scale comparison of bibliographic data sources: Scopus, web of science, dimensions, Crossref, and Microsoft academic. Quantitative Science Studies. 2021;**2**(1):20-41

[85] Mongeon P, Paul-Hus A. The journal coverage of web of science and Scopus: A comparative analysis. Scientometrics. 2016;**106**(1):213-228

[86] Aghimien D, Aigbavboa CO, Chan DWM, Aghimien EI. Determinants of cloud computing deployment in South African construction organisations using structural equation modelling and machine learning technique. Engineering, Construction and Architectural Management. 2022 (ahead-of-print). DOI: 10.1108/ECAM-05-2022-0464

[87] Attencia G, Mattos C. Adoption of digital technologies for asset management in construction projects. Journal of Information Technology in Construction (ITcon). 2022;**27**:619-629

[88] Badi S, Ochieng E, Nasaj M, Papadaki M. Technological, organisational and environmental determinants of smart contracts adoption: UK construction sector viewpoint. Construction Management and Economics. 2021;**39**(1):36-54

[89] Besklubova S, Skibniewski MJ, Zhang X. Factors affecting 3D printing technology adaptation in construction. Journal of Construction Engineering and Management. 2021;**147**(5):04021026

[90] Cai S, Ma Z, Skibniewski MJ, Guo J. Construction automation and robotics: From one-offs to follow-ups based on practices of Chinese construction companies. Journal of Construction Engineering and Management. 2020;**146**(10):05020013

[91] Chaurasia SS, Verma S. Strategic determinants of big data analytics in the AEC sector: A multi-perspective framework. Construction Economics and Building. 2020;**20**(4):63-81

[92] Dashti B, Viljevac-Vasquez R. Exploring use and perception of augmented- and virtual reality in the Swedish AEC industry [PhD thesis]. Stockholm, Sweden: Royal Institute of Technology; 2020

[93] Gan XL, Chang RD, Langston C, Wen T. Exploring the interactions among factors impeding the diffusion of prefabricated building technologies. Engineering, Construction and Architectural Management. 2019;**26**(3):535-553

[94] Jadhav DS. Understanding artificial intelligence adoption, implementation, and use in small and medium enterprises in India [PhD thesis]. Minneapolis, Minnesota: Walden University; 2021

[95] Katebi A, Homami P, Najmeddin M. Acceptance model of precast concrete components in building construction based on technology acceptance model (TAM) and technology, organization, and environment (TOE) framework. Journal of Building Engineering. 2022;**45**:103518

[96] Li C, Zhang Y, Xu Y. Factors influencing the adoption of blockchain in the construction industry: A hybrid approach using PLS-SEM and fsQCA. Buildings. 2022;**12**(9):1349. Available from: https://www.mdpi.com/2075-5309/12/9/1349

[97] Lu Y, Deng Y. What drives construction practitioners' acceptance of intelligent surveillance systems? An extended technology acceptance model. Buildings. 2022;**12**(2):104. Available from: https://www.mdpi.com/2075-5309/12/2/104

[98] Muylle L. Technology readiness and adoption of 3D printing in the

construction industry [master in business engineering: Operations management]. Universiteit Gent; 2019. Available from: https://libstore.ugent.be/fulltxt/RUG01/002/784/400/RUG01-002784400_2019_0001_AC.pdf

[99] Na S, Heo S, Han S, Shin Y, Roh Y. Acceptance model of artificial intelligence (AI)-based technologies in construction firms: Applying the technology acceptance model (TAM) in combination with the technology–organisation–environment (TOE) framework. Buildings. 2022;**12**(2):90. Available from: https://www.mdpi.com/2075-5309/12/2/90

[100] Pan M, Pan W. Understanding the determinants of construction robot adoption: Perspective of building contractors. Journal of Construction Engineering and Management. 2020;**146**(5):04020040

[101] Pan M, Pan W. Determinants of adoption of robotics in precast concrete production for buildings. Journal of Management in Engineering. 2019;**35**(5):05019007

[102] Umar T. Key factors influencing the implementation of three-dimensional printing in construction. Proceedings of the Institution of Civil Engineers—Management, Procurement and Law. 2021;**174**(3):104-117

[103] Wang X, Liu L, Liu J, Huang X. Understanding the determinants of blockchain technology adoption in the construction industry. Buildings. 2022;**12**(10):1709. Available from: https://www.mdpi.com/2075-5309/12/10/1709

[104] Wu H, Zhong B, Li H, Guo J, Wang Y. On-site construction quality inspection using blockchain and smart contracts. Journal of Management in Engineering. 2021;**37**(6):04021065

[105] Yuan M, Li Z, Li X, Luo X, Yin X, Cai J. Proposing a multifaceted model for adopting prefabricated construction technology in the construction industry. Engineering, Construction and Architectural Management. 2023;**30**(2):755-786. DOI: 10.1108/ECAM-07-2021-0613

[106] Chen Y, Yin Y, Browne GJ, Li D. Adoption of building information modeling in Chinese construction industry. Engineering, Construction and Architectural Management. 2019;**26**(9):1878-1898

[107] Juan YK, Lai WY, Shih SG. Building information modeling acceptance and readiness assessment in Taiwanese architectural firms. Journal of Civil Engineering and Management. 2017;**23**(3):356-367

[108] Lee S, Yu J. Discriminant model of BIM acceptance readiness in a construction organization. KSCE Journal of Civil Engineering. 2017;**21**(3):555-564

[109] Li J, Greenwood D, Kassem M. Blockchain in the built environment and construction industry: A systematic review, conceptual models and practical use cases. Automation in Construction. 2019;**102**:288-307

[110] Ma G, Jiang S, Jia J. Investigating the adoption of social media in the construction industry: Empirical evidence from project teams in China. Engineering, Construction and Architectural Management. 2022;**29**(10):3948-3969

[111] Park S, Yu H, Menassa CC, Kamat VR. A comprehensive evaluation of factors influencing acceptance of robotic assistants in field construction work. Journal of Management in Engineering. 2023;**39**(3):04023010

[112] Tran Q, Nazir S, Nguyen TH, Ho NK, Dinh TH, Nguyen VP, et al. Empirical examination of factors influencing the adoption of green building technologies: The perspective of construction developers in developing economies. Sustainability. 2020;**12**(19):8067. Available from: https://www.mdpi.com/2071-1050/12/19/8067

[113] Tran Q, Zhang C, Sun H, Huang D. Initial adoption versus institutionalization of E-procurement in construction firms: An empirical investigation in Vietnam. Journal of Global Information Technology Management. 2014;**17**(2):91-116

[114] Arnold C, Veile JW, Voigt KI. What drives Industry 4.0 adoption? An examination of technological, organizational, and environmental determinants. In: International Association for Management of Technology (IAMOT). Birmingham, United Kingdom; 2018

[115] Chandra S, Kumar KN. Exploring factors influencing organizational adoption of augmented reality in E-commerce: Empirical analysis using technology–organization–environment model. Journal of Electronic Commerce Research. 2018;**19**(3):237-265

[116] Ghaleb EAA, Dominic PDD, Fati SM, Muneer A, Ali RF. The assessment of big data adoption readiness with a technology–organization–environment framework: A perspective towards healthcare employees. Sustainability. 2021;**13**(15):8379. Available from: https://www.mdpi.com/2071-1050/13/15/8379

[117] Iranmanesh M, Lim KH, Foroughi B, Hong MC, Ghobakhloo M. Determinants of intention to adopt big data and outsourcing among SMEs: Organisational and technological factors as moderators. Management Decision. 2023;**61**(1):201-222

[118] Malak J. An analysis of the technological, organizational, and environmental factors influencing cloud adoption [PhD thesis]. Minneapolis, Minnesota: Walden University; 2016

[119] Tsai CA, Yeh CC. Understanding the decision rules for 3D printing adoption. Technology Analysis & Strategic Management. 2019;**31**(9):1104-1117

[120] Zhang Y, Sun J, Yang Z, Wang Y. Critical success factors of green innovation: Technology, organization and environment readiness. Journal of Cleaner Production. 2020;**264**:121701

[121] Chen X, Chang-Richards AY, Pelosi A, Jia Y, Shen X, Siddiqui MK, et al. Implementation of technologies in the construction industry: A systematic review. Engineering, Construction and Architectural Management. 2022;**29**(8):3181-3209

[122] Rashvand P, Majid MZA. Critical criteria on client and customer satisfaction for the issue of performance measurement. Journal of Management in Engineering. 2014;**30**(1):10-18

[123] Rogers EM, Shoemaker FF. Communication of Innovations; a Cross-Cultural Approach. New York: The Free Press; 1971

[124] Wu P, Zhao X, Baller JH, Wang X. Developing a conceptual framework to improve the implementation of 3D printing technology in the construction industry. Architectural Science Review. 2018;**61**(3):133-142

[125] Schuh G, Anderl R, Dumitrescu R, Krüger A, Hompel MT. Industry 4.0 maturity index: Managing the digital

transformation of companies – Update 2020. Acatech Study. 2020

[126] Eiris R, Gheisari M. Evaluation of small UAS acquisition costs for construction applications. In: Proceedings of the Joint Conference on Computing in Construction (JC3). Vol. 1. Heraklion, Greece; 2017. p. 931. Available from: http://itc.scix.net/paper/lc3-2017-195

[127] Elghdban MG, Azmy NB, Zulkiple AB, Al-Sharafi MA. Factors affecting the adoption of advanced IT with specific emphasis on building information Modeling based on TOE framework: A systematic review. International Journal of Advanced Science and Technology. 2020;**29**(4):3314-3333

[128] Krämer S, Bredekamp H. Culture, technology, cultural techniques – Moving beyond Text1. Theory, Culture & Society. 2013;**30**(6):20-29

[129] Piccoli G, Pigni F. Information Systems for Managers with Cases. Edition 4.0. Burlington, VT, USA: Prospect Press; 2019

[130] Ukobitz DV. Organizational adoption of 3D printing technology: A semisystematic literature review. Journal of Manufacturing Technology Management. 2021;**32**(9):48-74

[131] Bou Hatoum M, Piskernik M, Nassereddine H. A holistic framework for the implementation of big data throughout a construction project lifecycle. In: Tateyama K, Ishii K, Inoue F, editors. Proceedings of the 37th International Symposium on Automation and Robotics in Construction (ISARC). Kitakyushu, Japan: International Association for Automation and Robotics in Construction (IAARC); 2020. pp. 1299-1306

[132] Schillewaert N, Ahearne MJ, Frambach RT, Moenaert RK. The adoption of information technology in the sales force. Industrial Marketing Management. 2005;**34**(4):323-336

[133] Dargham SA, Hatoum MB, Tohme M, Hamzeh F. Implementation of integrated project delivery in Lebanon: Overcoming the challenges. In: Proc 27th Annual Conference of the International Group for Lean Construction (IGLC). Dublin, Ireland; 2019. pp. 917-928

[134] Arabshahi M. Developing a governance framework to assist with the adoption of sensing technologies in construction [PhD thesis]. Curtin University; 2021. Available from: http://hdl.handle.net/20.500.11937/84210

[135] Turk Ž. Interoperability in construction–Mission impossible? Developments in the Built Environment. 2020;**4**:100018

[136] Avram MG. Advantages and challenges of adopting cloud computing from an enterprise perspective. Procedia Technology. 2014;**12**:529-534

[137] Domlyn AM, Wandersman A. Community coalition readiness for implementing something new: Using a Delphi methodology. Journal of Community Psychology. 2019;**47**(4):882-897

[138] Scaccia JP, Cook B, Wandersman A. Building organizational readiness (capacities x motivation) for implementation: A research synthesis of the empirical evidence. SocArXiv. 2020. DOI: 10.31235/osf.io/84cjq

[139] Hamzeh F, González VA, Alarcon LF, Khalife S. Lean Construction 4.0: Exploring the challenges of development in the AEC industry. In: Proc 29th Annual Conference of the International Group for Lean

Construction (IGLC). Lima, Peru; 2021. pp. 207-216. Available from: http://www.iglc.net/papers/details/1881

[140] Dadi G, Nassereddine H, Taylor T, Griffith R, Ramadan B. Technological capabilities of departments of transportation for digital project management and delivery. In: National Cooperative Highway Research Program Project 20-05, Synthesis Topic 52-19. Washington DC, USA: The National Academies Press; 2022. (National Cooperative Highway Research Program Project 20-05, Synthesis Topic 52-19; vol. National Cooperative Highway Research Program Project 20-05, Synthesis Topic 52-19). DOI: 10.17226/26738

[141] ECSO. Digitalisation in the Construction Sector. Bruxelles/Brussel, Belgium: European Construction Sector Observatory; 2021. p. 159

[142] Pargoo NS, Ilbeigi M. A scoping review for cybersecurity in the construction industry. Journal of Management in Engineering. 2023;**39**(2):03122003

[143] Perera S, Nanayakkara S, Rodrigo MNN, Senaratne S, Weinand R. Blockchain technology: Is it hype or real in the construction industry? Journal of Industrial Information Integration. 2020;**17**:100125

[144] Bhattacharya S, Momaya KS. Actionable strategy framework for digital transformation in AECO industry. Engineering, Construction and Architectural Management. 2021;**28**(5):1397-1422

[145] Ghobakhloo M, Fathi M, Iranmanesh M, Maroufkhani P, Morales ME. Industry 4.0 ten years on: A bibliometric and systematic review of concepts, sustainability value drivers, and success determinants. Journal of Cleaner Production. 2021;**302**:127052

[146] Xu Y, Zhou Y, Sekula P, Ding L. Machine learning in construction: From shallow to deep learning. Developments in the Built Environment. 2021;**6**:100045

[147] Laudon KC, Laudon JP. Management Information Systems: Managing the Digital Firm. 13th ed. London, England: Pearson; 2012

[148] Kotter JP, Akhtar VA, Gupta G. Is your organization surviving change-or thriving in it. Harvard Business Review. 2021. Available from: https://hbr.org/2021/08/is-your-organization-surviving-change-or-thriving-in-it

[149] Liker JK. The Toyota Way: 14 Management Principles from the World's Greatest Manufacturer. 2nd ed. New York City, New York, USA: McGraw-Hill; 2021

[150] Das P, Perera S, Senaratne S, Osei-Kyei R. Paving the way for industry 4.0 maturity of construction enterprises: A state of the art review. Engineering, Construction and Architectural Management. 2023;**30**(10):4665-4694

[151] Duarte CM d M, Picchi FA. Key elements to enable systemic innovation in construction firms. Ambiente Construído. 2021;**21**(4):385-405

[152] Razkenari M, Fenner A, Shojaei A, Hakim H, Kibert C. Perceptions of offsite construction in the United States: An investigation of current practices. Journal of Building Engineering. 2020;**29**:101138

[153] Salama T, Moselhi O, Al-Hussein M. Modular industry characteristics and barriers to its increased market share. In: Modular and Offsite Construction (MOC) Summit Proceedings. Hollywood, FL, USA; 2018. pp. 8-15

[154] Martins R, Oliveira T, Thomas MA. Assessing organizational adoption of information systems outsourcing. Journal of Organizational Computing and Electronic Commerce. 2015;**25**(4):360-378

[155] JBKnowledge. Construction Technology Report. JBKnowledge; 2021. p. 73. Report No.: 10. Available from: https://contechreport.com/

[156] Klinc R, Turk Ž. Construction 4.0—Digital transformation of one of the oldest industries. Economic & Business Review. 2019;**21**(3):393-410

[157] Hwang BN, Huang CY, Wu CH. A TOE approach to establish a green supply chain adoption decision model in the semiconductor industry. Sustainability. 2016;**8**(2):168

[158] Hung BQ, Nham NTH, Ha LT. The importance of digitalization in powering environmental innovation performance of European countries. Journal of Innovation & Knowledge. 2023;**8**(1):100284

[159] Garg A, Goel P, Sharma A, Rana NP. As you sow, so shall you reap: Assessing drivers of socially responsible investment attitude and intention. Technological Forecasting and Social Change. 2022;**184**:122030

[160] Kumar V. Transformative marketing: The next 20 years. Journal of Marketing. 2018;**82**(4):1-12

[161] Xu X, Lu Y, Vogel-Heuser B, Wang L. Industry 4.0 and industry 5.0—Inception, conception and perception. Journal of Manufacturing Systems. 2021 Oct;**1**(61):530-535

[162] Breque M, Nul LD, Petridis A. Industry 5.0: Towards a sustainable, human-centric and resilient European industry. Directorate-General for Research and Innovation. 2021:48

[163] Leng J, Sha W, Wang B, Zheng P, Zhuang C, Liu Q, et al. Industry 5.0: Prospect and retrospect. Journal of Manufacturing Systems. 2022;**65**:279-295

[164] Huang S, Wang B, Li X, Zheng P, Mourtzis D, Wang L. Industry 5.0 and society 5.0—Comparison, complementation and co-evolution. Journal of Manufacturing Systems. Jul 2022;**1**(64):424-428

[165] Ikudayisi AE, Chan APC, Darko A, Adedeji YMD. Integrated practices in the architecture, engineering, and construction industry: Current scope and pathway towards industry 5.0. Journal of building. Engineering. 2023;**73**:106788

[166] Yitmen I, Almusaed A, Alizadehsalehi S. Investigating the causal relationships among enablers of the construction 5.0 paradigm: Integration of operator 5.0 and society 5.0 with human-centricity, sustainability, and resilience. Sustainability. 2023;**15**(11):9105. Available from: https://www.mdpi.com/2071-1050/15/11/9105

Chapter 4

# Perspective Chapter: Transportation 5.0 – From Cyber-Physical Transportation Systems to Cyber-Physical-Social Transportation Systems

*Zhitao Ma, Shizi Ma and Sheng Wang*

## Abstract

This chapter describes the Transportation 5.0 paradigm, providing ideas for the transformation of the transportation industry from Industry 4.0 to Industry 5.0. Transportation 5.0 is based on parallel intelligence (PI) as the theoretical foundation, with artistic societies-computational experiences-parallel execution (ACP) as the basic method, and cyber-physical-social transportation systems (CPSTS) as the framework, enabling the transportation system to smoothly transition to an ethical, responsible, and sustainable intelligent transportation paradigm. Firstly, the CPSTS framework was proposed, and the theories followed and goals pursued by Transportation 5.0 were explored. The social nature of intelligent transportation systems was explained. Furthermore, key supporting technologies for Transportation 5.0, including a series of enabling technologies for parallel transportation robots, were provided. Then, the application of Transportation 5.0 in the fields of transportation was demonstrated. At the same time, the challenges and potential research directions of Transportation 5.0 were explored.

**Keywords:** Industry 5.0, Transportation 5.0, cyber-physical-social systems, intelligent transportation, parallel intelligence

## 1. Introduction

The proposal of Transportation 5.0 can be traced back to 2017 or even earlier [1], and it is worth noting that it is still 3 years since the European Commission proposed "Industrial 5.0" in September 2020. However, with the continuous development of the Transportation 5.0 paradigm, we have found that the Transportation 5.0 paradigm and the Industrial 5.0 paradigm are similar in many aspects [2]. Therefore, we can further develop Transportation 5.0 as the transportation paradigm of the Industrial 5.0 era. Therefore, based on Dr. Wang's research, this chapter further redefines Transportation 5.0 from four perspectives: its objectives, theoretical basis, basic

 

| Reference | Sustainable | Society-centered | Communication | Vehicle manufacturing |
|---|---|---|---|---|
| [1] | Y | Y | N | N |
| [2] | Y | Y | N | N |
| [3] | Y | Y | N | N |
| [4] | Y | N | N | N |
| [5] | Y | N | Y | N |
| [6] | N | Y | Y | N |

**Table 1.**
*Comparison of research on Transportation 5.0 (Y: yes, N: no).*

methods, and framework, in order to make it more in line with the development requirements of Industry 5.0.

Dr. Wang was the first to introduce CPSS into the Transportation 5.0 paradigm and pointed out that the transportation system is using methods such as ACP and PI theory to present a sustainable and social-centric trend [3]. Meanwhile, in the context of Industry 5.0, travel, as a major application scenario in transportation systems, also has a sustainable trend [4]. Furthermore, it is undeniable that communication technology, as the fundamental technology applied to Transportation 5.0, should also be given special attention to how to make communication in the Transportation 5.0 paradigm more sustainable [5, 6]. Furthermore, a comparison of existing studies on Transportation 5.0 is presented in **Table 1**.

Transportation systems can be divided into four main categories: road vehicles, railways, aviation, and ocean transportation. It is worth noting that in the United States, highway transportation uses approximately 84% of all transportation energy. Therefore, due to space limitations, this chapter focuses on the Transportation 5.0 framework based on unmanned vehicles and drones, which does not deny the irreplaceable role of railway and ocean transportation in transportation systems. The current transportation system consists of many subsystems, which may lead to the collapse of the entire system if all subsystems are embedded into the system for operation, or if there is disharmony between subsystems. For example, early research on vehicle route planning (VRP) focused on the efficiency and economy of transportation systems [7]. However, environmentalists are more concerned about the sustainability of transportation systems [8] and the final routes provided by the two systems can be said to run counter to each other.

The transportation system is a social and technological system composed of transportation infrastructure (highways, railways, stations, parking lots, etc.), vehicles, and humans. Therefore, it is necessary to introduce technical ethics into Transportation 5.0. In addition, the uncertainty and complexity of the transportation system caused by human activities and social operations also need to be considered in the Transportation 5.0 paradigm. Industry 5.0 puts forward requirements for the elasticity, sustainability, and people-oriented nature of industrial systems [9]. The Cyber-Physical System CPS framework, as the core technology of Industry 4.0, focuses on how to use technological means to deeply integrate physical space and cyberspace, while neglecting the people-oriented nature of technology. Prior to the proposal of Industry 5.0, relevant researchers had conducted a preliminary exploration of the people-oriented approach.

In order to meet the requirement of "people-oriented", the concept of "Cognitive" was introduced based on the CPS framework, and the cognitive cyber-physical system (C-CPS) was proposed, aiming to make the framework meet the requirements of the Human Rights Council [10, 11]. In addition, another framework is human cyber-physical systems (HCPS) or cyber-physical human systems (CPHS), which attempts to introduce the concept of "Human" into CPS and establish a people-oriented CPS framework [12, 13]. Another similar framework is Cyber-physical-social systems (CPSS), which is also proposed for human-machine symbiotic systems, aiming to study the impact of human and social factors on large-scale complex systems [14]. Although the above three frameworks have a certain degree of application in different fields, in existing research, the main application fields of C-CPS and CPHS still remain in industrial fields such as factories, production lines, and manufacturing [10–13], rather than in the transportation field where human beings are highly involved. The "social system" in CPSS better reflects the impact of the entire human society on the system.

Therefore, in order to reasonably present the impact of the entire human society on the transportation system, this chapter selects CPSS as the framework and proposes cyber-physical-social transportation systems (CPSTS) based on CPSS, providing an overall overview of Transportation 5.0. Summarize and provide eight aspects that the transportation system should focus on under the Transportation 5.0 paradigm, namely efficiency, reliability, sustainability, service, social equity, economic benefits, and fulfilling ethics and responsibilities. Based on the theory of parallel intelligence, a transportation system based on unmanned vehicles and multimodal transportation modes was designed, which further demonstrates how CPSTS operates using advanced sensing, communication, and automation equipment. Furthermore, the main application scenarios of CPSTS are presented, based on the transportation scenarios of connected automated vehicle (CAV) and unmanned aerial vehicle (UAV). In addition, some other technologies and systems related to the Transportation 5.0 paradigm have been described.

## 2. Framework of Transportation 5.0

According to the smart park logistics system and power grid inspection system established based on CPSS [9, 15], this chapter establishes a Transportation 5.0 paradigm based on parallel intelligence (PI) theory, ACP as the basic method, and CPSTS

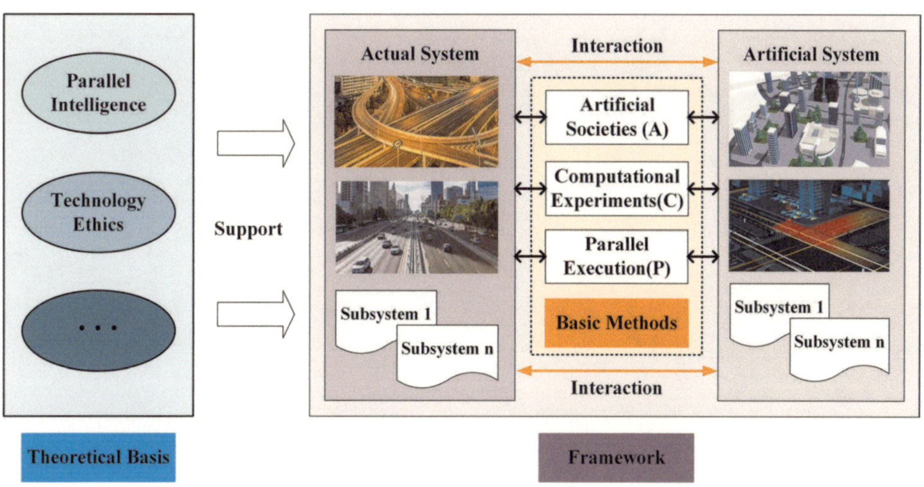


**Figure 1.**
*Overview of Transportation 5.0.*

as the framework. **Figure 1** shows the overall overview of the Industry 5.0 paradigm. As previously mentioned, CPSS, as a variant of CPS, aims to introduce "social system" into CPS. PI theory is a theory about systems science that mainly studies and describes the interaction and collaborative behavior of various components in complex systems.

The definition of PI theory is as follows:

*Definition 1:* Each subsystem in a complex large-scale system is interdependent and can interact with each other in real time. When the system is running, each subsystem runs simultaneously and does not follow a linear time series.

The core concept of PI theory is parallelism, that is, parallel operation and parallel interaction. Parallel operation refers to the ability of various parts of a system to operate and process information simultaneously, without the need to follow a strict sequence. Parallel interaction refers to the interaction and interaction between various components in a system, forming a common whole that can significantly improve the efficiency and stability of the system.

The ACP method is a method used to study complex large-scale systems. This method combines parallel computing techniques in computer simulation and PI theory to simulate and analyze large-scale complex systems through parallel execution and computational experiments. The ACP method first constructs an artificial system that maps the entire physical social world to the cyber world. Furthermore, a series of computational experiments were designed and executed to simulate and analyze the behavior and dynamic changes of large-scale complex systems. Finally, through advanced internet technology, real-time transmission of experimental results from the artificial world to the real world for parallel operation.

## 2.1 Cyber-physical-social transportation system framework

**Figure 2** shows the framework of CPSTS. CPSTS consists of three systems: social system, physical system, and artificial system. The software transportation robot (shown in **Figure 2** as a software vehicle) serves as the carrier of CPSTS and is responsible for performing artificial system design-related experiments and transmitting the experimental results in real-time to the real world. To ensure the availability of experimental results, it is necessary to ensure the accuracy and reliability of the

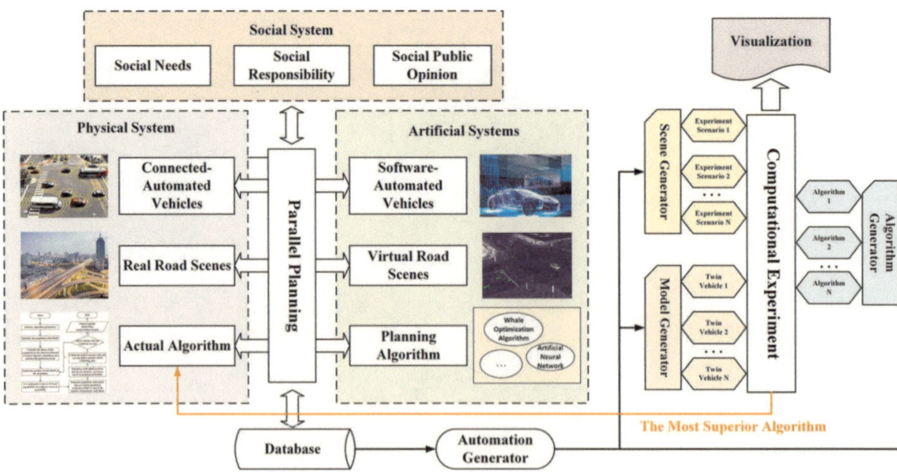


**Figure 2.**
*Framework of cyber-physical-social transportation systems.*

relevant scene models in the scene library. This requires real-time, comprehensive, and accurate modeling of the entire transportation system. The data in the database includes traffic flow, average speed, vehicle type, crowd density, and other traffic data.

## 2.2 Evaluation indicators of CPSTS

The eight areas that the transportation system should focus on under the Transportation 5.0 paradigm are efficiency, reliability, sustainability, service, social equity, economic benefits, and fulfilling ethics and responsibilities [16, 17].

### *2.2.1 Efficiency and reliability of CPSTS*

The CPSTS will use advanced sensing devices to transmit relevant data in real-time to artificial systems, monitoring traffic flow, road conditions, and traffic signals. Therefore, the efficiency of CPSTS under the Transportation 5.0 paradigm can be optimized by utilizing perception technology, real-time data, and intelligent algorithms for traffic management. In addition, CPSTS can provide personalized traffic navigation and route optimization functions for humans, improve the efficiency and convenience of public transportation, and reduce accidents and malfunctions. CPSTS has the ability to operate stably in different situations and provide accurate and reliable traffic information and services, with robust reliability. Therefore, CPSTS needs to have strong data collection and processing capabilities, redundant backup capabilities for multi-source data, real-time monitoring, and fault detection capabilities. It is worth pointing out that the disaster recovery speed and emergency response speed of the transportation system are also indicators for evaluating the reliability of CPSTS.

### *2.2.2 Service level and sustainability of CPSTS*

CPSTS aims to provide users with higher service quality and satisfaction, thereby improving the service level of the system. More specifically, CPSTS can provide more timely services, both in logistics and transportation, while ensuring the safety of passengers, goods, and vehicles. On this basis, CPSTS can provide a comfortable and convenient passenger experience, while ensuring service accessibility and coverage. The sustainability of the transportation system can be reflected in several directions such as vehicle development, infrastructure construction, and route planning. CPSTS uses energy-efficient technologies and facilities to reduce energy consumption. For example, measures such as introducing new energy vehicles, improving the efficiency of vehicle power systems, and improving traffic signal control systems can reduce vehicle exhaust pollution and energy consumption. In addition, CPSTS can reduce traffic demand and congestion by optimizing the layout of transportation roads and urban design.

### *2.2.3 Social equity and economic benefits of CPSTS*

CPSTS can ensure that all members of society have equal access to transportation services and opportunities, without unfair impacts due to differences in personal background, income level, or geographical location. CPSTS can ensure that transportation services are easily accessible to all populations, have wide coverage within the city, and have reasonable and equal costs. Differentiated fare policies, it will not cause excessive pressure on economically disadvantaged populations. At the same time, the design of CPSTS should take into account the needs of various groups of people, including the elderly, disabled people, and other special groups. For example, setting up accessible facilities, and providing convenient user interfaces and information transmission methods to ensure that they have equal access to transportation services. Furthermore, through technological means, the ineffective driving distance during transportation can be reduced, thereby reducing transportation costs for enterprises and ensuring their economic benefits.

#### *2.2.4 The moral and social responsibilities that CPSTS needs to fulfill*

CPSTS will better fulfill relevant ethical and social responsibilities, including (1) data privacy and protection responsibilities. System operators should take necessary security measures to protect user data from illegal acquisition, abuse, or leakage, and comply with relevant data privacy laws and regulations. (2) Fairness and equal responsibility, CPSTS should treat all users fairly during its operation, without discrimination against any specific group, and ensure the fair distribution of transportation resources and services. (3) Safety and risk management responsibilities, CPSTS should take necessary measures to prevent traffic accidents, and promptly handle and report accident events to ensure the safety and reliability of the system.

## 3. Enabling technology of Transportation 5.0

### 3.1 Parallel transportation robots

Because the supporting theory of CPSTS is the PI theory, parallel transportation robots are considered carriers of the Traffic 5.0 paradigm. As previously mentioned, this chapter focuses on CPSTS based on unmanned vehicles and drones. Therefore, parallel robots can be specifically divided into two categories: parallel autonomous vehicles and parallel UAVs. Eq. (1) shows the components of parallel transportation robots.

$$\begin{aligned} \text{Parallel Transportation Robot} = & \sum \text{Physical Transportation Robot} \\ & + \sum \text{Software Transportation Robot} \\ & + \sum \text{Database of Scenarios} \end{aligned} \tag{1}$$

Parallel robots are a combination of physical robots, software robots, artificial experimental systems, the Internet of Things, and databases. Parallel transportation robots have added virtual control and parallel execution compared to ordinary machine robots.

### 3.2 Vehicle road collaboration technology

With the development of technologies such as unmanned aerial vehicles (UAVs) and intelligent connected vehicles (CAVs). It can be foreseen that in the future, clean transportation vehicles such as CAVs and UAVs will be widely used in transportation systems. Therefore, **Figure 3** shows the cutting-edge technologies used in CPSTS

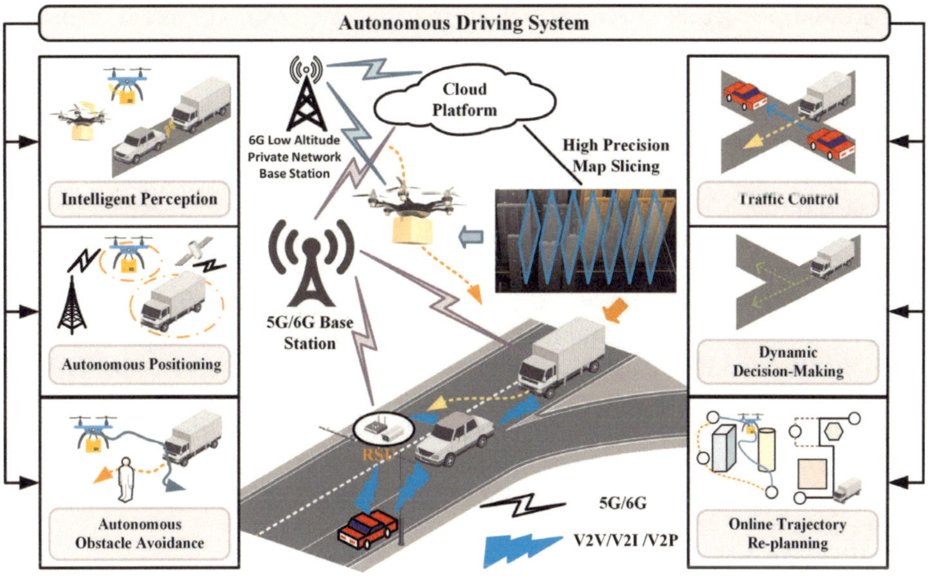


**Figure 3.**
*Cutting-edge technologies used in CPSTS.*

based on CAVs and UAVs. CPSTS and its subsystems use a large number of sensors, so networked sensor technology is important in 10 minutes. Networked sensor technology provides guarantees for data collection and transmission throughout the entire smart city. In this section, we will briefly introduce airborne sensors such as LiDAR, millimeter wave radar, ultrasonic radar, and cameras. On this basis, we introduced several technologies used in parallel transportation systems, including road side unit (RSU) and cellular vehicle-to-everything (C-V2X) communication.

Airborne sensors: LiDAR obtains target status information in the environment, including speed, distance, and other information, by transmitting and receiving laser beam signals; millimeter wave radar determines the distance between vehicles and targets by sending and receiving millimeter wave signals; ultrasonic radar is mainly used to identify obstacles within a short distance range; cameras are mainly used for pedestrian detection, signal lights, traffic sign recognition, and other work. It should be pointed out that ultrasonic radar is susceptible to physical conditions such as vehicle speed; millimeter microwave radar is more suitable for extreme weather conditions (such as rain, snow, and dust), but it is not easy to penetrate obstacles.

Road side unit: as the carrier of DSRC technology, RUS provides a hardware foundation for communication between roads and vehicles. During the working process, RSU obtains relevant information about various traffic participants (including all vehicles and pedestrians) and traffic signs through sensors such as radar and cameras and then broadcasts information to all vehicles within its coverage through the vehicle's On-board unit (OBU). It mainly includes five types of messages: Road Side Information (RSI), Basic Safety Message (BSM), Signal phase timing message (SPAT), Road Safety Message (RSM), and Map Message (MAP). It should be pointed out that in scenes with many obstacles, DSRC's communication performance may decrease due to the limitations of line-of-sight transmission technology.

C-V2X communication: as shown in **Figure 1**, C-V2X communication is mainly divided into four categories: vehicle-to-pedestrian (V2P), vehicle-to-vehicle (V2V), vehicle-to-infrastructure (V2I), and vehicle to network (V2N). At present, many V2X modules support the IEEE 802.11p standard DSRC and the 3GPP Release 14/15/16 standard C-V2X communication methods. During system operation, CAV and UAV receive signals sent by the cloud platform through 4G/5G networks and use software CAV/UAV to download algorithms on the built-in computer of the physical CAV/UAV to control themselves. In addition, a 5G pan low-altitude private network can be established through 5G base stations to solve the problems of airspace signal coverage and private transmission, thus achieving UAV network connectivity. Through the above technologies, CPSTS has the ability to connect and process data.

CAV/UAV intelligent perception: CAV intelligent perception refers to the perception of its own vehicle information, other vehicle information, and environmental information around the vehicle through various sensors, including cameras, LiDAR, gyroscopes, etc.; the intelligent perception of UAVs is also based on various sensors such as LiDAR, in order to obtain UAV's own state information, other UAV's state information, and surrounding environmental information. After the onboard sensors obtain this information, they transmit it to the parallel transportation system through the base station.

CAV/UAV automatic positioning: automatic positioning refers to the post-processing of automatic perception results, in which the UAV or CAV determines its accurate position relative to the external environment. In complex urban driving scenarios, the geometric shape of the road requires that the accuracy error of CAV positioning should not exceed 0.10 m and 0.17 deg. The current CAV/UAV positioning methods used include the Global Navigation Satellite System (GNSS), point cloud map positioning (also known as visual SLAM positioning), radar and camera fusion positioning, and vehicle networking positioning.

CAV/UAV automatic obstacle avoidance: the main purpose of CAV/UAV automatic obstacle avoidance is to reduce the incidence of accidents during driving, thereby avoiding losses to human society. It can be divided into the following two categories. The first type is obstacle avoidance between CAV/UAV and static obstacles such as buildings; The second type is CAV/UAV for obstacle avoidance against other dynamic obstacles such as pedestrians and birds.

CAV traffic control: CAV traffic control is based on the information of all traffic participants in complex scenes (such as intersections), and plans and controls all vehicles in the scene through a manager. When a vehicle approaches an intersection, it sends a vehicle status signal to the manager, who plans the driving route and speed for all vehicles within the same time period at the intersection based on the urgency of the task being performed by the vehicle (such as an ambulance).

CAV autonomous decision-making: during the CAV driving process, there are many route options between two points. We have established a traction model and a road damage model for CAVs to calculate the energy consumption required for each CAV to travel on each road section and the damage caused to the road surface by each CAV when passing through each road section. CAV will make independent decisions based on the following indicators: energy consumption of CAV; CAV damage to the road surface; real-time congestion situation of road sections; and the number of pedestrians on the road section.

CAV trajectory planning: based on the global path of CAV, in parallel transportation systems, we also need to consider local path planning of CAV to provide the complete driving trajectory of CAV. The local path planning of CAVs mainly includes three parts: CAV autonomous obstacle avoidance, CAV traffic control, and CAV autonomous decision-making.

UAV trajectory planning: the main steps include mobilizing the software UAV physical model in the database, mobilizing the algorithms in the algorithm library, and planning the flight trajectory of the drone based on multi-objective functions to minimize energy consumption during operation.

### 3.3 Energy conservation and emission reduction technology

In order to further improve the sustainability of parallel distribution systems, we consider CPSTS consisting of various types of vehicles, including electric trucks, hybrid trucks, and fuel trucks. Due to the need for charging during the use of electric trucks and hybrid electric trucks, this provides opportunities for the use of renewable energy technologies and further reduces the harm of CPTLS to the environment. We adopt a solar power generation model and install solar panels in the warehouse (also known as the distribution center) to power the vehicles and UAVs in CPSTS. The specific schematic diagram is shown in **Figure 4**.

During the operation of the system, CPSTS determines the number of customers it serves based on their emergency situation and the storage of solar panels installed in the warehouse. If the electricity demand of existing customers' vehicles exceeds the amount of electricity stored in the solar panels, external power sources are connected to charge the CAV and UAV. The top of the CAV is also equipped with solar panels, which can provide some electricity to the UAV. When the UAV is not in service, it can supply electricity, which to some extent extends the working hours of the UAV.

### 3.4 Intelligent vehicle design based on digital twins

At present, most sustainable solutions are based on vehicle control or vehicle path selection, neglecting the impact on the overall transportation environment. However, as connected autonomous electric vehicles are the main driving force of modern

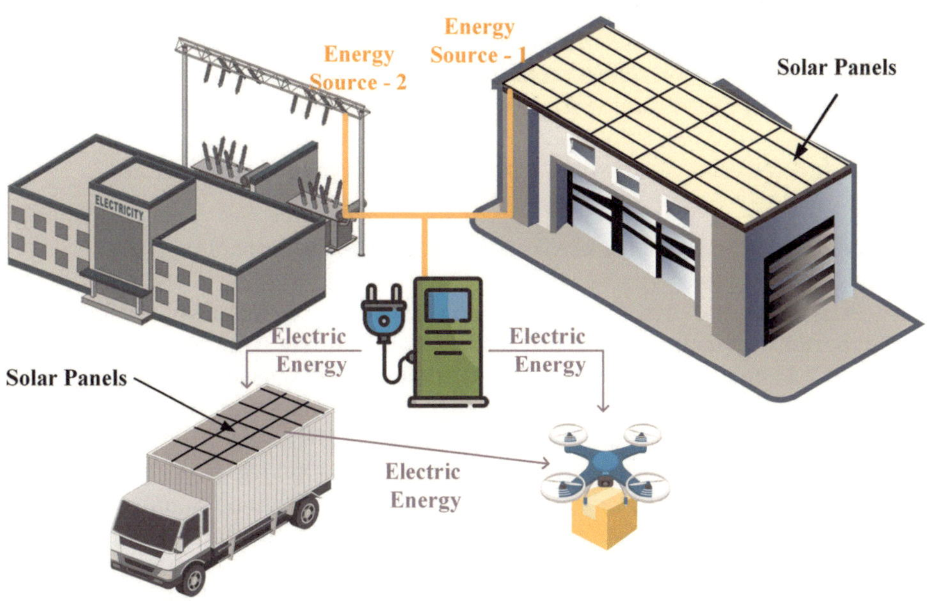


**Figure 4.**
*CPSTS power source schematic diagram.*

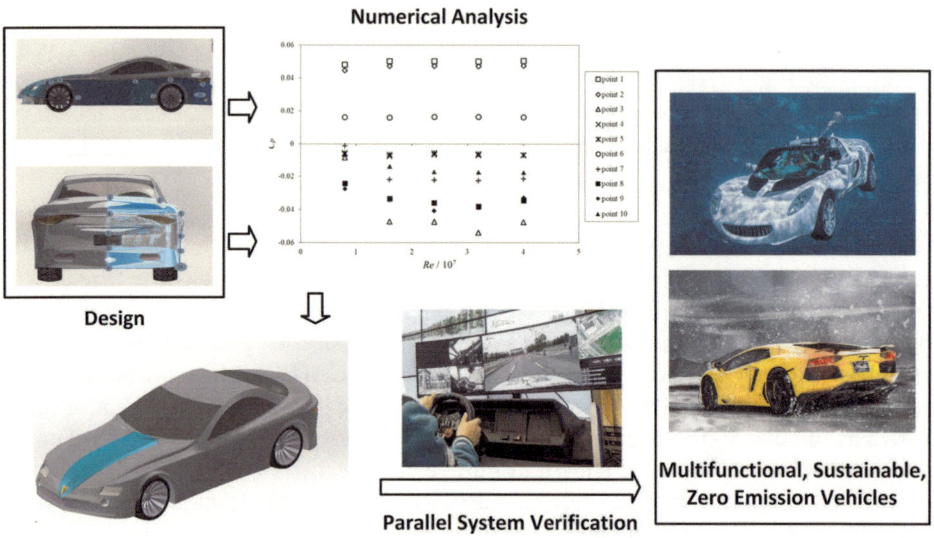


**Figure 5.**
*A vehicle design framework based on PI theory and parallel testing.*

transportation systems, automakers are also reassessing the sustainability of their value chains. Specifically, in terms of intelligent vehicle design, reference [18] aims to accurately predict the production capacity of the production line by establishing a digital twin system for the automotive production line. This work proposes a CPS system based on Digital Twin (DT), which establishes a digital twin production line by analyzing the operating process of the current car body production line. Reference [19] established a digital twin system for body control in automotive manufacturing enterprises, aiming to improve the development efficiency of CPS for automotive manufacturing. Based on the above research, this chapter establishes a vehicle design framework based on PI theory and parallel testing, as shown in **Figure 5**. On the other hand, the energy conservation and emission reduction of intelligent vehicles in the design stage can also be recovered from the vertical vibration process during vehicle movement, and corresponding vertical vibration energy recovery systems can be designed. In addition, hydrogen fuel cells and electric road systems also deserve further attention.

### 3.5 Simulation techniques for environmental and social impacts

The simulation and measurement technology of environmental and social impacts, as an important technology in parallel distribution planning systems, distinguishes CPS from CPSS and is the core of CPSTS. This technology is used in CPSTS to evaluate the impact of the system on the environment, its harm to human society, and the degree of wear and tear of the system on infrastructure. In addition, in the autonomous driving subsystem, this technology is also used for vehicle-pedestrian autonomous obstacle avoidance. In CPSTS, we calculate the environmental impact of the entire system during operation by calculating the energy consumption and greenhouse gas emissions of all CAVs and UAVs in the entire system. Among them, greenhouse gas emissions include direct emissions from autonomous vehicles during driving. In addition, the electricity generated by solar energy in CPSTS may not be sufficient to power the entire system, so greenhouse gas emissions also include the greenhouse gas emissions generated by the electricity obtained from external sources (such as greenhouse gas emissions from thermal power generation). Furthermore, we evaluate the impact of the overall system on society through the accident risk of Occupational Safety and Health, CAV, and UAV, as well as the threat to pedestrians posed by the system.

Social behavior modeling is a dynamic model of pedestrian behavior based on "social forces" and elements such as pedestrian intentions, actions, and attributes. This model is of great significance in predicting pedestrian trajectories during vehicle-pedestrian obstacle avoidance. Among them, "social force" refers to the interaction between pedestrians, pedestrians, and obstacles, that is, the impact on pedestrians in the process of interacting with the environment. When predicting pedestrian trajectories based on social behavior models, methods such as neural networks, adversarial theory, and reinforcement learning are often used.

## 4. Application of Transportation 5.0 paradigm

The application of CPS in logistics systems has been described, and relevant researchers have combined CPS technology with various aspects of the logistics system, aiming to monitor the entire logistics system and assist relevant personnel in decision-making [20]. The difference is that in the future, the demand for multimodal transportation in smart cities will continue to grow, so Transportation 5.0 will definitely adopt multimodal transportation modes. Therefore, this chapter demonstrates the superiority of multimodal transportation solutions in terms of logistics delivery time efficiency compared to traditional VRP problems. This chapter selects a single-vehicle delivery problem with 21 consumers (also known as customers) for case analysis. Considering that one of the main application scenarios of CPSTS is for the last-mile delivery to cities, the maximum speed of vehicles and the speed limit imposed by urban areas are taken into account, and the driving speed of vehicles is set at 40 km/h; The flight speed of the UAV is set at 80% of the maximum flight speed of the Horsefly drone, which is 16 m/s. The specific solution results are shown in **Figure 6**.

In **Figure 6(a)** and **(b)** are the results of using swarm intelligence algorithms to solve traditional VRP problems and joint delivery problems, respectively. The simulation experiment results show that the CAV and UAV joint delivery scheme designed in the chapter saves delivery time compared to the traditional VRP delivery mode when the delivery customer points are the same. **Figure 6(c)** shows the results of three-dimensional trajectory planning for delivery drones based on the I-GSO algorithm.

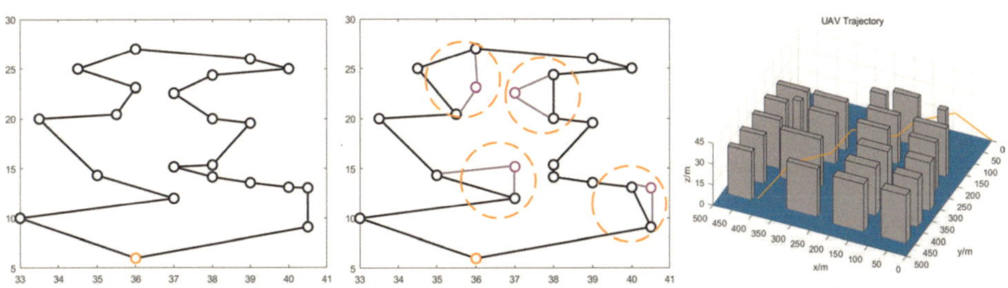


(a) (b) (c)

**Figure 6.**
*Comparison between multimodal transportation systems and traditional VRP.*

## 5. Conclusions

This chapter describes the paradigm of Transportation 5.0. Firstly, it describes the basic framework of CPSTS, aiming to further highlight the people-oriented goal of Transportation 5.0, thereby enabling the transportation system to smoothly transition to an ethical, responsible, and sustainable intelligent transportation paradigm. In addition, eight aspects of the transportation system under the Transportation 5.0 paradigm, including efficiency, reliability, sustainability, service, social equity, economic benefits, and fulfilling ethics and responsibilities, are presented. In addition, key enabling technologies for Transportation 5.0 have been provided, including parallel robot technology, vehicle road collaboration technology, energy conservation and emission reduction technology, intelligent vehicle design based on digital twins, and simulation and measurement technologies for environmental and social impacts. Finally, the application of Transportation 5.0 in the logistics field was demonstrated. Compared with existing work, this article provides a more comprehensive introduction to the Transportation 5.0 paradigm. However, there are still some shortcomings. In the future research process, the focus will be on studying multimodal transportation systems that combine air transportation, ocean transportation, rail transportation, and road transportation, in order to provide ideas for the development of Transportation 5.0.

## Conflict of interest

The authors declare no conflict of interest.

## Author details

Zhitao Ma[1], Shizi Ma[2] and Sheng Wang[3]*

1 Shenzhen Zhongwe Electronics Co., Ltd, Shenzhen, China

2 Coventry University, Coventry, England

3 Harbin Institute of Technology (Weihai), Weihai, China

*Address all correspondence to: 2200510129@stu.hit.edu.cn

## References

[1] Wang F-Y, Zhang JJ. Transportation 5.0 in CPSS: Towards ACP-based society-centered intelligent transportation. In: 2017 IEEE 20th International Conference on Intelligent Transportation Systems (ITSC); 16-19 Oct. 2017; Yokohama, Japan. New York: IEEE; 2017. pp. 762-767. DOI: 10.1109/ITSC.2017.8317905

[2] Wang F-Y et al. Transportation 5.0: The DAO to safe, secure, and sustainable intelligent transportation systems. IEEE Transactions on Intelligent Transportation Systems. 2023;**24**(10): 10262-10278. DOI: 10.1109/TITS.2023.3305380

[3] Chen Y, Zhang H, Wang F-Y. Society-centered and DAO-powered sustainability in Transportation 5.0: An intelligent vehicles perspective. IEEE Transactions on Intelligent Vehicles. 2023;**8**(4):2635-2638. DOI: 10.1109/TIV.2023.3264585

[4] Qahtan S, Alsattar HA, Zaidan AA, Pamucar D, Deveci M. Integrated sustainable transportation modelling approaches for electronic passenger vehicle in the context of industry 5.0. Journal of Innovation & Knowledge. 2022;**7**(4):100277. DOI: 10.1016/j.jik.2022.100277

[5] Khan WU, Ihsan A, Nguyen TN, Ali Z, Javed MA. NOMA-enabled backscatter communications for green transportation in automotive-industry 5.0. IEEE Transactions on Industrial Informatics. 2022;**18**(11):7862-7874. DOI: 10.1109/TII.2022.3161029

[6] Wang F-Y, Chen B. Crowdsensing intelligence: Advancing trustworthy, intelligent, interactive, and cooperative sensing and computing for Transportation 5.0. IEEE Transactions on Intelligent Vehicles. 2023;**8**(8):3963-3967. DOI: 10.1109/TIV.2023.3311089

[7] Liu H, Sun Y, Pan N, Li Y, An Y, Pan D. Study on the optimization of urban emergency supplies distribution paths for epidemic outbreaks. Computers & Operations Research. 2022;**146**:105912. DOI: 10.1016/j.cor.2022.105912

[8] Xia F, Rahim A, Kong X, Wang M, Cai Y, Wang J. Modeling and analysis of large-scale urban mobility for green transportation. IEEE Transactions on Industrial Informatics. 2018;**14**(4): 1469-1481. DOI: 10.1109/TII.2017.2785383

[9] Ma S, Liu H, Pan N, Wang S. Study on an autonomous distribution system for smart parks based on parallel system theory against the background of industry 5.0. Journal of King Saud University-Computer and Information Sciences. 2023;**35**(7):101608. DOI: 10.1016/j.jksuci.2023.101608

[10] Mizanoor Rahman SM. Cognitive Cyber-Physical System (C-CPS) for Human-Robot Collaborative Manufacturing. In: 2019 14th Annual Conference System of Systems Engineering (SoSE); 19-22 May 2019; Anchorage, AK, USA. Vol. 2019. New York; IEEE. pp. 125-130. DOI: 10.1109/SYSOSE.2019.8753835

[11] Sangaiah AK, Wang X, Lin Y-B, Jianwei N, Yuan X. Guest editorial cognitive cyber-physical systems with AI based solutions in medical informatics. IEEE Journal of Biomedical and Health Informatics. 2023;**27**(2):586-587. DOI: 10.1109/JBHI.2023.3234603

[12] Zhou J, Zhou Y, Wang B, Zang J. Human–cyber–physical systems

(HCPSs) in the context of new-generation intelligent manufacturing. Engineering. 2019;**5**(4):624-636. DOI: 10.1016/j.eng.2019.07.015

[13] Gupta S, Epiphaniou G, Maple C. AI-augmented usability evaluation framework for software requirements specification in cyber physical human systems. Internet of Things. 2023;**23**: 100841. DOI: 10.1016/j.iot.2023.100841

[14] Yilma BA, Panetto H, Naudet Y. Systemic formalisation of Cyber-Physical-Social System (CPSS): A systematic literature review. Computers in Industry. 2021;**129**:103458. DOI: 10.1016/j.compind.2021.103458

[15] Liu H et al. Study on UAV parallel planning system for transmission line project acceptance under the background of Industry 5.0. IEEE Transactions on Industrial Informatics. 2022;**18**(8):5537-5546. DOI: 10.1109/TII.2022.3142723

[16] Fleming CH, Leveson NG. Early concept development and safety analysis of future transportation systems. IEEE Transactions on Intelligent Transportation Systems. 2016;**17**(12): 3512-3523. DOI: 10.1109/TITS.2016.2561409

[17] Muratori M et al. Exploring the future energy-mobility nexus: The transportation energy & mobility pathway options (TEMPO) model. Transportation Research. Part D, Transport and Environment. 2021; **98**:102967. DOI: 10.1016/j.trd.2021.102967

[18] Son YH et al. Digital twin–based cyber-physical system for automotive body production lines. International Journal of Advanced Manufacturing Technology. 2021;**115**(1–2):291-310. DOI: 10.1007/s00170-021-07183-3

[19] Xie G, Yang K, Xu C, Li R, Hu S. Digital twinning based adaptive development environment for automotive cyber-physical systems. IEEE Transactions on Industrial Informatics. 2022;**18**(2):1387-1396. DOI: 10.1109/TII.2021.3064364

[20] Liu Y, Tao X, Li X, Colombo AW, Hu S. Artificial intelligence in smart logistics cyber-physical systems: State-of-the-arts and potential applications. IEEE Transactions on Industrial Cyber-Physical Systems. 2023;**1**:1-20. DOI: 10.1109/TICPS.2023.3283230

Chapter 5

# Perspective Chapter: Nano and Society 5.0 – Advancing the Human-Centric Revolution

*Basma El Zein, Ali Elrashidi, Mohanad Dahlan, Ahmed Al Jarwan and Ghassan Jabbour*

## Abstract

The chapter "*Nano and Society 5.0: Advancing the Human-Centric Revolution*" delves into the profound implications of nanotechnology within the context of Society 5.0, a visionary concept that seeks to harmoniously merge technological progress with human-centric ideals. Society 5.0 envisions a world where technology enhances life quality for individuals and society, with nanotechnology playing a crucial role in this transformation. This chapter explores the role of nanotechnology in Society 5.0, highlighting its potential in personalized healthcare, real-time health monitoring, sustainability, and education. Nanotechnology enables precision medicine, enabling tailored treatments and diagnostics. It also revolutionizes energy generation, storage, and materials science, contributing to environmentally conscious construction practices. Nanotechnology-driven innovations address global challenges such as water purification and resource conservation. In education, nanotechnology inspires future generations, particularly in STEM disciplines, and supports accessible and inclusive learning environments. However, ethical considerations regarding privacy, equitable access, and responsible governance must be considered as nanotechnology becomes a central focus in this human-centric revolution. This chapter highlights the role of nanotechnology in shaping society toward a future where technology aligns with core values, demonstrating its potential to be a transformative force, propelling Society 5.0 into a new era of innovation, inclusivity, and human betterment.

**Keywords:** nanotechnology, Society 5.0, human-centric, STEM, nano revolution, nanomaterials, waste management, renewable energy, clean environment, clean water, nanosensors, health and well-being

## 1. Introduction

In the tapestry of societal evolution, the concept of Society 5.0 stands as a beacon, illuminating a path where technological progress converges with human values to amplify the well-being of individuals and propel societal advancement [1–3]. Unlike its predecessors, Society 5.0 transcends mere industrial and technological growth, prioritizing the harmonious integration of cutting-edge innovations for the benefit of humanity. At its essence, Society 5.0 envisions a world where technology is not just a means to an end but a powerful force that elevates the human experience [4, 5].

At the heart of this transformative vision lies an unwavering commitment to human-centric principles. Society 5.0 places the well-being of individuals and the collective advancement of society at the forefront of its objectives. It strives for a seamless integration of technology into our daily lives, enhancing our capabilities, fostering inclusivity, and addressing societal challenges. In this epoch, the revolution is not merely technological; it is fundamentally human-centric [6–10].

Central to the realization of Society 5.0 is the catalytic role of nanotechnology. Operating at the infinitesimally small scale of atoms and molecules, nanotechnology emerges as a key enabler, weaving intricate threads that connect technological prowess with the fundamental fabric of human needs. It is within the realm of nanotechnology that we discover the tools and mechanisms to unlock unprecedented possibilities, fundamentally altering the landscape of healthcare, sustainability, education, and beyond [11–13].

In recent reserchs, many researchers are attempting to use nanotechnology for illness diagnosis, treatment, and prevention since they are aware of the advantages of nanomedicine. For the upcoming generation of medical scientists, there are potential applications in the design of medical instruments and procedures [14]. A growing amount of commentary has been made about how STEM (science, technology, engineering, and math) fields will be affected and how their roles in higher education will be redefined. This has included a thorough analysis of how university-industry partnerships will change as a result of each party adapting to the other's expanded role [15].

Zero hunger, excellent health and wellbeing, affordable and clean energy, clean water and sanitation, ethical consumption and production, and climate action are all possible with the aid of nanotechnology [16].

In this chapter, we embark on a journey to explore the symbiotic relationship between nanotechnology and the aspirations of Society 5.0. As we navigate through the intricate web of nanoscale marvels, we unravel the ways in which this transformative technology becomes the lynchpin in advancing the human-centric revolution envisioned by Society 5.0. From personalized healthcare solutions to sustainable practices and inclusive education, nanotechnology emerges as a silent architect, shaping the contours of a future where technology is not just a means to progress but a conduit for a more humane and enlightened society.

### 1.1 Society 5.0

In the ever-evolving narrative of human civilization, each societal epoch marks a distinct chapter in our collective journey. As we stand at the precipice of a new era, the concept of Society 5.0 emerges as a compelling vision, transcending traditional paradigms of societal development. Society 5.0 envisions a future where the seamless integration of advanced technologies not only propels economic growth but, more fundamentally, serves as a catalyst for the enhancement of human well-being and societal advancement [1, 17, 18].

At its core, Society 5.0 is a response to the growing imperative to harmonize the unprecedented capabilities of technology with the innate needs and aspirations of humanity. Unlike previous industrial revolutions that primarily focused on economic and industrial progress, Society 5.0 represents a paradigm shift—a departure from the mechanistic to the human-centric. The emphasis is on the holistic development of individuals and society, recognizing that technology's true measure lies not in its sophistication but in its ability to enrich lives [19–27].

The focal point of Society 5.0 is a relentless commitment to human well-being. It envisions a society where technology, guided by ethical principles and a profound understanding of human needs, becomes a transformative force for good. From healthcare to education, from urban planning to environmental sustainability, the primary objective is to create a society that is not just technologically advanced but, more importantly, humanely advanced [28–33].

Society 5.0 perceives technology not as an end in itself but as a means to elevate the human experience. It envisions a society where technology acts as an empowering tool, fostering inclusivity, enhancing individual capabilities, and collectively addressing the most pressing challenges of our time. As we delve into the nuances of Society 5.0, we embark on a journey to understand how this vision unfolds, with a keen focus on the profound ways in which technology becomes a cornerstone for societal advancement and, ultimately, the well-being of humanity [34, 35].

Furthermore, Industry 5.0 employs a blend of technological advancements and organizational ideas to create and oversee supply chains and operations as robust, sustainable, and people-focused systems. Although the concept of Industry 5.0 has been clarified, nothing is known about how it will affect supply chains and future operations [36]. Despite the perception that Industry 4.0 will advance sustainable development, a number of pressing sustainability issues have been disregarded or misinterpreted by the movement, giving rise to the Industry 5.0 agenda. Although most people agree that Industry 5.0 has desired sustainability characteristics, little is known about how this agenda may actually bring about sustainable transformation [37].

Moreover, the emergence of ChatGPT has marked a shift in the field of Artificial Intelligence from Algorithmic Intelligence to Linguistic Intelligence. In this new era, real-time and online interactions between humans and machines, as well as between genuine and artificial entities, are crucial and dynamic [38].

### 1.2 Nanotechnology overview: unveiling the world at the nanoscale

Nanotechnology, an intricate and revolutionary field, ushers us into a realm where the manipulation of matter occurs at the nanoscale. At its essence, nanotechnology is the science, engineering, and application of materials and devices with structures, properties, and performance characteristics that emerge at the scale of nanometers. A nanometer, denoted as one billionth of a meter, is a scale so minuscule that it ventures into the realm of individual atoms and molecules [39–42].

To put this into perspective, the diameter of a human hair is approximately 80,000–100,000 nanometers. At the nanoscale, materials exhibit unique properties and behaviors that differ markedly from their macroscale counterparts. These properties stem from the quantum effects that dominate at such dimensions, providing a playground for innovation and exploration.

Nanotechnology encompasses a spectrum of applications, from nanomaterials to nanodevices, and it extends across various scientific disciplines, including physics, chemistry, biology, and engineering. The ability to engineer and manipulate materials at the atomic and molecular level grants unprecedented control over their properties. Researchers and engineers delve into this microscopic world with the aim of

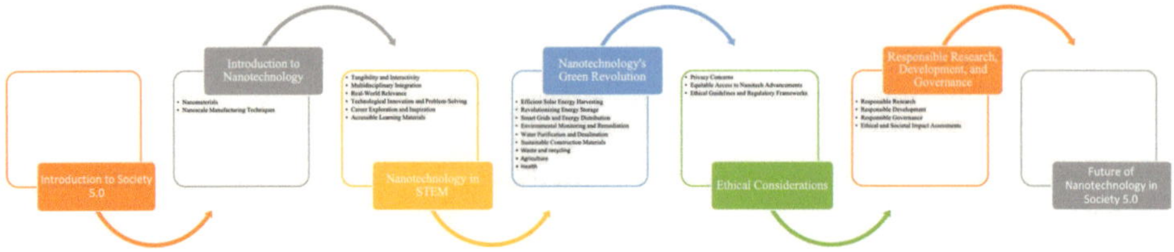


**Figure 1.**
*The chapter approach.*

harnessing its potential to revolutionize industries, from healthcare and electronics to energy and materials science [43–45].

In the chapters that follow, we embark on a journey into the world of nanotechnology, exploring its fundamental principles, applications, and, most importantly, its transformative role within the paradigm of Society 5.0. As we navigate this intricate landscape [46–48], we uncover the promise and potential that nanotechnology holds in advancing the human-centric revolution using Artificial Intelligence (AI) [49], shaping a future where the infinitesimally small becomes the foundation for monumental progress [50].

**Figure 1** illustrates the structure of the paper and the title of the paper.

## 2. Methodology

This review paper utilizes a comprehensive analysis of existing literature to explore and synthesize key insights into the role of nanotechnology in advancing the principles of Society 5.0. The methodology involves a thorough examination of academic articles, books, and reports to extract relevant information on nanomaterials, nanoscale manufacturing techniques, educational applications, environmental sustainability, and ethical considerations.

A scoping review was conducted to identify and analyze scholarly works related to nanotechnology and its intersections with Society 5.0.

Information was extracted from the selected literature (the articles with relevance to Nanotechnology principles, applications, and their alignment with Society 5.0 goals) focusing on key themes related to (Nanomaterials, Manufacturing Techniques, Green Revolution, Resource Efficiency, and Ethical Considerations).

The extracted data were then synthesized to provide a cohesive narrative on how nanotechnology aligns with the principles of Society 5.0. The synthesis includes case studies and discussions on the transformative potential, challenges, and future prospects of nanotechnology in fostering a human-centric technological revolution.

## 3. Key principles and concepts in nanotechnology: unveiling nanomaterials and manufacturing techniques

Nanotechnology, operating at the scale of nanometers, introduces a myriad of principles and concepts that redefine the properties and behavior of materials. Two foundational aspects of nanotechnology are nanomaterials and nanoscale manufacturing techniques, each playing a pivotal role in the innovation and transformation this field promises [51–54].

### 3.1 Nanomaterials

Nanomaterials represent the building blocks of nanotechnology. At the nanoscale, materials exhibit distinct properties due to quantum effects and increased surface-to-volume ratios. Several types of nanomaterials exist, each offering unique characteristics:

- *Nanoparticles*: particles with dimensions in the nanometer range, often used for their enhanced reactivity and unique optical, electronic, or magnetic properties.

- Nanotubes and nanowires: cylindrical structures with diameters at the nanoscale, possessing exceptional strength and conductivity. Carbon nanotubes, for example, exhibit remarkable mechanical and electrical properties.

- *Nanocomposites*: materials composed of a combination of nanoscale constituents, offering a synergistic combination of properties from different components.

- *Nanocolloids*: stable suspensions of nanoparticles in a liquid medium, used in various applications such as drug delivery and imaging.

Understanding and manipulating these nanomaterials is fundamental to unlocking their potential in diverse fields, ranging from medicine to electronics.

### 3.2 Nanoscale manufacturing techniques

Nanoscale manufacturing techniques enable the precise design and assembly of nanomaterials into functional structures. Several key techniques have emerged to manipulate matter at the nanoscale [55–58]:

- Top-down approaches: involves reducing the size of larger structures to nanoscale dimensions. Techniques such as lithography use this method to etch or pattern materials at the nanoscale.

- Bottom-up approaches: assembling nanoscale structures from individual atoms or molecules. Self-assembly processes, like molecular nanotechnology, leverage this approach.

- Chemical vapor deposition (CVD): depositing thin films of material on a substrate, commonly used in the semiconductor industry to create nanoscale layers.

- Molecular beam epitaxy (MBE): precisely depositing individual atoms or molecules to create thin films with specific properties.

- Template-assisted methods: using templates or molds to guide the assembly of nanoscale structures. Electrospinning and nanoimprinting fall under this category.

These manufacturing techniques empower scientists and engineers to sculpt materials with unparalleled precision, enabling the creation of nanodevices and nanosystems that form the backbone of innovations in Society 5.0.

In the sections ahead, we will delve deeper into the applications and implications of nanomaterials and manufacturing techniques, exploring how these fundamental principles contribute to the advancement of the human-centric revolution envisioned by Society 5.0.

## 4. Nanotechnology as an educational catalyst in STEM disciplines: inspiring the next generation of innovators

Nanotechnology, with its capacity to unveil the mysteries of the nanoscale world, offers a powerful educational tool to captivate the minds of students and ignite their curiosity in STEM (Science, Technology, Engineering, and Mathematics) disciplines. By incorporating nanotechnology into educational curricula, educators can stimulate interest, foster critical thinking, and prepare the next generation of innovators for the challenges and opportunities of a technologically advanced future [59–62].

1. *Tangibility and interactivity*: nanotechnology provides a tangible and interactive platform for learning. Hands-on activities, experiments, and demonstrations involving nanoscale materials and devices allow students to directly engage with scientific concepts. This experiential learning approach not only deepens their understanding of complex STEM principles but also instills a sense of wonder and curiosity.

2. *Multidisciplinary integration*: nanotechnology inherently spans multiple scientific disciplines, seamlessly integrating concepts from physics, chemistry, biology, and engineering. This multidisciplinary nature mirrors the collaborative environment prevalent in real-world STEM applications. Educators can leverage nanotechnology to break down traditional disciplinary silos and promote a holistic understanding of STEM subjects.

3. *Real-world relevance*: nanotechnology's impact extends into various industries, from healthcare to electronics and materials science. By highlighting real-world applications, educators can demonstrate the practical relevance of STEM disciplines. This connection to tangible, real-world problems not only enhances students' motivation but also illustrates how STEM knowledge can be harnessed to address global challenges.

4. *Technological innovation and problem-solving*: nanotechnology encourages a mindset of innovation and problem-solving. Students engaging with nanotechnology learn to think critically, creatively, and analytically. They develop the skills needed to tackle complex problems and design novel solutions, fostering an entrepreneurial spirit essential for the rapidly evolving landscape of technology and industry.

5. *Career exploration and inspiration*: integrating nanotechnology into STEM education provides students with insights into potential career paths. Exposure to cutting-edge technologies and the impact of nanotechnology on various indus-

tries can inspire students to pursue STEM-related careers. Guest lectures, industry partnerships, and field trips to nanotechnology facilities further enhance the connection between classroom learning and future career possibilities.

6. *Accessible learning materials*: advancements in educational technology and online resources make nanotechnology accessible to a wide range of students. Virtual labs, simulations, and online courses enable learners to explore nanoscale phenomena and experiments beyond the constraints of traditional classroom settings, fostering a more inclusive and flexible educational experience.

Incorporating nanotechnology into STEM education not only enhances the quality of learning but also cultivates a generation of STEM enthusiasts equipped with the skills and mindset needed to navigate the complexities of our technologically driven world. As we look toward the future, the educational integration of nanotechnology stands as a cornerstone in preparing students to contribute meaningfully to the ongoing human-centric revolution in Society 5.0 [63, 64].

Nanotechnology, with its capacity to revolutionize how we perceive and interact with matter at the smallest scales, holds significant potential in promoting accessible and inclusive learning environments in STEM (Science, Technology, Engineering, and Mathematics) education. By leveraging the transformative potential of nanotechnology, we move closer to a future where equal opportunities for quality STEM education are extended to every learner, fostering a diverse and empowered generation of individuals ready to contribute to the human-centric revolution in Society 5.0.

## 5. Nanotechnology's green revolution: advancing clean energy generation and storage

Nanotechnology stands at the forefront of a green revolution, driving innovations that hold the potential to transform how we generate and store clean energy. In the pursuit of sustainability goals, nanotechnology is catalyzing breakthroughs across various domains, ushering in a new era of efficiency, affordability, and environmental responsibility [65, 66].

*Efficient solar energy harvesting: nanoscale photovoltaics*: nanotechnology is enhancing the efficiency of solar cells through the development of advanced photovoltaic materials. Innovations like perovskite solar cells and quantum dot solar cells leverage nanoscale materials to capture and convert sunlight into electricity more effectively. This leads to higher energy yields and a reduced reliance on traditional, less sustainable energy sources.

*Revolutionizing energy storage: nanomaterials in batteries*: nanotechnology is transforming energy storage solutions, particularly in batteries. Nanomaterials, such as nanostructured electrodes and nanocomposite materials, enhance the capacity, charge/discharge rates, and lifespan of batteries. This innovation not only supports renewable energy integration but also contributes to the development of more efficient electric vehicles.

*Smart grids and energy distribution: nanogrids and nanosensors*: nanotechnology plays a role in the development of smart grids and energy distribution systems. Nanogrids, equipped with nanosensors, enable precise monitoring and control of energy distribution. This enhances grid stability, reduces energy losses, and accommodates the decentralized nature of renewable energy sources like solar and wind.

*Efficient lighting solutions: nanophotonics for LEDs*: nanotechnology is advancing lighting solutions through nanophotonics. Nanomaterials are integrated into Light Emitting Diodes (LEDs), resulting in more energy-efficient lighting with enhanced brightness and color control. This contributes to energy conservation and aligns with sustainability goals in the field of illumination.

*Energy-efficient building materials: nanomaterials in construction*: nanotechnology is influencing the development of energy-efficient building materials. Nanomaterials like aerogels and phase-change materials enhance insulation properties, regulating temperature and reducing the need for heating or cooling. This leads to more sustainable and energy-efficient buildings.

*Clean fuel production: nanocatalysts for hydrogen production*: nanocatalysts play a role in clean fuel production, particularly in hydrogen generation through water splitting. Nanotechnology enhances the efficiency of catalytic processes, making the production of clean fuels more viable and sustainable.

*Environmental monitoring and remediation: nano-enabled environmental sensors*: nanotechnology contributes to environmental sustainability by enabling the development of nanoscale sensors for real-time environmental monitoring. These sensors can detect pollutants and facilitate targeted remediation efforts, ensuring a cleaner and healthier environment.

The integration of nanotechnology into clean energy generation and storage aligns with global sustainability goals, offering solutions that not only address current energy challenges but also contribute to the mitigation of environmental impacts. As nanotechnology continues to advance, it promises to play a pivotal role in achieving a more sustainable and eco-friendly energy landscape [67, 68].

## 6. Nanomaterials: catalysts for resource efficiency and environmental sustainability

Nanomaterials, operating at the nanoscale, have emerged as pivotal agents in revolutionizing resource efficiency and mitigating environmental impact. Their unique properties and applications span various industries, offering innovative solutions that align with the goals of sustainability. Here's a closer look at the role of nanomaterials in advancing resource efficiency and reducing environmental impact [69–72]:

1. *Water purification and desalination: nanofiltration membranes*: nanomaterials, such as graphene oxide and carbon nanotubes, are integral to the development of advanced nanofiltration membranes. These membranes exhibit superior filtration properties, enabling efficient removal of contaminants from water sources. Nanotechnology contributes to sustainable water management by improving desalination processes and enhancing access to clean water.

   *Case study: graphene-based nanofiltration membranes*: graphene-based nanofiltration membranes have shown remarkable efficiency in water purification processes. In a case study, researchers developed membranes composed of graphene oxide to selectively filter out contaminants, including heavy metals and organic pollutants, from water sources. The high permeability and selective filtration properties of these nanomaterial-based membranes contribute to sustainable water treatment practices.

2. *Efficient energy harvesting and storage*: nanomaterials in batteries and supercapacitors: nanotechnology enhances the performance of energy storage devices through the incorporation of nanomaterials in batteries and supercapacitors. Nanostructured electrodes and materials increase energy storage capacity, charge/discharge rates, and overall efficiency. This promotes the transition to clean and renewable energy sources while reducing reliance on traditional energy systems with higher environmental footprints.

   *Case study: nanomaterials in lithium-sulfur batteries*: nanotechnology plays a crucial role in advancing sustainable energy storage solutions. In a case study, researchers applied nanomaterials, such as nanostructured sulfur composites, in lithium-sulfur batteries. This innovation enhances the energy storage capacity and cycling stability of the batteries, making them more efficient and sustainable for renewable energy storage applications.

3. *Lightweight and high-strength materials: nanocomposites*: nanomaterials contribute to the development of nanocomposites, which are lightweight yet possess high strength and durability. These materials find applications in industries such as automotive and aerospace, leading to the production of lighter vehicles and structures. The use of nanocomposites reduces the overall material consumption and enhances resource efficiency.

4. *Waste management and recycling: nanomaterials for selective adsorption:* nanomaterials, including nanoparticles and nanocomposites, can be designed for selective adsorption of pollutants and contaminants. This capability is utilized in waste management and recycling processes, allowing for the targeted removal of specific pollutants from waste streams. Nanotechnology aids in the creation of more efficient and environmentally friendly recycling methods.

   *Case study: nanomaterials for targeted pollutant removal in wastewater*: nanotechnology is employed in waste management through the development of nanomaterials for targeted pollutant removal. In a case study, researchers utilized nanomaterials with high adsorption capacities to selectively capture specific pollutants from industrial wastewater. This approach enhances the efficiency of wastewater treatment processes, contributing to more sustainable and eco-friendly waste management practices.

5. *Enhanced agricultural practices: nanopesticides and nanofertilizers*: nanomaterials play a role in agriculture by improving the efficiency of pesticides and fertilizers. Nanoformulations enable targeted delivery of agrochemicals, reducing the overall quantity required and minimizing environmental runoff. This precision in agricultural practices enhances resource efficiency and reduces the ecological impact of conventional farming.

   *Case study: nanofertilizers for crop yield improvement*: nanotechnology contributes to sustainable agriculture through the development of nanofertilizers. In a case study, researchers explored the use of nanomaterials to encapsulate and deliver nutrients to plants more efficiently. This nanotechnology-enabled approach enhances nutrient uptake by crops, reduces fertilizer runoff, and improves overall agricultural sustainability by optimizing resource use.

6. *Air quality improvement: nanomaterials in catalysis*: nanocatalysts contribute to air quality improvement through applications in catalytic converters. These catalysts facilitate more efficient and complete combustion of pollutants in vehicle emissions, reducing the release of harmful substances into the atmosphere.

   *Case study: nanocatalysts in automobile catalytic converters*: nanocatalysts are employed in catalytic converters to mitigate air pollution from vehicle emissions. In a case study, researchers developed nanocatalysts with enhanced surface areas and catalytic activities, leading to more efficient conversion of harmful pollutants into less toxic substances. This nanotechnology application contributes to improved air quality and aligns with sustainable practices in the automotive industry.

7. *Sustainable construction materials: nanomaterials in concrete*: nanotechnology enhances the properties of construction materials like concrete. The incorporation of nanomaterials improves the strength, durability, and self-healing capabilities of concrete, leading to longer-lasting structures. This extension of material lifespan contributes to resource efficiency in the construction industry.

   *Case study: nanomaterials in self-healing concrete*: nanotechnology contributes to eco-friendly construction practices through the development of self-healing concrete. In a case study, nanomaterials, such as nanoparticles of calcium carbonate or other healing agents, were incorporated into the concrete mix. These nanoparticles react with water and carbon dioxide in the air, filling microcracks in the concrete and enhancing its durability. This innovation not only reduces the need for frequent maintenance and repairs but also extends the lifespan of structures, aligning with sustainability goals in the construction industry.

By harnessing the unique properties of nanomaterials, industries can optimize processes, reduce waste, and enhance the performance of various materials and systems. This, in turn, fosters resource efficiency and contributes to a more sustainable and environmentally friendly approach to manufacturing, agriculture, energy, and waste management. As nanotechnology continues to advance, its role in promoting resource efficiency and reducing environmental impact will become increasingly pronounced [73, 74].

These case studies illustrate how nanotechnology applications are making significant strides in promoting sustainability across diverse sectors. From water purification to construction materials and renewable energy storage, nanomaterials are proving to be instrumental in advancing eco-friendly practices and contributing to a more sustainable and resilient future (**Table 1**) [75, 76].

These case studies exemplify how nanotechnology applications align with the goals of Society 5.0, fostering a future where technology is harnessed for the benefit of individuals and society. From personalized healthcare to sustainable solutions and inclusive education, nanotechnology serves as a catalyst for positive societal transformation in alignment with the principles of Society 5.0.

| | Application | Case study |
|---|---|---|
| Precision medicine | Targeted drug delivery systems | In the field of oncology, nanotechnology has facilitated the development of targeted drug delivery systems. Nanoparticles are engineered to deliver chemotherapy directly to cancer cells, minimizing damage to healthy tissues. This precision medicine approach aligns with the Society 5.0 goal of personalized healthcare, enhancing treatment efficacy while reducing side effects. |
| Environmental sustainability | Nanomaterials for water purification | Nanotechnology plays a pivotal role in addressing water scarcity. Nanomaterials like graphene oxide and carbon nanotubes are employed in advanced filtration systems, removing contaminants at the molecular level. These nanotech solutions contribute to sustainable water management, aligning with Society 5.0's focus on environmental stewardship and resource efficiency. |
| Smart energy solutions | Nanomaterials in solar cells | Nanotechnology enhances the efficiency of solar cells through the development of nanomaterial-based photovoltaics. Innovations like perovskite solar cells leverage nanoscale materials to capture and convert sunlight into electricity more effectively. This aligns with Society 5.0's commitment to sustainable energy sources and smart technologies. |
| Inclusive education | Nanotechnology in educational tools | Nanotechnology is integrated into educational tools, making STEM subjects more accessible. For instance, nanoscale experiments conducted through virtual laboratories provide interactive and inclusive learning experiences. This aligns with Society 5.0's goal of education for all, leveraging technology to create inclusive learning environments. |
| Health monitoring | Wearable nanosensors | Nanosensors embedded in wearable devices offer continuous health monitoring, providing real-time data on physiological parameters. These nanodevices empower individuals to take proactive measures for their well-being. This aligns with the Society 5.0 vision of personalized healthcare and emphasizes the role of technology in enhancing individual and community health. |
| Inclusive innovation | Nanotechnology in 3D printing | Nanotechnology contributes to inclusive innovation through advancements in 3D printing. Nanomaterials enhance the precision and versatility of 3D-printed structures, making the technology more accessible for customized manufacturing, prosthetics, and affordable housing solutions. This aligns with Society 5.0's commitment to technological inclusivity and diverse applications. |

**Table 1.**
*Furthermore, some additional real-world case studies: nanotechnology applications enabling Society 5.0 goals.*

## 7. Analysis

At the nanoscale, nanomaterials unveil a realm of unique properties dictated by quantum effects. This intrinsic behavior becomes a linchpin in the harmonious merger of technological progress with human-centric ideals. Nanoparticles, nanotubes, and nanocomposites, acting as the fundamental building blocks, are diversified tools that can be precisely tailored for specific applications, from medicine to electronics. This diversity opens avenues for materials designed to enhance human well-being, exemplified by the use of nanocomposites in sustainable construction—a clear alignment with the principles of Society 5.0.

Nanoscale manufacturing techniques, including top-down and bottom-up approaches, provide unprecedented precision in designing and assembling nanomaterials. This precision is indispensable for crafting nanodevices, contributing substantially to innovations in Society 5.0. It signifies that nanotechnology is not merely an advancement but a conduit to address societal challenges. For instance, the deployment of nanogrids and nanosensors in energy distribution embodies an application that ensures efficient and sustainable energy practices, reflecting the commitment to societal advancement and the enhancement of human life.

In the realm of education, nanotechnology brings forth tangible and interactive learning experiences, inviting students to directly engage with the nanoscale world. This hands-on approach aligns seamlessly with the human-centric vision of Society 5.0, encouraging active participation in the learning process. The real-world relevance of nanotechnology in STEM education prepares students for the challenges of a technologically advanced future, ensuring that education is not merely knowledge-centric but also aligned with the skills essential for societal progress. The transformative potential of nanotechnology is further realized by revolutionizing learning materials, promoting accessibility, and inclusivity. By leveraging nanotechnology in educational tools, it extends the vision of equal opportunities for quality STEM education to every learner, fostering a diverse and empowered generation in line with the principles of Society 5.0.

In the domain of clean energy, nanotechnology-driven innovations address global sustainability goals by offering solutions that are efficient, affordable, and environmentally responsible. This alignment with the human-centric ideals of Society 5.0 signifies that technological progress contributes not only to societal well-being but also to environmental harmony. The deployment of nanotechnology-enabled environmental sensors underscores a commitment to environmental responsibility, actively monitoring and remediating environmental issues—a testament to technology as a transformative force for good in alignment with Society 5.0's vision.

Nanomaterials, acting as catalysts for resource efficiency, play a pivotal role in optimizing processes, reducing waste, and enhancing the performance of various materials and systems. This resource efficiency contributes to a more sustainable approach to manufacturing, resonating with the goals of Society 5.0 to create a society that is not only technologically advanced but also environmentally conscious. The diverse applications of nanomaterials, spanning water purification to lightweight and high-strength materials, demonstrate their instrumental role in promoting sustainability across different sectors—a testament to Society 5.0's emphasis on using technology to address societal challenges and improve the quality of life for individuals.

These interconnected sections underscore how nanotechnology, with its foundational principles and diverse applications, serves as a linchpin in advancing the human-centric revolution envisioned by Society 5.0. By seamlessly integrating nanotechnology into various facets of society, from education to clean energy, the transformative potential of technology is harnessed for the benefit of individuals and society as a whole, aligning harmoniously with the core ideals of Society 5.0.

The concept of nanotechnology within the context of Society 5.0 is clearly illustrated in **Figure 2**, which shows the implications and their relationship with human-centric approaches.

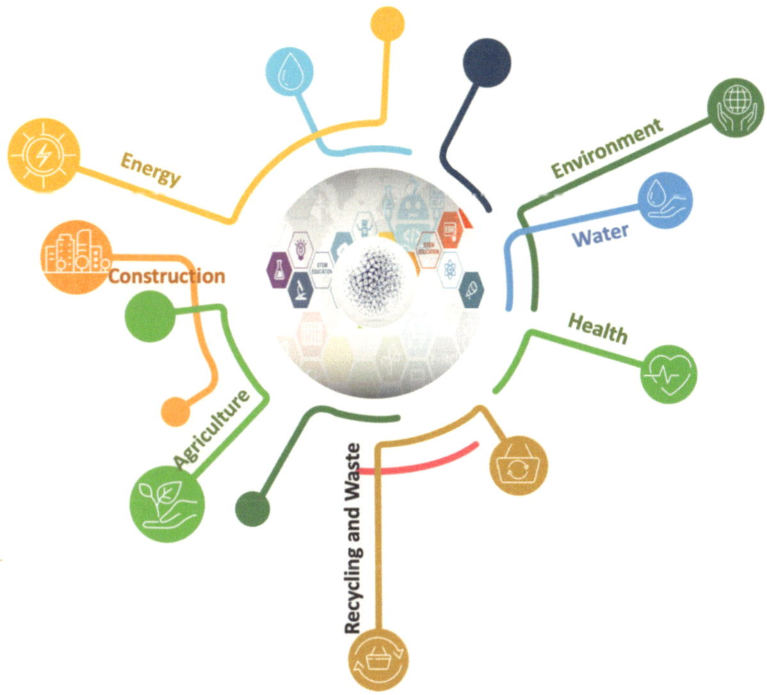


**Figure 2.**
*The concept of nanotechnology within the context of Society 5.0.*

## 8. Navigating ethical considerations in nanotechnology: balancing progress with responsibility

Nanotechnology's transformative potential brings forth a host of ethical considerations that demand careful attention as we venture into this realm of innovation. Addressing concerns related to privacy and equitable access to nanotech advancements is crucial to ensuring that the benefits of nanotechnology are ethically harnessed for the collective well-being of society [77–81].

1. *Privacy concerns*

   - *Nanoscale surveillance technologies*: the precision of nanoscale sensors and devices raises concerns about the potential for intrusive surveillance. Tiny sensors capable of collecting highly detailed data may inadvertently encroach upon personal privacy. Striking a balance between leveraging nanotechnology for beneficial applications, such as in healthcare monitoring, and safeguarding individual privacy requires robust ethical frameworks and regulations.

   - *Data security and ownership*: as nanotechnology generates vast amounts of data, questions surrounding data security and ownership come to the forefront. Ensuring that individuals have control over their personal data and that comprehensive security measures are in place is imperative. Ethical guidelines should address the responsible handling, storage, and sharing of nanotech-generated data to prevent unauthorized access and potential misuse.

2. *Equitable access to nanotech advancements*

   - *Technological disparities*: there is a risk that nanotechnology advancements may exacerbate existing technological disparities, creating a divide between those who have access to cutting-edge nanotech applications and those who do not. Ensuring equitable distribution and access to nanotechnological benefits requires proactive efforts to bridge technological gaps, particularly in education and resource allocation.

   - *Global equity*: the global landscape introduces challenges related to international equity. Developing nations may face barriers in adopting and benefiting from nanotechnology due to resource limitations or a lack of infrastructure. Ethical considerations should drive collaborative efforts to transfer technology responsibly, ensuring that the advantages of nanotechnology reach diverse populations globally.

3. *Ethical guidelines and regulatory frameworks*

   - *Transparent research practices*: nanotechnology research should uphold transparency in methodologies and outcomes. Ethical guidelines should emphasize the importance of clear communication about potential risks and benefits to stakeholders, fostering trust between the scientific community, policymakers, and the public.

   - *Community engagement*: inclusive decision-making processes and community engagement are essential for navigating the ethical terrain of nanotechnology. Ensuring that diverse voices are heard helps in identifying potential ethical concerns and tailoring solutions that reflect the values and perspectives of the communities affected by nanotech advancements.

4. *Responsive regulations*: regulatory frameworks must evolve to keep pace with nanotechnological advancements. Adaptable regulations should strike a balance between fostering innovation and safeguarding ethical principles. Regular assessments and updates to regulations will be crucial in addressing unforeseen ethical challenges that may arise as nanotechnology continues to progress.

In the pursuit of a responsible and ethical integration of nanotechnology into society, stakeholders from scientific communities, regulatory bodies, and the public must collaboratively design and implement frameworks that ensure privacy is protected, access is equitable, and the potential benefits of nanotechnology are realized without compromising ethical values. By doing so, we can harness the potential of nanotechnology to contribute positively to Society 5.0 while upholding ethical standards that respect individual rights and promote societal well-being [82, 83].

## 9. Upholding responsibility in nanotechnology: navigating research, development, and governance in Society 5.0

As nanotechnology unfolds as a driving force in the transition to Society 5.0, the principles of responsible research, development, and governance become paramount. This nascent field's transformative potential requires a conscientious approach to ensure that its benefits align with the human-centric vision of Society 5.0 while mitigating potential risks and ethical concerns [84–88].

1. *Responsible research*

    - *Nanosafety and risk assessment*: responsible research in nanotechnology necessitates a rigorous commitment to nanosafety and risk assessment. Understanding the potential environmental and health impacts of nanomaterials is crucial. Researchers must adopt comprehensive safety protocols, considering the unique characteristics of nanoscale materials, to prevent unintended consequences and ensure the well-being of both humans and ecosystems.

    - *Open collaboration and knowledge sharing*: encouraging open collaboration and knowledge sharing is essential for responsible nanotechnology research. Embracing a culture of transparency promotes collective learning, helps identify potential risks early in the research phase, and facilitates the development of ethical guidelines that govern nanotechnology applications.

2. *Responsible development*

    - *Ethical design and application*: in the development phase, responsible practices involve integrating ethical considerations into the design and application of nanotechnological solutions. Thoughtful design choices, considering societal impacts and potential unintended consequences, contribute to the development of technologies that align with the principles of Society 5.0.

    - *Inclusive innovation*: responsible development requires an inclusive approach to innovation. Ensuring that the benefits of nanotechnology are accessible to diverse populations promotes societal equity. This inclusivity extends to addressing the needs of marginalized communities and fostering solutions that enhance overall well-being.

3. *Responsible governance*

    - *Regulatory frameworks and compliance*: governance plays a pivotal role in ensuring responsible nanotechnology deployment. Establishing and enforcing regulatory frameworks that oversee nanotechnology applications is critical. Regulatory bodies should adapt swiftly to technological advancements, maintaining a balance between fostering innovation and safeguarding against potential risks.

    - *International collaboration and standards*: given the global nature of nanotechnology, responsible governance involves international collaboration and the development of shared standards. Collaborative efforts facilitate the exchange of best practices, address regulatory gaps, and ensure a harmonized approach to responsible nanotechnology development on the global stage.

- *Public engagement and ethical discourse*: incorporating public engagement and ethical discourse into governance processes is vital. Public input helps shape policies that reflect societal values, and ethical discussions provide a platform for diverse perspectives to be considered. This transparency fosters a sense of trust and accountability in the governance of nanotechnology.

4. *Ethical and societal impact assessments*

- *Assessing ethical implications*: integrating ethical and societal impact assessments into the research and development lifecycle is integral to responsible governance. These assessments help identify potential ethical challenges, unintended consequences, and societal implications, enabling informed decision-making and course corrections where necessary.

- As Society 5.0 unfolds, the responsible integration of nanotechnology becomes a cornerstone for shaping a future where technological progress harmonizes with human values. By prioritizing responsible research, development, and governance, stakeholders can navigate the complex landscape of nanotechnology in a manner that upholds ethical standards, aligns with the human-centric vision of Society 5.0, and ensures the long-term well-being of individuals and society as a whole [89–91].

## 10. The future nexus: nanotechnology and the human-centric revolution of Society 5.0

As we peer into the future, the trajectory of nanotechnology unfolds as a linchpin in the realization of Society 5.0's human-centric revolution. The transformative potential of nanotechnology is poised to propel advancements that will reshape the way we live, work, and interact with the world, further aligning with the principles set forth by Society 5.0 [92–94].

- *Enhanced healthcare paradigms: nanomedicine and personalized therapies*: nanotechnology is poised to revolutionize healthcare with personalized and targeted treatments. Nanoscale drug delivery systems, precise diagnostics, and therapeutic interventions tailored to individual genetic profiles will usher in an era where healthcare is truly personalized, preventive, and patient-centric.

- *Integrated Internet of Nano-Things (IoNT): seamless connectivity at the nanoscale*: the integration of nanosensors into the Internet of Things (IoT) forms the Internet of Nano-Things (IoNT). This interconnected network of nanoscale devices will enable real-time monitoring and data exchange at the molecular level. IoNT applications will range from environmental sensing to health monitoring, contributing to a smarter and more responsive society.

- *Revolutionizing energy landscapes: nanotechnology in energy storage*: future energy solutions will be shaped by nanotechnology, particularly in the development of advanced energy storage systems. Nanomaterials will enhance the efficiency and storage capacity of batteries and supercapacitors, supporting the widespread adoption of renewable energy sources and contributing to a sustainable and decentralized energy landscape.

- *Nanotechnology-enabled AI and robotics: synthesis of nanotechnology, AI, and robotics*: the synergy between nanotechnology, artificial intelligence (AI), and robotics will give rise to intelligent nanobots capable of performing intricate tasks at the molecular level. This convergence will underpin advancements in fields such as precision manufacturing, targeted drug delivery, and autonomous systems, furthering the augmentation of human capabilities.

- *Nano-ethics and responsible development: ethical guidelines for nanotechnology*: the future of nanotechnology within Society 5.0 demands a robust ethical framework. As nanotech applications become more pervasive, ethical considerations will center around issues such as data privacy, environmental impact, and equitable access. Responsible governance, stakeholder engagement, and ongoing discourse will be pivotal in navigating these ethical complexities.

- *Educational empowerment and lifelong learning: nanotechnology in lifelong education*: nanotechnology's educational impact will extend to lifelong learning, providing accessible and engaging educational tools. Virtual reality-enhanced nano-education platforms will allow individuals to explore the nanoscale world, fostering a continuous learning mindset and ensuring that the benefits of nanotechnology are accessible to all.

- *Global collaboration for societal progress: international cooperation in nanotech research*: the future of nanotechnology in Society 5.0 hinges on global collaboration. Nations, research institutions, and industry leaders will collaborate to share knowledge, best practices, and resources. This collaborative spirit will accelerate breakthroughs, drive innovation, and address global challenges such as healthcare disparities, climate change, and resource management [95, 96].

As nanotechnology continues to evolve, its integration into the fabric of Society 5.0 holds the promise of a future where technology is not just a tool but an enabler of human well-being, societal advancement, and harmonious coexistence with the environment. By embracing the principles of responsible research, development, and governance, society can navigate the unfolding nanotechnological landscape, shaping a future that embodies the human-centric revolution envisioned by Society 5.0.

## 11. Conclusion

In the exploration of "Nano and Society 5.0: Advancing the Human-Centric Revolution," we embark on a journey through the intersection of nanotechnology and the visionary paradigm of Society 5.0. This chapter delves into the profound implications of nanotechnology as a catalyst for transformative change, aligning with the core tenets of a society that places human well-being at its epicenter.

As we navigate the landscapes of nanoscience and its integration into the fabric of Society 5.0, a narrative of promise unfolds. Nanotechnology emerges not merely as a scientific discipline but as a beacon guiding the evolution of a society that prioritizes human needs, aspirations, and inclusivity. The synergy between nano-scale innovation and the overarching goals of Society 5.0 accentuates the potential to reshape how we live, work, learn, and connect with our surroundings.

The amalgamation of nanotechnology and Society 5.0 paints a canvas where precision meets purpose. In the pursuit of advancing the human-centric revolution, nanotechnology stands as a linchpin, offering solutions that transcend traditional boundaries. From personalized medicine and sustainable energy solutions to inclusive education and accessible technologies, the applications of nanotechnology resonate with the ethos of Society 5.0—a society that embraces technological advancements to elevate the human experience.

As we reflect on the case studies, discussions, and explorations within this chapter, it becomes evident that nanotechnology is not merely a tool but an integral part of the narrative unfolding in our pursuit of a better future. The concept of Society 5.0, characterized by the harmonious integration of technology and humanity, finds an ally in nanotechnology—a silent force propelling the human-centric revolution into new realms of possibility.

However, as we chart this course toward a future shaped by nano-driven innovations, a conscious acknowledgment of ethical considerations and responsible governance becomes paramount. Navigating the transformative potential of nanotechnology demands a commitment to ensuring equitable access, safeguarding privacy, and fostering a culture of transparency and inclusivity.

In conclusion, the synergy between nanotechnology and Society 5.0 embodies the spirit of progress intertwined with human values. This chapter serves as a testament to the collaborative efforts of scientists, innovators, policymakers, and society at large, collectively steering toward a future where technology empowers individuals, fosters inclusivity, and propels the human-centric revolution envisioned by Society 5.0 into the forefront of our shared reality. As we stand on the precipice of this transformative era, the partnership between nano and Society 5.0 holds the promise of a future where the human experience is not just enriched but fundamentally redefined.

*DOI: http://dx.doi.org/10.5772/intechopen.1004221*

**Author details**

Basma El Zein[1*], Ali Elrashidi[1], Mohanad Dahlan[2], Ahmed Al Jarwan[3] and Ghassan Jabbour[4]

1 Electrical Engineering Department, College of Engineering, University of Business and Technology, Jeddah, Saudi Arabia

2 College of Business Administration, University of Business and Technology, Jeddah, Saudi Arabia

3 Global Council for Tolerance and Peace, Valetta, Malta

4 Canada Research Chair in Engineered Advanced Materials and Devices, Faculty of Engineering, University of Ottawa, Ottawa, ON, Canada

*Address all correspondence to: basma@ieee.org

## References

[1] Rojas C, Peñafiel G, Buitrago D, Romero C. Society 5.0: A Japanese concept for a superintelligent society. Sustainability. 2021;**13**(12):6567

[2] Potočan V, Mulej M, Nedelko Z. Society 5.0: Balancing of Industry 4.0, economic advancement and social problems. Kybernetes. 2020;**50**:794-811

[3] Takakuwa S, Veza I, Celar S. Industry 4.0′ in Europe and East Asia. Vienna, Austria: DAAAM International Vienna; 2018. pp. 0061-0069

[4] Berawi MA. Managing Nature 5.0 in industrial Revolution 4.0 and Society 5.0 era. International Journal of Technology. 2019;**10**:222

[5] Aldabbas M, Xie X, Teufel B, et al. Future security challenges for smart societies: Overview from technical and societal perspectives. In: IEEE-2020 8th International Conference on Smart Grid and Clean Energy Technologies (ICSGCE-2020). Sara-wak, Malaysia: Ei Compendex, Scopus Waterfront Hotel in Kuching; 2020

[6] Calzada I, Cobo C. Unplugging: Deconstructing the Smart City. Social Science Electronic Publishing. 2015;**22**(1):23-43

[7] Mavrodieva AV, Shaw R. Disaster and climate change issues in Japan's Society 5.0 – A discussion. Sustainability. 2020;**12**(5):12

[8] Roblek V, Meko M, Bach MP, et al. The interaction between internet, sustainable development, and emergence of Society 5.0. Data. 2015;**5**(3):80

[9] Shiroishi Y, Uchiyama K, Suzuki N. Better actions for Society 5.0: Using AI for evidence-based policy making that keeps humans in the loop. Computer. 2019;**52**(11):73-78

[10] Zengin Y, Naktiyok S, Kaygn E, et al. An investigation upon Industry 4.0 and Society 5.0 within the context of sustainable development goals. Sustainability. 2015;**13**. Article ID: 2682

[11] Gelfert A. Nanotechnology as ideology: Towards a critical theory of converging technologies. Science, Technology and Society. 2012;**17**(1):143-164

[12] Grinin L, Grinin A. Global technological transformations. Globalistics and Globalization Studies. 2013:98-128

[13] Jain V, Jain S, Mahajan S. Nanomedicines based drug delivery systems for anti-cancer targeting and treatment. Current Drug Delivery. 2015;**12**(2):177-191

[14] Verma V, Thakur P. Nanotechnology in natural world and its application in medical sector. Recent Innovative Trends in Interdisciplinary Research Areas. 2023;**2**:17

[15] Neubauer E. Redefining the role of the university and the social sciences within the emergent structures of Society 5.0. In: Transformation of Higher Education in the Age of Society 5.0: Trends in International Higher Education. Cham: Springer International Publishing; 2023. pp. 9-22

[16] Bhattacharya S, Arkadyuti S. Application of nanotechnology for eco-friendly and sustainable economic development. Diversity and Applications of New Age Nanoparticles. IGI Global. 2023:1-24

[17] Deguchi A, Hirai C, Matsuoka H, Nakano T, Oshima K, Tai M, et al. What is Society 5.0? In: Society 5.0: A People-Centric Super-Smart Society. Singapore: Springer; 2020. pp. 1-23

[18] Smuts H, Smith A. Collaboration of human and machine for knowledge work: an organisational transformation framework for data-driven decision-making. In: Lee ZWY, Chan TKH, Cheung CMK, editors. Information Technology in Organisations and Societies: Multidisciplinary Perspectives from AI to Technostress. Bingley, UK: Emerald Publishing Limited; 2021. pp. 25-59

[19] Zengin Y, Naktiyok S, Kaygın E, Kavak O, Topçuoğlu E. An investigation upon Industry 4.0 and Society 5.0 within the context of sustainable development goals. Sustainability. 2021;**13**:2682

[20] Roblek V, Meško M, Bach MP, Thorpe O, Šprajc P. The interaction between internet, sustainable development, and emergence of Society 5.0. Data. 2020;**5**:80

[21] Konno N, Schillaci CE. Intellectual capital in Society 5.0 by the lens of the knowledge creation theory. Journal of Intellectual Capital. 2021;**22**:478-505

[22] Yıkılmaz İ. New era: The transformation from the Information Society to Super Smart Society (Society 5.0). In: Mert G, Şen E, Yılmaz O, editors. Data, Information and Knowledge Management. Istanbul, Turkey: Nobel Publishing Group; 2020. pp. 85-112

[23] Deguchi A. From smart city to Society 5.0. In: Society 5.0: A People-Centric Super-Smart Society. Singapore: Springer; 2020. pp. 43-65

[24] Serpa S, Ferreira CM. Society 5.0 and sustainability digital innovations: A social process. Journal of Organizational Culture, Communications and Conflict. 2019;**23**:1-14

[25] Lisitsyn AB, Chernukha IM, Nikitina MA. Development of a personalized meat product using structural-parametric modeling. Theory and Practice of Meat Processing. 2019;**4**:11-18

[26] Gonokami M, Nakanishi H. Interview: Creating knowledge collaboratively to forge a richer society tomorrow—An innovation ecosystem to spearhead social transformation. In: Society 5.0: A People-Centric Super-Smart Society. Singapore: Springer; 2020. pp. 145-154

[27] Deguchi A, Karasawa K. Issues and Outlook. In Society 5.0: A People-Centric Super-Smart Society. Singapore: Springer; 2020. pp. 155-173

[28] Gladden ME. Who will be the members of society 5.0? Towards an anthropology of technologically posthumanized future societies. Social Science. 2019;**8**:148

[29] Bryndin E. System synergetic formation of Society 5.0 for development of vital spaces on basis of ecological economic and social programs. Annals of Ecology and Environmental Science. 2018;**1**:12-19

[30] Pater RL, Cristea SL. Correlation "sustainability–functions–competitiveness" for products in Society 5.0. In: Prostean G, Villahoz JJL, Brancu L, Bakacsi G, editors. Innovation in Sustainable Management and Entrepreneurship. Cham, Switzerland: Springer; 2020. pp. 63-77

[31] Carayannis EG, Dezi L, Gregori G, Calo E. Smart environments and techno-centric and human-centric innovations

for industry and Society 5.0: A quintuple helix innovation system view towards smart, sustainable, and inclusive solutions. Journal of the Knowledge Economy. 2021;**13**:926-955

[32] Sołtysik-Piorunkiewicz A, Zdonek I. How Society 5.0 and Industry 4.0 ideas shape the open data performance expectancy. Sustainability. 2021;**13**:917

[33] Bruno S. The challenges of localization, the market, skills and knowledge. In: Society 5.0: Industry of the Future, Technologies, Methods and Tools. Hoboken, NJ, USA: Wiley; 2018. pp. 191-208

[34] Tyagi A, Dananjayan S, Agarwal D, Thariq HF. Blockchain—Internet of things applications: Opportunities and challenges for Industry 4.0 and Society 5.0. Sensors. 2023;**23**(2). Article ID: 947

[35] Wahyuningtyas R, Disastra G, Rismayani R. Toward cooperative competitiveness for community development in economic Society 5.0. Journal of Enterprising Communities: People and Places in the Global Economy. 2023;**17**(3):594-620

[36] Ivanov D. The Industry 5.0 framework: Viability-based integration of the resilience, sustainability, and human-centricity perspectives. International Journal of Production Research. 2023;**61**(5):1683-1695

[37] Ghobakhloo M, Iranmanesh M, Morales ME, Nilashi M, Amran A. Actions and approaches for enabling industry 5.0-driven sustainable industrial transformation: A strategy roadmap. Corporate Social Responsibility and Environmental Management. 2023;**30**(3):1473-1494

[38] Wang FY, Yang J, Wang X, Li, Han QL. Chat with chatgpt on industry 5.0: Learning and decision-making for intelligent industries. IEEE/CAA Journal of Automatica Sinica. 2023;**10**(4):831-834

[39] Mechler A et al. Nanoscale velocity–Drag force relationship in thin liquid layers measured by atomic force microscopy. Applied Physics Letters. 2004;**85**:3881-3883

[40] Snow ES et al. Atomic force microscopy using single-wall C nanotube probes. Journal of Vacuum Science & Technology B. 2002;**B20**:822-827

[41] Stachewicz U et al. Enhanced wetting behavior at electrospun polyamide nanofiber surfaces. Langmuir. 2011;**27**(6):3024-3029

[42] Goldbart O et al. Diameter-dependent wetting of tungsten disulfide nanotubes. Proceedings of the National Academy of Sciences of the United States of America. 2016;**113**(8):13624-13629

[43] Steitz R et al. Nanobubbles and their precursor layer at the interface of water against a hydrophobic substrate. Langmuir. 2003;**19**(6):2409-2418

[44] Zhao B et al. In situ measurement of contact angles and surface tensions of interfacial nanobubbles in ethanol aqueous solutions. Soft Matter. 2016;**12**:3303-3309

[45] Jia Y et al. Identification of surface nanobubbles and resolving their size-dependent stiffness. Science China Physics, Mechanics & Astronomy. 2020;**63**. Article ID: 294614

[46] Tai VC, Che HX, Kong XY, Ho KC, Ng WM. Decoding iron oxide nanoparticles from design and development to real world application in water remediation. Journal of Industrial and Engineering Chemistry. 2023;**127**:82-100

[47] Mohapatra J, Nigam S, George J, Arellano AC, Wang P, Liu JP. Principles and applications of magnetic nanomaterials in magnetically guided bioimaging. Materials Today Physics. 2023;**32**:101003

[48] Malhotra K, Hrovat D, Kumar B, Qu G, Houten JV, Ahmed R, et al. Lanthanide-doped upconversion nanoparticles: Exploring a treasure trove of nir-mediated emerging applications. ACS Applied Materials & Interfaces. 2023;**15**(2):2499-2528

[49] Widjaja G, Kumar A, Chandrasekar V, Shankar BB, Nayak BB. Artificial intelligence and the contributions of nanotechnology to the biomedical sector. Handbook of Research on Advanced Functional Materials for Orthopedic Applications. 2023:65-92

[50] Hossain N, Mobarak MH, Mimona MA, Islam MA, Hossain A, Zohur FT, et al. Advances and significances of nanoparticles in semiconductor applications–A review. Results in Engineering. 2023;**19**:101347

[51] Gomez-Gonzalez MA, Koronfel MA, Goode AE, Al-Ejji M, Voulvoulis N, Parker JE, et al. Chemical evolution of CoCrMo wear particles: An in Situ characterization study. ACS Nano. 2019;**13**:11049

[52] Federici S et al. Anal. Nanoplast. Microplast. Food Additives & Contaminants: Part A: Chemistry, Analysis, Control, Exposure & Risk Assessment. Foreword. 2022;**1**:282

[53] Khalid MF et al. Nanoparticles: The plant saviour under abiotic stresses. Nanomaterials. 2022;**12**(21):3915

[54] Khan ST et al. Engineered nanomaterials in soil: Their impact on soil microbiome and plant health. Plants. 2021;**11**(1). Article ID: 109

[55] Moore K, Wei W. Applications of carbon nanomaterials in perovskite solar cells for solar energy conversion. Nano Materials Science. 2021;**3**(3):276-290

[56] Muhammad I et al. Mechanisms regulating the dynamics of photosynthesis under abiotic stresses. Frontiers in Plant Science. 2020;**11**:11

[57] Murali M et al. Fate, bioaccumulation and toxicity of engineered nanomaterials in plants: Current challenges and future prospects. Science of the Total Environment. 2022;**811**. Article ID: 15229

[58] Pereira ES, Oliveira HC, Fraceto LF, Santaella C. Nanotechnology potential in seed priming for sustainable agriculture. Nanomaterials. 2021;**11**(2). Article ID: 267

[59] Taylor A, Jones G. Proportional reasoning ability and concepts of scale: Surface area to volume relationship in science. International Journal of Science Education. 2009;**31**:1231-1247

[60] Tomasik J, Jin S, Hamers R, Moore J. Design and initial evaluation of an online nanoscience course for teachers. Journal of Nano Education. 2009;**1**:48-69

[61] Toumey C, Baird D. Nanoliteracy: Nurturing understandings of nanotechnology and societal interactions with nanotech. In: Sweeney AE, Seal S, editors. Nanoscale Science and Engineering Education. USA: American Scientific Publishers, University of Central Florida; 2008. pp. 577-589

[62] Tretter T, Jones MG, Andre T, Negishi A, Minogue J. Conceptual boundaries and distances: Students' and experts' concepts of the scale of scientific phenomena. Journal of Research in Science Teaching. 2008;**43**:282-319

[63] Tretter T, Jones MG, Minogue J. Accurary of scale conception in science: Mental maneuverings across many orders of spatial magnitue. Journal of Research in Science Teaching. 2006;**43**:1061-1065

[64] Zenner GM, Crone WC. Introducing nanotechnology and society issues into the classroom. In: Sweeney AE, Seal S, editors. Nanoscale Science and Engineering Education. USA: American Scientific Publishers, University of Central Florida; 2008. pp. 621-647

[65] Smith GB. SPIE Proceedings [SPIE SPIE NanoScience + Engineering - San Diego, California] Nanostructured Thin Films IV-Green Nanotechnology. San Diego, California, United States: SPIE Digital Library; 2011. p. 8104

[66] Chen H, Liu T, Meng Y, Cheng Y, Lu J, Wang H. Novel graphene oxide/aminated lignin aerogels for enhanced adsorption of malachite green in wastewater. Colloids and Surfaces A: Physicochemical and Engineering Aspects. 2020;**253**:603

[67] Ghosh S, Ramaprabhu S. Green synthesis of transition metal nanocrystals encapsulated into nitrogen-doped carbon nanotubes for efficient carbon dioxide capture. Carbon. 2019;**141**:692-703

[68] Leo VV, Singh BP. Prospectus of nanotechnology in bioethanol productions. Green nanotechnology for biofuel production. Biofuel and Biorefinery Technologies. 2018;**5**:129-139

[69] Colvin VL. The potential environmental impact of engineered nanomaterials. Nature Biotechnology. 2003;**10**:1166-1170

[70] Hoffmann MR, Martin ST, Choi W, Bahenmann DW. Environmental applications of semiconductor photocatalysis. Chemical Reviews. 1995;**95**:69

[71] Kamat PV, Meisel D. Nanoscience opportunities in environmental remediation. Comptes Rendus Chimie. 2003;**6**:999-1007

[72] Li XQ, Elliott DW, Zhang WX. Zero-valent iron nanoparticles for abatement of environmental pollutants: Materials and engineering aspects. Critical Reviews in Solid State and Materials Sciences. 2006;**31**:111-122

[73] Obare SO, Meyer GJ. Nanostructured materials for environmental remediation of organic contaminants in water. Environmental Science and Health, Part A. 2004;**39**:2549

[74] Pirkanniemi K, Sillanpaa M. Heterogeneous water phase catalysis as an environmental application: A review. Chemosphere. 2002;**48**:1047-1060

[75] Tratnyek PG, Johnson RL. Nanotechnologies for environmental cleanup. Nano Today. 2006;**1**(2):44-48

[76] Zhang WX. Nanoscale iron particles for environmental remediation: An overview. Journal of Nano Research. 2003;**5**:323-332

[77] Arksey H, O'Malley L. Scoping studies: Towards a methodological framework. International Journal of Social Research Methodology. 2005;**8**(1):19-32

[78] Bowman DM, Gatof J. Reviewing the regulatory barriers for nanomedicine: Global questions and challenges. Nanomedicine. 2015;**10**(21):3275-3286

[79] Brady AP, Neri E. Artificial intelligence in radiology – Ethical considerations. Diagnostics. 2020;**10**(4):231-239

[80] Glenn LM, Boyce JS. Regenerative nanomedicine: Ethical, legal, and social issues. In: Navarro M, Planell JA, editors. Methods in Molecular Biology. Clifton: Humana Press; 2012. pp. 303-316

[81] Jaremko JL, Azar M, Bromwich R, Lum A, Cheong LHA, Gibert M, et al. Canadian association of radiologists white paper on ethical and legal issues related to artificial intelligence in radiology. Canadian Association of Radiologists Journal. 2019;**70**(2):107-118

[82] Meetoo D. Nanotechnology: Is there a need for ethical principles? The British Journal of Nursing. 2009;**18**(20):1264-1268

[83] McHale JV. Nanomedicine and the EU: Some legal, ethical and regulatory challenges. Maastricht Journal of European and Comparative Law. 2009;**16**(1):65-88

[84] Aerni P. Exploring the roots of the old GMO narrative and why young people have started to ask critical questions. In: Ricroch A, Chopra S, Kuntz M, editors. Plant Biotechnology. Berlin, Germany: Springer; 2021. pp. 227-304

[85] Douglas CM, Stemerding D. Challenges for the European governance of synthetic biology for human health. Life Sciences, Society and Policy. 2014;**10**(1):6-18

[86] Florin MV, Bürkler MT. Introduction to the IRGC Risk Governance Framework. Lausanne, Switzerland: EPFL; 2017

[87] Greer SL, Wismar M, Figueras J. Strengthening Health System Governance: Better Policies, Stronger Performance, European Observatory on Health Systems and Policies, Maidenhead. Maidenhead: Open University Press; 2016

[88] Greer SL, Vasev N, Jarman H, Wismar M, Figueras J. It's the Governance, Stupid! Tapic: A Governance Framework to Strengthen Decision Making and Implementation. Geneva, Switzerland: WHO; 2020

[89] Kuzma J, Gould F, Brown Z, Collins J, Delborne J, Frow E, et al. A roadmap for gene drives: Using institutional analysis and development to frame research needs and governance in a systems context. Journal of Responsible Innovation. 2018;**5**(1):S13-S39

[90] Oye KA. Proactive and Adaptive Governance of Emerging Risks: The Case of DNA Synthesis and Synthetic Biology. Geneva: International Risk Governance Council; 2012

[91] Roco MC, Harthorn B, Guston D, Shapira P. Innovative and responsible governance of nanotechnology for societal development. In: Nanotechnology Research Directions for Societal Needs in 2020. Dordrecht: Springer; 2020. pp. 561-617

[92] Onik MM, Miraz MH, Kim CS. A recruitment and human resource management technique using blockchain technology for industry 4.0. In: Smart Cities Symposium. Bahrain: University of Bahrain; 2018. pp. 1-6

[93] Sheridan TB. Human–robot interaction: Status and challenges. Human Factors. 2016;**58**(4):525-532

[94] Kent MD, Kopacek P. Do we need synchronization of the human and robotics to make industry 5.0 a success story? In: The International Symposium for Production Research. Turkey: Springer; 2020. pp. 302-311

[95] Demir KA, Döven G, Sezen B. Industry 5.0 and human-robot co-working. Procedia Computer Science. 2019;**158**:688-695

[96] Longo F, Padovano A, Umbrella S. Value-oriented and ethical technology engineering in industry 5.0: A human-centric perspective for the design of the factory of the future. Applied Sciences. 2020;**10**(12):4182

Section 3

# Emerging Paradigms and Sustainable Practices

Chapter 6

# Digital Entrepreneurship in the Fourth Industrial Revolution and beyond

*Nompumelelo Mbhele and Andrisha Beharry-Ramraj*


## Abstract

The nature of the confusion that underpins entrepreneurial processes and outcomes and the strategies for addressing it have been changed due to the Fourth Industrial Revolution brought about by the development of digital technologies. Technology is the main force behind digital entrepreneurship. The Fourth Industrial Revolution's technological development is both a limitation and a turning point for digital entrepreneurship. Most importantly, it has been assumed that the Fourth Industrial Revolution will provide additional drivers for the future of digital entrepreneurship. The purpose of this chapter was to compile the most recent research on digital entrepreneurship, investigate how the Fourth Industrial Revolution's digital transformation has affected this field, and explore how the COVID-19 pandemic has affected it. The study conducted an evidence-based literature review on digital entrepreneurship, using a qualitative analysis method and content analysis. The research found that digital businesses were unaffected by Covid-19 due to their familiarity with digital methods and business models. Covid-19 benefited digital entrepreneurs by allowing them to pivot to new markets and segments quickly. However, it also threatened their survival due to disruptions in their business model and supply chain. The study suggests that digital entrepreneurship in the Fourth Industrial Revolution is promising to continue.


**Keywords:** digital, entrepreneurship, technologies, transformation, COVID-19

## 1. Introduction

Today's world is drastically changing, particularly concerning information and communication technologies (ICT). This change shows how quickly evolving digital technologies with novel functionalities alter market dynamics and standard business strategies, structures, and practices [1]. According to Hai et al. [2], this subject is currently the most debated due to the recent explosion in the adoption of digital technology. Everyone is impacted by digital transformation, and in most fields, the power of digital technology can be applied to all facets of an organization, mainly digital businesses. Organizations are being forced to change how they operate due to the global digital transformation, which includes artificial intelligence (AI), blockchain technology, and the Internet of Things. The COVID-19 pandemic forced many companies to adopt a new way of trading their goods and services to customers. Digital tools such as social media, big data, mobile, and cloud solutions were used. Because digital tools enabled entrepreneurs to operate remotely during the COVID-19 pandemic, digital entrepreneurship was regarded as the best business practice. Many issues that plagued other industries during the pandemic did not affect digital businesses.

According to Pananond et al. [3] and WIR [4], digitalization will fundamentally change how companies operate in globally interconnected value chains, both in terms of production and organization. The sector of digital entrepreneurship will considerably gain from this. "A few examples of the new technologies that are part of the digital transformation are the Internet of Things (IoT), artificial intelligence (AI), robotics-enabled automation, cloud, augmented reality (AR), virtual reality (VR), platform-based technologies, e-commerce, fintech, blockchain, and 3D printing" ([2], p. 10). When combined, globalization and cross-border connectivity enable organizations to operate throughout a wider region. However, these changes offer a financial chance for corporate operations to be restored, allowing for local production and consumption.

As earlier studies on using digital transformation in entrepreneurship only examined scattered phenomena related to it, digital entrepreneurship has needed more conceptual discussion and improvement. Some important fundamental questions are mainly ignored in the current literature. For example, what impact is digital technologies having on entrepreneurship? What sets digital entrepreneurship apart from traditional forms of entrepreneurship? The COVID-19 pandemic's consequences on digital entrepreneurship in the context of the Fourth Industrial Revolution and how they will continue to be felt after. These queries will be addressed in this chapter.

### 1.1 Background

The First Industrial Revolution in 1765 was led by steam engines. Steam engines played a crucial role in transforming various industries, such as textile manufacturing, mining, and transportation. They provided a more efficient and reliable source of power, leading to increased production and economic growth. Following the First Industrial Revolution, the Second Revolution in 1870 was driven by electricity and oil-based power. It was characterized by advancements in electricity, oil-based power, and other key technologies. Electricity played a significant role in this revolution. Thomas Edison's development of practical electrical systems, including the incandescent light bulb and the electric power distribution, was a breakthrough. This led to the widespread adoption of electric lighting, which transformed industries and urban areas, improving productivity and quality of life. The Third Revolution in 1969 was supported by electronics and information technology. Today, new technologies have been introduced, like Internet of Things (IoT), Artificial Intelligence, Big Data, and many more. In addition, in the late 1960s, advancements in integrated circuit (IC) technology that had been made in earlier years were maintained. ICs got more potent, more compact, and more reasonably priced. More intricate and advanced electronic devices have been made possible by the growing integration and downsizing of electronic components. As a result, more compact and effective computers, calculators, and communication systems were created. These new technologies are shaping what is being called the Fourth Industrial Revolution. The Fourth Industrial Revolution is characterized by the fusion of physical, digital, and biological systems, and it is expected to have a profound impact on almost every industry and aspect of society. One of the key pillars of the Fourth Industrial Revolution is the Internet of Things (IoT).

### 1.2 Problem statement

The COVID-19 pandemic has changed how businesses in all industries and regions operate for years. As a result of the changes brought about by the pandemic, enterprises have accelerated the digitization of their business controls, interactions with their supply chains, and customer relationships. Companies that were accustomed to operating in a free COVID-19 world have found this to be complicated. Even when there is no pandemic, dealing with changes in the workplace environment can be stressful for teams and individuals. It was easier and more accessible for digital entrepreneurs familiar with digital businesses. The pandemic developed a setting that will continue to support technological advancement and innovation. According to Hai et al. [2] and Nambisan [5], digital entrepreneurship is crucial, particularly in light of the COVID-19 crisis. Creating new business activities, enhancing business analytics, and quickly communicating with many customers are benefits of digital business. The development of new techniques and technologies may result from the expansion of digital entrepreneurship. In these COVID-19 times, this is critical to every business.

The introduction of untapped technological advances into various business and advancement fields, such as “mobile computing, cloud computing, social media, 3D printing, and information analytics” ([6], p. 5), in recent years has altered the nature of the tall flimsiness in entrepreneurship and its causes as well as the approaches to managing such vulnerability. This has resulted in various research queries on digital entrepreneurship at the connection of digital technologies and entrepreneurship that demand careful consideration of digital technologies and their unique qualities in shaping entrepreneurial activities during and after. The development of digital transformation is accelerating at this time, and it is impacting how organizations are evolving. Its consequences are still being defined. Therefore, the chapter aims to interpret and discover how people perceive digital transformation and how their minds change. It also highlights the good things that have happened due to the process and successes in digital entrepreneurship.

## 2. Theoretical framework

Digital entrepreneurship involves identifying new opportunities in the digital realm, creating and launching digital businesses, or transforming traditional businesses into digital ones. Digital entrepreneurs leverage emerging technologies such as artificial intelligence, machine learning, big data analytics, cloud computing, and the Internet of Things (IoT) to streamline processes, enhance customer experience, and drive growth. This literature review studies the various aspects of digital entrepreneurship including its definition, characteristics, and challenges.

### 2.1 Digital entrepreneurship

The rise of digital platforms and entrepreneurial ecosystems has significantly impacted innovation and entrepreneurship. However, the advantages entrepreneurs derive from these settings are widely recognized, and research on the technical upheavals that give rise to digital entrepreneurship is still pending [7], according to Scarborough and Cornwall [8]. Entrepreneurship is the process of starting a new business in the face of the possibility of failure and uncertainty of the business to generate income and growth by identifying significant opportunities and assembling the necessary resources to take advantage of them. According to Duan, Kotey, and Sandhu [9], entrepreneurs play a crucial role in the economy by creating jobs, making products, and offering customer services. Entrepreneurship is the solution to people's unemployment, especially youth unemployment. There are many benefits to entrepreneurship, including creating employment opportunities that will help address socioeconomic issues like poverty and unemployment, which will, in turn, lower crime rates as more people find work. Scarborough and Cornwall [8] simply that successful entrepreneurs take every possible measure to improve their chances of success. Vineela [1] suggests that understanding every concept related to entrepreneurship is crucial for becoming a successful entrepreneur. Every entrepreneur needs to stay current on changes in the market and customer tastes and preferences to compete in the marketplace and reach business objectives. Utilizing contemporary digital tools and software can sometimes be necessary to communicate with customers and boost the value of products. Because digital entrepreneurship stems from entrepreneurship, the chapter began by explaining the concept of entrepreneurship.

Digital entrepreneurship is the intelligent adaptation of impactful digitalization to business. It is changing how business operations are done innovatively [5, 10]. "Digital entrepreneurship is at the heart of the digital economy, which is hailed as one of the most significant economic developments since the industrial revolution" ([10], p. 2; [11], p. 4). Zaheer et al. [10] suggest that digital entrepreneurship is making digital profit entrepreneurially using a set of available alternative digital enablers to support effective digital data acquisition, processing, supply, and utilization, according to a broad definition by Zhao and Collier [11], "digital entrepreneurship" refers to developing new businesses and changing existing ones through innovative digital technologies.

According to Sahut et al. [12], there are several definitions of "digital entrepreneurship," and the research contributions fall broadly into two categories. The first one is investigating whether and how digitization alters entrepreneurship and the traditional process of starting a new business. The second is the research on new venture creation in the digital economy and entrepreneurial opportunities made possible by technological innovation in the sector (digital technologies as both enablers and outputs). Simply put, "the offer of digital products or services across electronic networks" is what digital entrepreneurship entails [13]. Digital entrepreneurship emphasizes entrepreneurship's transition to the digital age. In light of this, digital entrepreneurship has been classified under numerous business categories, including production, sales, logistics, trade, business management, and operation [9]. DE improved the innovation of business models and procedures as well.

The Australian Innovation System Report [14] suggests that the values of entrepreneurial organizations have primarily been commended for their ability to create jobs and promote unused innovations. According to Zhao and Collier [11], this is changing as the experience and understanding of the digital economy develop, putting business owners and the businesses they found in a unique position to capitalize on new opportunities, adopt cutting-edge technologies, and reshape competition by entering untapped markets. The novel application of digital technologies for entrepreneurship has received more attention in recent developments in entrepreneurship research. For example, multinational software entrepreneurs in Iceland use social networking sites to grow their networks and spot business opportunities. Academic Research in digital entrepreneurship faces some difficulties despite expanding quickly. Confusion is brought on by the dynamic terminology used in the field. They use various terms from emerging terminology interchangeably as trends come and go. For instance, the term "Internet entrepreneurship" was first used in the field in 2000–2001; it later evolved into "e- and "cyber" entrepreneurship around 2004, and now, it seems, we have settled on "digital entrepreneurship" [10].

### *2.1.1 Importance of digital entrepreneurship*

The importance of digital entrepreneurship must be addressed in these times when technology is advancing. Traditional businesses need to pay attention to adapting to the trend. Digital business is different from conventional business. Digital enterprises use many models to run their businesses [12]. According to Zaheer et al. [10], digital entrepreneurs are the ones who are in charge of the business model and the company culture in this era. In order to provide supply resilience in the face of the COVID-19 pandemic, digital transformation has been crucial, according to Niu et al. [15]. Brands that have gone digital can now modify their order and supply volumes based on outbreak forecast information. This emphasizes the importance of digital entrepreneurship in these times when technology is advancing. For traditional businesses to survive in this digital age, they will need to adapt and change with the times. Digital businesses use many different business models, which can be challenging for traditional businesses to keep up with. Traditional businesses will need to learn to use digital tools and platforms if they want to compete in this era.

### *2.1.2 Communication with consumers*

"Expectations from consumers and investors, as well as the potential for greater economic and social benefits, are driving digital transformation and innovation in digitalization" ([16], p. 2). Digital entrepreneurship helps rebuild unused businesses by creating technologically advanced products and services, eventually resulting in a faster rate of financial development. As a result, an open approach that energizes and supports business should be considered essential for financial growth. Vineela [1] articulates that the interaction between a buyer and a seller is simple because digital entrepreneurship is linked to using digital systems for all business operations. Compared to other communication modes, communication via the Internet is simple. Purchasing goods and products online is the most convenient option for consumers. People nowadays prefer buying things online rather than shopping in stores. As a result of the ease of purchasing, the number of customers can be increased.

### *2.1.3 Competitiveness of the market*

According to Chaffey and Ellis-Chadwick [17], keeping up with the competition is essential in every business. A business can increase its customer base and compete on a more competitive level by using digital marketing. Digital technology is crucial for every business to meet the challenges of the market and expand its operations. It has revolutionized how businesses operate and has made it easier for companies to reach a broader range of customers. It is easy to make digital marketing strategies for businesses. However, making the right decisions can be difficult, especially when choosing the right digital marketing agency.

### *2.1.4 Affordability*

Flyverbom et al. [18] suggest that business websites should provide as many services as possible to convert visitors into efficient customers and, as a result, consumers. Different entrepreneurs approach this in different ways, but the common goal for all is high sales for their company [19]. As a result, a well-designed website for any business can serve as a platform to achieve this goal. According to Peukert [19], digital technology is viable financially. This means that digital marketing is very inexpensive. The costs differ depending on the type of marketing strategy employed. As a result, the use of digital technologies can automatically reduce costs.

### *2.1.5 Digital ecosystem*

The existence of a digital ecosystem is required for digital entrepreneurship. "The digital ecosystem" is at the core of the "Digital Entrepreneurial Ecosystem" framework, which Sussan and ACS [20] first introduced" ([21], p. 6). A digital ecosystem is defined by Li et al. [22] as a self-organizing, scalable, and sustainable system composed of heterogeneous digital entities and their interrelationships concentrating on interactions between many entities to increase system functionality, gain advantages and promote knowledge transfer, internal and transnational collaboration, and system innovation. Thanks to digital technology, businesses can create new services and products and adapt to their customers' needs. New business models, new business models, and new business models can all emerge from digital ecosystems. Hence, the digital ecosystem is essential to businesses [9]. The context of the digital ecosystem is typically used when talking about digital ecosystems. A collection of digital assets that are connected and form a sophisticated network is known as a digital ecosystem. The foundation of digital entrepreneurship is the existence or growth of a digital ecosystem.

### *2.1.6 Digital management*

According to Tsvetkov et al. [23], businesses must implement a digital management strategy if they want to stay competitive and relevant in the rapidly evolving digital world. A digital management strategy will assist companies in locating and seizing opportunities and controlling the risks brought on by digitization. Businesses must have a thorough understanding of their target market, the needs of their customers, and the best ways to use digital tools to satisfy those needs to develop an effective digital management strategy [18]. Tsvetkov et al. [23] define digital management as using digital tools to manage businesses using digitization as their operating framework. It encompasses various activities, including digital marketing, asset management, rights management, and supply chain management. By leveraging digital tools and technologies, businesses can achieve efficiencies and scale that were impossible in the past. The goal of digital management is to create customer value and manage business processes through the use of digital technologies. This is done by creating a digital strategy and roadmap that outlines the company's goals and how they will be achieved. Additionally, digital management includes the implementation of digital marketing campaigns, using social media to engage customers, and using data analytics to understand customer behavior.

## 2.2 A concept for studying digital entrepreneurship

According to Zhao and Collier [11], emerging concepts like digital entrepreneurship are distinct from traditional and general entrepreneurship, which has been studied for years. Each of the five "pillars" identified by the European Commission [24] in its conceptual model of digital entrepreneurship is important to consider when analyzing it. These are (1) Digital business environment and ICT market; (2) Digital knowledge base and ICT market; (3) Access to finance; (4) Digital skills and e-leadership; and (5) Entrepreneurial Culture. According to the European Commission [24], the framework was developed to allow businesses and entrepreneurs to grow their companies in a welcoming environment while encouraging originality and creativity. Encouraging the development of online businesses will lead to the creation of new employment opportunities. Consumers will adopt technology more readily in an environment where it is readily available, claims Bisht et al. [25]. Entrepreneurs should promote a culture of market creation rather than concentrating on market development. There is a huge amount of untapped value-creation potential at the bottom of the pyramid. This leads to the need for the advancement of the framework to keep up with the trend and provide a more effective way of engaging in the digital technology business. In order to study this new phenomenon in a comprehensive and integrative way, Zhao and Collier [11] proposed an approach to study the relationships among variables in a hypothetical process of digital entrepreneurship. They created a new conceptual framework.

According to Zhao and Collier [11], three theories, namely the social network theory, the social capital theory, and the institutional theory, were chosen by the authors as the theoretical foundations for their model because of digital entrepreneurship's social and networked nature. Social capital and social networks frequently seem to interact as digital entrepreneurship develops. For instance, OSS communities for open-source software are drawing entrepreneurs to the communities to share knowledge and innovate to generate and reap economic benefits. Relationships between individuals in a social network have the potential to develop into or lead to significant sources of social capital, according to the central claim of the social capital theory (e.g., information, knowledge, and resources). The performance of an individual or company's innovation also depends on where they are in the network.

Their developed theory reflects the interaction between the three approaches and the five main factors influencing digital entrepreneurship. The authors argue that social capital is the most important of the three theories and that this theory has emerged as the most important to the industry. The authors say that the most crucial thing social capital does is provide a basis for entrepreneurship, which has been a critical factor in the growth of the digital marketing industry. In addition, the authors' prior work on social capital in the context of developers and entrepreneurs sheds light on the important social factors for digital entrepreneurs (**Figure 1**).

According to Zhao and Collier [11], this model makes use of these theories to investigate how social networks at the individual, institutional, and societal levels, as well as social capital both online and offline, influence the discovery and exploration of digital opportunities as well as the results of entrepreneurial endeavors. It guarantees that social and economic organizations are operating efficiently. With the help of

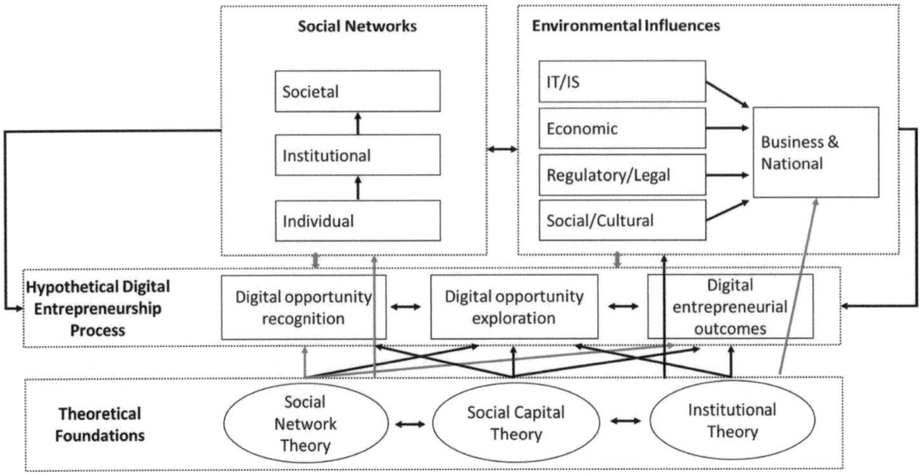


**Figure 1.**
*Conceptual framework for study of digital entrepreneurship. Source: Zhao and Collier [11].*

this model, it can specifically look into how social networks and social capital interact to influence the growth and results of digital entrepreneurship.

## 2.3 Problems with digital entrepreneurship

Without a doubt, digital business is booming, and the ICT market is expanding rapidly. However, there are still some issues that must be addressed. One of the most serious issues is that digital businesses are not immune to cybercrime. Cybercrime can harm a company's reputation, finances, and physical security [26]. There is also no doubt that the new innovative changes offer a range of great opportunities for the ICT industry in digital entrepreneurship. However, in order to seize them, the industry will have to evolve. "The Gartner 2018 CIO Agenda survey shows that anxiety about being disrupted by digital business is a main concern of CIOs". The shift of the industry or change can lead to cultural anxiety. This is because it calls for a significant change in behaviors and how things are done. As much change is good in business, but it comes with consequences. According to Matar [27], change is essential for businesses to succeed. To change, organizations first need to understand the challenges they face and how to overcome them. With the right mindset, embracing digital business can help mitigate the risks associated with change. By doing so, organizations can create a more efficient and effective workplace and better serve their customers. They are confident that embracing digital business can turn the threat into an opportunity for the industry.

## 2.4 Digital transformation and the Fourth Industrial Revolution

The Fourth Industrial Revolution is receiving much attention from society. It has impacted many aspects of our lives. Moavenzadeh [28] stated that digital transformation is expected to change many proceedings within the business sector. "The Fourth Industrial Revolution refers to the technological transformation society is undergoing in the 21st Century" ([29], p. 3). According to Ross and Maynard [29], when Klaus

Schwab, the founder of the World Economic Forum, used the phrase "Fourth Industrial Revolution," he was referring to a period characterized a technological revolution. "This shift in technological innovation is creating a vast ecosystem of interconnected, complex, and dynamic interaction between humans and the built environment" ([30], p. 8). According to WIR [4], the Fourth Industrial Revolution is defined by four main aspects: the digitization of products and services, the emergence of new digital business models, the spread of digital connectivity, and the development of new technologies such as artificial intelligence (AI), robotics, and the Internet of Things (IoT). The Fourth Industrial Revolution has three main characteristics. The three main trends in technology are as follows: (1) the convergence of digital, biological, and physical systems; (2) the rapid advancement of processing and storage power; and (3) the introduction of novel technologies like 3D printing, robots, and artificial intelligence. "The change is being fueled by the exponential rise of digital technologies."

Technologies that are becoming more and more integrated into daily life include augmented reality (AR), artificial intelligence (AI), the Internet of Things (IoT), and driverless cars ([30], p.10; [2], p. 17). In Tang et al.'s [31] study, it was found that distributed innovation enhances business performance in digital innovation. It also partially mediates the positive link between distributed innovation and performance in digital innovation. Additionally, IT-enabled capabilities positively influence the connection between distributed innovation and digital innovation opportunities. Moreover, IT-enabled capabilities play a positive role in this relationship.

During the First Industrial Revolution, production was automated through the utilization of steam power energy. The second produced enormous volumes using electric power. Digital transformation or technical advancement is a never-ending cycle of competing advancements rather than a linear one. One example of a new technology that emerged concurrently with the development of the vehicle, the aircraft, and nuclear power is the cell phone, the radio, and televisions. When it came to cars, the invention of the internal combustion engine facilitated the development of the vehicle. The phonograph and television inventions came first in the history of radio and television. Technological innovation and transformation happen faster than ever before in the Fourth Industrial Revolution [6]. Comparatively, in just two years, Instagram reached 100 million subscribers, while the interactive smartphone game Pokémon Go drew 100 m users in just one month. It took 75 years for 100 million users to adopt the telephone" ([32], p. 9). Kodama [6] asserts that the Fourth Industrial Revolution encompasses more than merely sophisticated, networked machinery and systems. Its range is far wider. "Because of the integration of these advances in technology and their connections across physical elements, electronic, and biological realms, the Fourth Industrial Revolution is fundamentally different from previous revolutions" ([2], p. 17).

According to Kodama [6], the Fourth Industrial Revolution will have a profound impact on employees, organizations, and society. Organizations today need to strike a balance between the benefits of technology advancement and new job and employment conceptions, as well as local and global power shifts, as work and the meaning of work change for employees. The Fourth Industrial Revolution will be driven more than ever by digitalization and vast smart ecosystems, according to the latest study. As a result, machine learning and artificial intelligence will grow in importance and become indispensable to our daily operations. As a result, companies and employees need to reevaluate what new types of work might involve and how they fit into the concepts of the modern workplace. According to Zhao and Collier [11], these technologies drive the digital economy by opening up a new spectrum of options with substantial potential economic value and the capacity to drastically reduce the cost of new initiatives. Alibaba.com is an excellent example; it has helped millions of Chinese individuals launch enterprises and created a large number of jobs.

Moavenzadeh [28] studied the Fourth Industrial Revolution and its future in the world. September 2015 found that "90% of the news that the general public reads will be produced by computers by 2025, according to 50% of media, entertainment, and information strategy officers. One hundred percent of insurance and asset management officers concur that an insurer's competitive positioning will depend on real-time sensor data streams by 2020. By 2030, most of our financial architecture will be supported by distributed ledger technology, according to 92% of banking and capital markets strategy officers. Fifty percent of institutional investors and sovereign fund strategy officers agree that by 2025, the majority of financial transactions, as well as management of important documents, will take place on blockchain architecture" ([28], p. 6). This emphasizes how important traditional need to adapt to digital businesses for them to keep up with the competition.

### 2.5 Digital entrepreneurship in the Fourth Industrial Revolution

The Fourth Industrial Revolution, brought in by the advancement of digital technologies, has altered the nature of the hesitation, which supports entrepreneurial processes, results, and methods for handling it. According to Budd et al. [33], the success of the Fourth Industrial Revolution is dependent on digital entrepreneurship. It creates, launches, manages, and controls business enterprises using new digital technologies. The Fourth Industrial Revolution's technological advances have created opportunities for entrepreneurs and businesses of all sizes. Digital entrepreneurship has benefited from the advancement of technology as they work with it.

According to Budd et al. [33] and Moavenzadeh [28] digital technologies are becoming more important in the entrepreneurial process. Budd et al. [33] and Matt et al. [34] suggest that as we become increasingly connected to technology, it is likely that new technologies will profoundly impact human societies and the economy. They enable the instant transfer of ideas and the sharing of resources, stimulating innovation and providing new opportunities. Digital entrepreneurs have leveraged the latest technologies to create new businesses and industries. Opportunities for digital entrepreneurship abound in the Fourth Industrial Revolution, characterized by the widespread use of digital technologies. According to Budd et al. [33] and Purbasari et al. [21], digital technologies have significantly impacted how businesses are conducted. In particular, Nambisan [5] articulates that digital technologies have allowed businesses to operate much faster and more accurately. This has resulted in a rise in the number of businesses competing in a global market. As a result, digital entrepreneurs have become more prevalent and are making a big difference in the current economy. This is seen as a good thing happening to the economy.

According to Budd et al. [33], the Fourth Industrial Revolution's technological development is both a limitation and a turning point for digital entrepreneurship. The technological development of the Fourth Industrial Revolution and the digital economy have been found to have several implications for digital entrepreneurship. The results of this study suggest that digital entrepreneurs should consider the following implications when developing their business models: technology developments can limit the ability of digital entrepreneurs to identify and exploit opportunities;

technology developments can provide digital entrepreneurs with new opportunities to exploit, and technology developments can provide digital entrepreneurs with the ability to create new business models that are not possible with existing technology.

### 2.6 The impact of COVID-19 on digital entrepreneurship in the Fourth Industrial Revolution

The devastating global pandemic caused by the COVID-19 virus that hit the world in 2020 affected people and businesses worldwide. The pandemic had extensive effects that were felt all over the world. According to Purbasari et al. [21], the COVID-19 outbreak has created a lot of vulnerability, especially regarding economic uncertainty. This includes the rate of recovery, government interference and agreements, changes in consumer behavior and how they affect exchange efficiency, contemporary business practices, R&D, human capital development, and other factors that impact efficiency over the medium and long term. A few governments implemented travel restrictions, social exclusion policies, and event cancellation guidelines to prevent the spread of widespread.

Digitized businesses were hit hard as people lost their jobs, some businesses were forced to close their jobs, and businesses shut down [33]. "The digital revolution has transformed many aspects of life. As of 2019, 67% of the global population had subscribed to mobile devices, of which 65% were smartphones, with sub-Saharan Africa experiencing the fastest growth. In 2019, 204 billion apps were downloaded, and 3.8 billion people actively used social media as of January 2020" ([33], p. 2). Businesses were forced to shut down within days, causing economies to contract and industries to collapse. In addition, companies that did not have the digital infrastructure to continue making money were left without the ability to hire workers. This resulted in the death of many small businesses, their jobs, their income, and their assets. The fall in the value of the USD Dollar made it more difficult to move money around. The global financial crisis led to a currency crisis, and many countries could not pay their bills. Some of these countries could not pay their debts, and many others were bankrupt.

In response to COVID-19, numerous digital technologies are being used. The types of technologies that are used are clearly shown in **Figure 2** on the next page. Because of the development of technologies, the Fourth Industrial Revolution made it simpler for digital entrepreneurs to run their businesses. Businesses can select a wide range of digital technologies for their operations. "These digital technologies include blockchain technology, the Internet of Things (IoT), big data analytics, artificial intelligence (AI) that uses deep learning, and next-generation telecommunication networks" ([35], p. 1).

Despite the negative effects the pandemic had on entrepreneurship, digital entrepreneurship has been greatly affected by the COVID-19 epidemic, according to Yáñez-Valdés and Guerrero [36], which has turned industries into digital solutions. In order to address social and economic challenges, digital entrepreneurship has given rise to projects in the fields of entertainment, banking, health, education, and digital payments. The crisis has altered the assessment of digital entrepreneurship, meaning that projects in the future will probably involve digital elements.

#### *2.6.1 Challenges*

The overall impact of the pandemic was felt from the beginning of the pandemic. Qermane and Mancha [37] imply that COVID-19 benefited digital entrepreneurs by

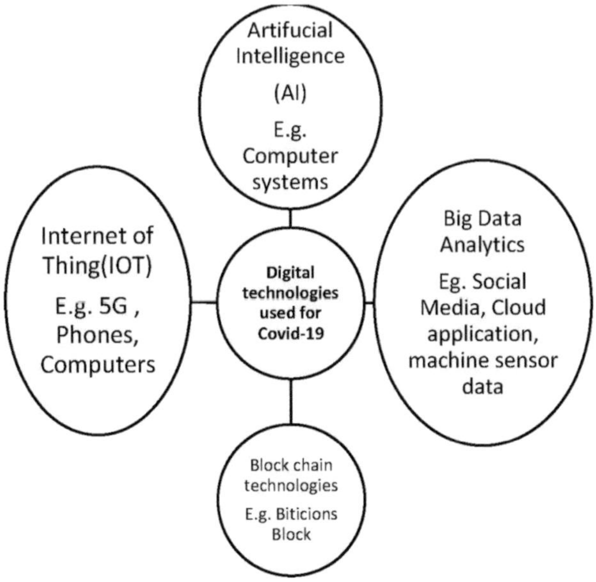


**Figure 2**
*The interconnected digital technologies used in digital entrepreneurship respond to COVID-19. Source: Schilirò [16].*

allowing them to quickly and effectively pivot to a new market and segment. However, COVID-19 also posed a threat to the survival of the businesses as it disrupted their business model and disrupted their supply chain. The pandemic was the result of the Fourth Industrial Revolution. According to Purbasari et al. [21], the Fourth Industrial Revolution was a key development in the history of capitalism. It led to the development of new technologies and new businesses. The Fourth Industrial Revolution also significantly impacted the economy and society. The impact of the Fourth Industrial Revolution was felt in many ways. There was a shift in how businesses were run and the economy was organized. There was a shift in the way people lived their lives and the way they interacted with each other. According to Budd et al. [33], many established businesses have been compelled to change to accommodate the new global order. They have found this to be difficult. Many people have lost their jobs, and many others have been forced to shut down traditional businesses or open new ones. Another issue was that with so many businesses going online, there was a lot of competition. For improvement in their businesses, digital businesses need to improve their marketing strategies.

### *2.6.2 Benefits*

The COVID-19 pandemic transformed business operations into digital [21, 37], according to Ross and Maynard. [29] and Purbasari et al. [21], digital businesses were unaffected because they were already familiar with digital methods of operation and their business model. The pandemic changed how people interacted with businesses, which caused a slew of issues. One of the issues businesses faced was that people were no longer willing to go to the business and buy the product because they could do so from home. However, this did not affect digital businesses as they are operating online, e.g., online shops and online services. "The digital revolution has transformed many aspects of life. As of 2019, 67% of the global population had subscribed to mobile devices, of which 65% were smartphones, with Sub-Saharan Africa experiencing the fastest growth. In 2019, 204 billion apps were downloaded, and 3.8 billion people actively used social media as of January 2020" ([33], p. 2). The DE benefited because customers' attention was on purchasing online and using technology for many activities in their lives.

### 2.7 Entrepreneurial resilience and advancement following the pandemic

The COVID-19 epidemic has caused a paradigm shift in the growth and recovery of entrepreneurship. According to Sharma et al. [38], companies need to focus on creative ways to recover, embrace socially rooted orientations, and implement best practices for crisis management. Readjusting the entrepreneurial orientation or developing a new kind of entrepreneurship is necessary for the post-crisis entrepreneurial revival. Using AI-CRM technology in family enterprises, creating an entrepreneurial environment through value co-creation, and investigating owner motives, stretched resources, and dynamic capacities for post-disaster recovery are a few examples [39]. To increase a company's resilience and competitiveness, it is necessary to pay closer attention to these new developments (**Table 1**).

Yáñez-Valdés and Guerrero [36] focus on small business owners and startups; this paper probably explores the difficulties faced by entrepreneurs during the COVID-19 epidemic, including supply chain interruptions, changes in customer behavior, financial restrictions, and regulatory concerns. With an emphasis on resilience building, innovation fostering, and long-term business model development, the article explores how entrepreneurs have responded to the challenges posed by the pandemic and offers insights and recommendations for entrepreneurs and policymakers to reconsider entrepreneurial strategies in response to the COVID-19 crisis.

In their analysis of the connection between entrepreneurship and COVID-19, Sharma et al. [38] hope to support business owners and other interested parties in their endeavors, both in navigating the post-pandemic environment they are currently in and in the event that other crises arise. According to their research, business owners should integrate best practices for crisis management, take a socially grounded approach, and concentrate on creative strategies to recover. Readjusting the entrepreneurial orientation or developing a new kind of entrepreneurship is necessary for the post-crisis entrepreneurial revival. Audretsch et al. [40] suggest that By facilitating diversification, adaptation, access to international markets, and knowledge sharing, digital transformation improves entrepreneurial resilience and increases a company's capacity to endure and expand in times of crisis. Mitsa and Lyakh [41] focus on small- to medium-sized businesses and how it is important for them to apply digital

| Author and year | Title | Journal |
|---|---|---|
| Yáñez-Valdés and Guerrero, [36] | Determinants and impacts of digital entrepreneurship: A pre-and post-COVID-19 perspective | Technovation |
| Sharma et al., [38] | Entrepreneurial challenges of COVID-19: Re-thinking entrepreneurship after the crisis | journal of Small Business Management |
| Audretsch et al., [40] | Resilience and digitally advanced entrepreneurship | Entrepreneurship & Regional Development |
| Mitsa and Lyakh [41] | Application of digital entrepreneurship platforms in small and medium-sized businesses | Actual Problems of Economics |

**Table 1**
*Recent significant studies regarding the adaptation of Digital Entrepreneurship to Industry 4.0.*

transformation in their businesses. As the world is moving rapidly, it is important to keep up with the trend.

## 3. Research methodology

This research aims to study the impact of COVID-19 on digital entrepreneurship in the Fourth Industrial Revolution and how it will be beyond. A qualitative analysis research method was used for this study. According to Bougie and Sekaran [42], qualitative research aims to gather and analyze non-numerical data to understand better ideas, opinions, or experiences (e.g., text). Using qualitative methods, you can learn more about concepts and experiences. For this study, secondary data sources were consulted. The chapter offers a comprehensive understanding of the field through a review of earlier research findings. Data were gathered for this study using secondary research techniques. A secondary research method is used to gather the information that has been published before. It is desk-top research. The information was gathered from various published sources, including books, journals, articles, case studies, and websites. A total of 50 journal articles, books, and publications were read, and 33 were used as a reference to the study.

Content analysis is the data collection and analysis of the content of a document. The content analysis aims to understand the meaning of textual data and information. Text mining aims to understand the meaning of the text (textual content) and the relationships between texts (relationships between the textual content and the relationships between texts). This method enabled the researcher to progress from dealing with gathered data to detecting patterns and developing new ideas. The information collected from journals, articles, books, and other sources was analyzed and organized to allow the researcher to identify patterns and develop new ideas.

## 4. Discussion of findings

### 4.1 The study of digital entrepreneurship

Digital entrepreneurship is the intelligent adaptation of impactful digitalization to business. It is changing how business operations are done innovatively [5, 10]. DE is a broad topic, and several authors define it similarly. These two authors defined it as an intelligent adaptation of digital technologies to entrepreneurship. "Digital entrepreneurship is at the heart of the digital economy, which is hailed as one of the most significant economic developments since the industrial revolution" ([10], p. 2; [11], p. 4). These authors studied and found that digital entrepreneurship contributes much to the economy by providing job opportunities to individuals. It has also been found that digital entrepreneurship has been classified under numerous business categories, including production, sales, logistics, trade, business management, and operation [9]. This is one of the importance of digital entrepreneurship. Enterprises use many models to run their businesses [12].

According to Zaheer et al. [10], digital entrepreneurs are the ones who are in charge of the business model and the company culture in this era. Overall, these authors suggest that it is very important for businesses to adopt the digital culture in order to survive. DE improved the innovation of business models and procedures as well. Purbasari et al. [21] suggest that an essential initiative for startups with a digital focus in the ecosystem of digital entrepreneurship is the intelligent adaptation of impactful digitalization to business. It changes how business operations are done innovatively [5, 10]. In the digital sector, technology has permeated every aspect of businesses. A digital ecosystem is defined by Li et al. [22] as a self-organizing, scalable, and sustainable system composed of heterogeneous digital entities and their interrelationships concentrating on interactions between many entities to increase system functionality, gain advantages and promote knowledge transfer, internal and transnational collaboration, and system innovation. The digital ecosystem plays a very important role in DE.

Digital entrepreneurship involves identifying new opportunities in the digital realm, creating and launching digital businesses, or transforming traditional businesses into digital ones. Digital entrepreneurs leverage emerging technologies such as artificial intelligence, machine learning, big data analytics, cloud computing, and the Internet of Things (IoT) to streamline processes, enhance customer experience, and drive growth. They understand the potential of these technologies to disrupt industries and create new markets. Through digital entrepreneurship, businesses can improve their operations by automating manual tasks, integrating systems, and analyzing data to make informed decisions. This can result in increased productivity, reduced costs, and improved customer satisfaction.

### 4.2 Digital entrepreneurship in industry 4.0

The dynamic landscape of digital entrepreneurship in the context of Industry 4.0, or the Fourth Industrial Revolution, is depicted in this section. It emphasizes how entrepreneurship may make use of cutting-edge digital technologies including cloud computing, big data analytics, machine learning, artificial intelligence, and the Internet of Things (IoT). The interconnected network of digital entities, which includes investors, startups, entrepreneurs, accelerators, and digital platforms, is referred to as the Digital Entrepreneurship Ecosystem. It stands for the cooperative atmosphere that fosters the growth of digital enterprise. Digital entrepreneurship is propelled by foundational technologies known as technological enablers. They enable business owners to spot fresh opportunities, develop original solutions, and upend established markets. Blockchain, IoT, AI, and data analytics are a few examples. Rethinking conventional company structures and developing fresh value propositions made possible by digital technologies are key components of digital entrepreneurship. The field of digital entrepreneurship is significantly impacted by the Fourth Industrial Revolution. It changes the entrepreneurial landscape and has an impact on the strategies and techniques used by digital entrepreneurs. It offers both opportunities and problems. Flexible and adaptive, successful digital entrepreneurs can navigate uncertainty and take advantage of new opportunities. Resilience and adaptability are critical in the face of disruptive technological breakthroughs and outside shocks like the COVID-19 pandemic.

### 4.3 To understand the digital transformation (Fourth Industrial Revolution) impacts on digital entrepreneurship

"The Fourth Industrial Revolution refers to the technological transformation society is undergoing in the 21st Century" ([29], p. 3). According to Kodama [6], There are more than just cutting-edge, networked devices and systems involved in the Fourth Industrial Revolution. Its scope is much wider. According to Budd et al. [33]

and Moavenzadeh [28], compared to earlier industrial revolutions in human history, the Fourth Industrial Revolution is a notable divergence. The convergence of several disruptive technologies, such as biotechnology, improved materials, robots, artificial intelligence, and the Internet of Things (IoT), is what distinguishes it. The distinctions between the digital, biological, and physical realms are becoming increasingly hazy due to the rapid advancement of these technologies and their interconnectivity across several domains. It has been found that digital entrepreneurs have been able to leverage the latest technologies to create new businesses and industries. This is an advantage to digital entrepreneurs. Opportunities for digital entrepreneurship abound in the Fourth Industrial Revolution, characterized by the widespread use of digital technologies [5]. According to Budd et al. [33] and Purbasari et al. [21], digital technologies have significantly impacted how businesses are conducted. In particular, digital technologies have allowed businesses to operate much faster and more accurately. This has led to an increase in the number of businesses that can compete in a global market. As a result, digital entrepreneurs have become more prevalent and are playing an essential role in the current economy.

### 4.4 Study COVID-19 pandemic impacts on digital entrepreneurship in the Fourth Industrial Revolution

In 2020, the COVID-19 virus unleashed a deadly global pandemic that impacted individuals and companies around the globe [2, 21]. Globally, the pandemic's wide-ranging consequences were felt. According to Hai et al. [2], there were both challenges and benefits of this outbreak to digital businesses. The outbreak significantly affected businesses in many ways, particularly for entrepreneurs. The fourth industrial Revolution, or Industry 4.0, brought about by the development of digital technologies, has altered the nature of the uncertainty that underlies entrepreneurial processes and results as well as the methods for addressing it. The pandemic has changed, forcing businesses to implement or adjust new business models. This has been a challenge to businesses. According to Purbasari et al. [21], the Fourth Industrial Revolution was a key development in the history of capitalism. It led to the development of new technologies and the creation of new businesses. According to Ross and Maynard [29] and Purbasari et al. [21], digital businesses were unaffected because they were already familiar with digital methods of operation and their business model. These authors articulate that because digital businesses were familiar with digital tools, it was not a challenge for them to adapt to the changes.

## 5. Recommendations for future research

This study looked at the most recent research on digital entrepreneurship, investigated how the Fourth Industrial Revolution's digital transformation has affected this field, and investigated how the COVID-19 pandemic has affected it. Future studies can examine how digital entrepreneurs can grow their companies and implement digital globalization. The transformation of digital entrepreneurship from Industry 4.0 toward Industry 5.0 could be introduced. Industry 5.0 could represent a shift toward more human-centered automation and the integration of technologies that enhance human creativity, decision-making, and problem-solving within the industrial landscape. It focuses a strong emphasis on human–machine cooperation while also addressing sustainability, moral issues, and the development of human potential in tandem with technology. And lastly, future research could be geared toward primary research since this one was based on secondary research.

Businesses that want to digitize their operations should invest in software, tools, and technology infrastructure. To increase productivity and streamline procedures, this involves implementing automation, artificial intelligence, data analytics, and cloud computing. Digital enterprise requires a strong online presence. To interact with clients and advertise their goods and services, businesses should concentrate on creating a user-friendly website, optimizing it for search engines, and utilizing social media channels.

Given the growing dependence of organizations on digital platforms, cybersecurity needs to be given top priority. Cyberthreats can be avoided by putting robust security measures in place, including as firewalls, encryption, and frequent security audits. This will safeguard sensitive data and consumer information.

## 6. Conclusion

In summarizing what has been mentioned above, the purpose of this chapter was to gather the most recent research on digital entrepreneurship, as well as a current list of the main ideas and strategies covered in the literature, to study digital entrepreneurship in the Fourth Industrial Revolution and beyond in response to COVID-19. A research roadmap pointing to additional research opportunities for academics working in the field was also suggested based on the results of the comprehensive literature review. An investigation of journal articles, book editions, and other Internet documentation was conducted to conduct an evidence-based literature review on digital entrepreneurship and the Fourth Industrial Revolution. Digital entrepreneurship in the Fourth Industrial Revolution is promising to look beyond. In response to COVID-19, numerous digital technologies are being used. Digital businesses are using digital technologies, which include "blockchain technology, the Internet of Things (IoT), big data analytics, artificial intelligence (AI) that uses deep learning, and next-generation telecommunication networks" ([35], p. 1). Digital entrepreneurship is responsible for managing and controlling a business or enterprise through the use of new digital technologies. The Fourth Industrial Revolution's technological advances have created opportunities for entrepreneurs and businesses of all sizes. Digital entrepreneurship has benefited from the advancement of technology as they work with it. According to Budd et al. [33] and Purbasari et al. [21], digital technologies have significantly impacted how businesses are conducted. In particular, digital technologies have allowed businesses to operate much faster and more accurately. This has led to an increase in the number of businesses that can compete in a global market. As a result, digital entrepreneurs have become more prevalent and play an important role in the current economy.

Moavenzadeh [28] studied the Fourth Industrial Revolution and its future in the world. September 2015 found that "90% of the news that the general public reads will be produced by computers by 2025, according to 50% of media, entertainment, and information strategy officers. One hundred percent of insurance and asset management officers concur that an insurer's competitive positioning will depend on real-time sensor data streams by 2020. By 2030, most of our financial architecture will be supported by distributed ledger technology, according to 92% of banking and capital markets strategy officers. Fifty percent of institutional investors and sovereign fund strategy officers agree that by 2025, the majority of financial transactions, as well as management of important documents, will take place on blockchain architecture" ([28], p. 6). This emphasizes how important it is for traditional businesses to adapt to digital businesses in order to keep up with the competition. The future is promising when it comes to digital entrepreneurship in the Fourth Industrial Revolution.

## Author details

Nompumelelo Mbhele and Andrisha Beharry-Ramraj*
University of KwaZulu-Natal, South Africa

*Address all correspondence to: beharrya@ukzn.ac.za

## References

[1] Vineela GS. Digital entrepreneurship. Research Scholar. 2018:441-448

[2] Hai TN, Van QN, Thi Tuyet MN. Digital transformation: Opportunities and challenges for leaders in the emerging countries in response to COVID-19 pandemic. Emerging Science Journal. 2021;**5**:21-36

[3] Pananond P, Gereffi G, Pedersen T. An integrative typology of global strategy and global value chains: The management and organization of cross-border activities. Global Strategy Journal. 2020;**10**(3):421-443

[4] WIR. UNITED World Investment Report 2020: International Production beyond the Pandemic. New York and Geneve: United Nations; 2020

[5] Nambisan S. Digital entrepreneurship: Toward a digital technology perspective of entrepreneurship. Entrepreneurship Theory and Practice. 2017;**41**(6): 1029-1055

[6] Kodama F. Learning mode and strategic concept for the 4th industrial revolution. Journal of Open Innovation: Technology, Market, and Complexity. 2018;**4**(3):32

[7] Paul J, Alhassan I, Binsaif N, Singh P. Digital entrepreneurship research: A systematic review. Journal of Business Research. 2023;**156**:113507

[8] Scarborough N, Cornwall J. Essentials of Entrepreneurship and Small Business Management. 9th ed. Upper Saddle River, NJ: Pearson Education Limited; 2019

[9] Duan C, Kotey B, Sandhu K. Ecosystem strategies for transnational digital entrepreneurship: A conceptual framework of three ecosystems. In: Disruptive Technology and Digital Transformation for Business and Government. IGI Global; 2021. pp. 1-23

[10] Zaheer H, Breyer Y, Dumay J. Digital entrepreneurship: An interdisciplinary structured literature review and research agenda. Technological Forecasting and Social Change. 2019;**148**:119735

[11] Zhao F, Collier A. Digital entrepreneurship: Research and practice. 2016

[12] Sahut JM, Iandoli L, Teulon F. The age of digital entrepreneurship. Small Business Economics. 2021;**56**(3): 1159-1169

[13] Kraus S, Palmer C, Kailer N, Kallinger FL, Spitzer J. Digital entrepreneurship: A research agenda on new business models for the twenty-first century. International Journal of Entrepreneurial Behavior & Research. 2018

[14] AIS. Australian Innovation System Report. In: Office of the Chief Economist, Department of Industry, Innovations, and Science. 2015. ISBN ISSN: 978-1-925092-61-5

[15] Niu B, Wang L, Yu X, Feng B. Data-driven analysis of digital entrepreneurship in medical supply resilience confronting the COVID-19 epidemic. Information Processing & Management. 2024;**61**(1):103502

[16] Schilirò D. Towards Digital Globalization and the Covid-19 Challenge. 2020

[17] Chaffey D, Ellis-Chadwick F. Digital Marketing: Strategy, Implementation & Practice. Pearson UK; 2019

[18] Flyverbom M, Leonardi P, Stohl C, Stohl M. Digital age the management of visibilities in the digital age—Introduction. International Journal of Communication. 2016;**10**:12

[19] Peukert C. The next wave of digital technological change and the cultural industries. Journal of Cultural Economics. 2019;**43**(2):189-210

[20] Sussan F, Acs ZJ. The digital entrepreneurial ecosystem. Small Business Economics. 2017;**49**(1):55-73

[21] Purbasari R, Muttaqin Z, Sari DS. Digital entrepreneurship in pandemic Covid 19 Era: The digital entrepreneurial ecosystem framework. Review of integrative business and economics research. 2021;**10**:114-135

[22] Li W, Du W, Yin J. Digital entrepreneurship ecosystem as a new form of organizing: The case of Zhongguancun. Frontiers of Business Research in China. 2017;**11**:1-21

[23] Tsvetkov VY, Shaytura SV, Ordov KV. Digital management railway. In: International Scientific and Practical Conference on Digital Economy (ISCDE 2019). Atlantis Press; 2019. pp. 846-850

[24] European Commission. European Commission (EC). In: Digital Transformation of European Industry and Enterprises; A report of the Strategic Policy Forum on Digital Entrepreneurship. 2015. Available from: http://ec.europa.eu/DocsRoom/documents/9462/attachments/1/translations/en/renditions/native [Accessed: 19 August 2022]

[25] Bisht S, Prakash N, Saraswat S, Srivastava S. Digital entrepreneurship and the bottom of the pyramid-A conceptual framework. International Journal on Recent Trends in Business and Tourism (IJRTBT). 2019;**3**(1):33-42

[26] Li Y, Liu Q. A comprehensive review study of cyber-attacks and cyber security; Emerging trends and recent developments. Energy Reports. 2021;**7**:8176-8186

[27] Matar AM. Change management and its role in enhancing the competitive advantage in the construction sector. Journal of University Studies for inclusive research. 2018;**1**(1):1-19

[28] Moavenzadeh J. The fourth industrial Revolution: Reshaping the future of production. In: World Economic Forum. Amsterdam: DHL Global Engineering & Manufacturing Summit; 2015. p. 57

[29] Ross P, Maynard K. Towards a fourth industrial revolution. Intelligent Buildings International. 2021;**13**(3):159-161

[30] Fletcher P. The Built Environment at the Eve of the Fourth Industrial Revolution. Through Ideas. 2016. Available from: https://www.throughideas.com/the-built-environment-at-the-eve-of-the-fourth-industrial-revolution/. [Accessed: 19 August 2022]

[31] Tang H, Yao Q, Boadu F, Xie Y. Distributed innovation, digital entrepreneurial opportunity, IT-enabled capabilities, and enterprises' digital innovation performance: A moderated mediating model. European Journal of Innovation Management. 2023;**26**(4):1106-1128

[32] Schulze E. Everything You Need to Know About the Fourth Industrial Revolution. 2019. Available from: https://www.cnbc.com/2019/01/16/fourth-industrial-revolution-explained-davos-2019.html. [Accessed: 19 August 2022]

[33] Budd J, Miller BS, Manning EM, Lampos V, Zhuang M, Edelstein M, et al. Digital technologies in the public health response to COVID-19. Nature Medicine. 2020;**26**(8): 1183-1192

[34] Matt C, Hess T, Benlian A. Digital transformation strategies. Business & Information Systems Engineering. 2015; **57**(5):339-343

[35] Ting D, Carin L, Dzau V, Wong TY. Digital technology and COVID-19. Nature Medicine. 2020;**26**(4):459-461. DOI: 10.1038/s41591-020-0824-5

[36] Yáñez-Valdés C, Guerrero M. Determinants and impacts of digital entrepreneurship: A pre-and post-COVID-19 perspective. Technovation. 2024;**132**:102983

[37] Qermane K, Mancha R. WHOOP, Inc.: digital entrepreneurship during the Covid-19 pandemic. Entrepreneurship Education and Pedagogy. 2021;**4**(3): 500-514

[38] Sharma GD, Kraus S, Liguori E, Bamel UK, Chopra R. Entrepreneurial challenges of COVID-19: Re-thinking entrepreneurship after the crisis. Journal of Small Business Management. 2024;**62** (2):824-846

[39] Chaudhuri R, Chatterjee S, Kraus S, Vrontis D. Assessing the AI-CRM technology capability for sustaining family businesses in times of crisis: The moderating role of strategic intent. Journal of Family Business Management. 2022. DOI: 10.1108/jfbm-12-2021-0153

[40] Audretsch DB, Belitski M, Caiazza R, Drapeau MD, Menter M, Wales WJ. Resilience and digitally-advanced entrepreneurship. Entrepreneurship & Regional Development. 2024;**36**(1–2): 1-9

[41] Mitsa V, Lyakh I. Application of digital entrepreneurship platforms in small and medium-sized businesses. Actual Problems of Economics. 2023. DOI: 10.32752/1993-6788-2022-1-262-6-11

[42] Bougie R, Sekaran U. Research Methods for Business: A Skill Building Approach. John Wiley & Sons; 2019

Chapter 7

# Perspective Chapter: Sustainable and Resilient ODeL Practices for the Industry 5.0 Paradigm – Application of Digitalization to Support Authentic Knowledge Creation

*Motshidisi Masilo*

## Abstract

Students' digital competency is key in open distance learning (ODeL) space. In addition, engagement in online interactive learning through social and cognitive networking is essential. This chapter reports the online facilitator's experiences on the sustainable and resilient learning practices in interactive ODeL classroom. It draws from the connectivism theory that emphasizes the importance of the students' abilities to live, work and thrive in the interconnected learning community. This qualitative autoethnographic case-study is an inquiry into the ODeL mathematics education students' interactive learning processes. A case study in this chapter takes the form of a story that is enhanced by theory and practices aligned with the researcher's experiences. The self-observation notes that the author has drafted from practices in own online classroom are connected to literature to explore the interactive practices in an ODeL context. Digitalization in teaching enhances students' connectivism practices for the Fourth Industrial Revolution (4IR). This enables students to connect socially and cognitively to acquire multidimensional thinking and in-depth learning to enhance authentic learning. In essence, the ODeL facilitator should apply sustainable teaching through digitalization to support students to adhere to interactive sustainable practices to flourish in the interactive learning systems, and to attain the industry 5.0 skills.

**Keywords:** authentic learning, connectivism, sustainability, resilience, mathematics education

## 1. Introduction

Societal values within the fourth industrial revolution (4IR) era align with beliefs that the usage of digital tools can support the inquisitive nature of those who learn. The necessary inquisitiveness enhances participation in social and cognitive networks that can benefit students to advance creative critical thinking and authentic learning. Facilitators of learning and students in the 4IR learning society must be equipped with appropriate values, knowledge, and practices to advance the industry 5.0 competences which is the envisaged future in education [1]. However, the appropriate values are viable through the set societal ethical standards. For example, even in online learning, through utilization of digital resources, originality or authenticity should be prioritized in knowledge creation to avoid plagiarism.

My narrative in this chapter departs from my concern of interactive learning practices in an ODeL learning context. It seems complicated for the current cohort of ODeL students to network through social and digital means and be able to develop authentic critical creative thinking. Currently, the 4IR means of digitalization in the education sphere are challenged with lack of originality, where students fail to maintain academic integrity practice, such as avoiding plagiarism. In this sense, the preparation of students for the industry 5.0 competencies is not possible. Through lack of originality and plagiarism practices, sustainable practices are not maintained in ODeL, focused on mathematics education in this chapter. The lack of sustainable practices in learning at an ODeL space hinder cognitive development that aligns with the needs of the workforce of the 5IR era. The present ODeL students are included as the workforce of the future in the 5IR. However, the concern in this chapter is that the student cohort that is trained and prepared for the demands of the 5IR is not coping well with interactive learning and in the education space that has a wealth of knowledge. This is because they rely on the existing information and knowledge, and they find it hard to transform and align their thinking and knowledge-creation abilities with the plethora of existing knowledge.

The purpose of this chapter is to give a perception of the online facilitator's experiences and insight into the sustainable practices in the online classroom of students who study mathematics teaching qualification. The group of students that were studied, were prospective teachers who were learning and were equipped with relevant skills to teach mathematics in the digital era. The following questions were asked in this chapter: What are my interpersonal experiences,

- in view of how sustainable and resilient learning practices are affected by a plethora of digital information leading to plagiarism?
- as an ODeL facilitator in supporting students to apply skills that can assist them to advance authentic knowledge creation?

The questions asked resonate with the notion of students' abilities to "live, work, and thrive in the interconnected community" [2]. This means that with a plethora of knowledge from social networks through digitalization, students should be able to evaluate the information at their exposure and use it to build a cognitive network that is original and authentic. Sharing my experience of ODeL facilitation to support sustainable and resilient mathematics education practices, is a way of addressing the culture of academic plagiarism elevated by the world of digital information, to propagate a call for the need for ethical practices in the 4IR era to advance the expertise needed in the future, that is, in the 5IR era. In the following sections, literature is discussed, and the theory of the digital age is engaged in a discourse on how students respond to digital network creation for sustainable social and cognitive networks.

## 2. Literature review

Literature in this chapter affirms that sustainable and resilient mathematics education encompasses the education processes that task facilitators with teaching skills that assist students in developing the necessary skills to learn along machines. Furthermore, the literature follows a discourse on the essence of digitalization in supporting sustainable and resilient mathematics education processes, the impact of digitalization on authentic learning, and academic plagiarism in digitized ODeL environments. The discourse leads to the synthesis that shows the influence of the current interactive learning practices as aligned with the impact on social and cognitive networks.

### 2.1 Sustainable and resilient mathematics education practices

The Education for Sustainable Development (ESD) mission is part of the targets of sustainable development in societies by 2030. Based on the United Nations (UN) ESD goals, ESD covers the development of values and transformative actions that lead to problem-solving, ability to recognize the needs for a sustainable society, acceptance of modern society, and ability to tackle problems in the immediate society [3]. Through ESD, educational activities must empower students as builders of the society. The ESD further promotes competencies, skills, and attitudes such as ability to think in multidimensional and integrative ways, communicate, and cooperate with other problem-solvers. In line with the right attitude through empowerment by the ESD, students need an attitude to respect relations and connections; as well as the attitude to participate proactively [3, 4]. The key facilitator actions necessary to empower the 4IR student with ESD competencies include transformative pedagogies that promote proactive, interactive, and in-depth learning. In addition, pedagogy that is ESD aligned must support activities that are aligned with students' experiences, and promote cooperative learning through group activities, allowing students to collaborate in doing investigations and completing academic discussions [3, 4]. The envisaged implementation of ESD and assumed students' response aligns with the student's ability to connect the acquired knowledge with inquiry characteristics such as critical thinking and exploration that promotes authenticity in knowledge production. Research has shown that inquiry in learning designates a process where students explore situations to discover real-world facts that will aid in problem-solving [5–8]. In addition, research confirms that learning by inquiry to achieve authentic learning, promotes a sustainable practice of inquiry-based learning (IBL) that is student-centered, promotes students' ability to ask critical questions as they learn, collect information, and examine it; produce solutions to problems, make decisions, rationalize conclusions, and take actions. The IBL-aligned teaching strategies engage students actively in an authentic scientific discovery process where they can identify the problem, explore the problem, and provide the solution [8]. IBL designates an appropriate skill for sustainable education.

Practices that involve learning by inquiry are possible through teaching, that is, through inquiry-based facilitation, teaching that orientates students to active thinking processes, how to think, and how to be thorough in critical thinking [7–10]. The inquiry-based driven teaching helps learners to inquire, formulate hypotheses, collect data, test the hypotheses, and ultimately formulate theories from their self-tested hypotheses. Such practices build mathematical resilience. Mathematical resilience refers to a positive approach to learning mathematics that supports students to overcome barriers they encounter when learning mathematics [11]. Considering this, this chapter refers to resilient ODeL mathematics education practices as students' ability to adapt to challenging problem-solving processes through digital networks to acquire authentic critical thinking and maintain sound ethical practices. Even when problem-solving seems difficult, resilient practices assist students in refraining from plagiarizing, but resorting to self-directedness urging inquisitiveness through asking pertinent questions. Resilient practices complemented by authentic learning through inquiry contribute sustainable mathematics education practices, that can help students to thrive in societal spaces that have ample knowledge that can be effortlessly accessed through social and digital networks. Furthermore, mathematical resilience implies that students must approach mathematical problem-solving with confidence and persistence, including a willingness to research, reflect, and discuss [11]. Sustainable and resilient practices of learning enable students to maintain originality and create authentic ideas out of the wide continuum of information they can access using digital technology.

### 2.2 The essence of digitalization in mathematics education

In education, digitalization refers to a process of translating text and images into a digital format that can be processed through a computer; and the tools for digitalization are outlined as computer, smartphone, internet, and more [12]. In addition, the ways of digitalization are outlined as sharing of online knowledge, digital support material, online social groups, and more [12]. Digitalization creates smart education systems, that can provide content around the world and create an interactive system for teaching and learning [13]. In addition, the authors argue that digitalization implicates an approach in artificial intelligence which is a mathematical code aligned with some algorithms; and can influence individuals' thinking. Artificial intelligence in educational settings implies smart robots programmed as teachers [13, 14]; which probably provides ample knowledge that prohibits critical inquiry for both teachers and learners. Sustainable digitalization should prioritize digital transformation when the existing ways of sustainability yield low results. Mathematics education in diverse societies yields lower production in terms of knowledge sustainability for problem-solving skills that can be applied to ailing societies, economies, and environments. Exposure to the digital world with all relevant information, has turned individuals who learn into dependable individuals rather than individuals who are able to inquire and explore the existing and current to better their skills of critical thinking and knowledge creation. Hence, reliance on existing sources of information that are forever transforming destroys authenticity and creative thinking. I maintain in this chapter that digitalization should instead increase the abilities of knowledge creation for example, that the complementarity of humans and machines for the industry 5.0 paradigm is viable where humans can create information that they can use to operate machines for machines to yield advanced models that humans can explain and apply. From the wide spectrum of information that is obtained from knowledgeable others and digital networks, individual students can apply inquiry-based practices of collecting information, examining, analysing, deducing, operating, and informing the machines with deduced data and allow the machines to act on the data to produce functional models. Such sustainable practices show resilience in the complementary role of an individual's interaction with digital technology in knowledge production. In this way, resilience yields authenticity impacted by understanding that digital transformation poses high demands of knowledge that will fit into the competitive social, economic, and environmental spaces we live in. Sustainable and resilient mathematics education practices of the digital era should not lead to despair and lack of thinking, but to integration that can enhance knowledge that is authentic to fit in the existing space of knowledge and strategies of realistic problem-solving.

### 2.3 The impact of digitalization on authentic learning

Authentic learning also referred to as deep learning, refers to engagement with diverse activities in learning, for example, reference to real-world problems with solutions, conducting case studies, learning through problem-based activities, and engagement in virtual communities of practice [10]. Relatively, authentic learning can be viable in mathematics education through usage of relevant authentic material. The probable authentic material for sustainable and resilient mathematics learning refers to modeling exercises that pose the real situation, thus learning in the real-world environment; ultimately, being able to analyse models and create real mathematical connotations [15–17]. Modeling in mathematics, that is, learning in the real world, creating and analysing models to create real-life models and new knowledge, contributes to autonomous and authentic learning. While the expectations are that authentic mathematics materials must improve knowledge-acquiring strategies to original strategies where humans must be able to learn along and inform machines, things turn vice versa as in the digital era, humans retrieve knowledge from the machines and present it as their own. Digital learning turned out to be an opportunity for cheating [18] and reproducing knowledge. Digital transformation in authentic mathematical modeling is aligned with the usage of computers to handle models, though, such may not lead to sophisticated results. The implication is that where machines fall short, humans are supposed to interact and bring in their expertise to aid the machine. Considering this, it means authentic learning is essential for digital transformation to prepare the students for the demands of industry 5.0. The machine should not be used to plagiarize but to enhance knowledge and production for the sustainability and resilience in education, social and economic spheres.

### 2.4 Academic plagiarism in digitalized ODeL environments

Plagiarism refers to claiming false authorship of information, also intellectual theft [19]. Concerns are raised about academic plagiarism that it has spread in many educational contexts, and it is difficult to understand, fight, and detect [20]. This chapter looked at plagiarism in the ODeL contexts on assignments that are formative or continuous assessment tasks. Academic plagiarism is influenced by different practices, and such contribute to mathematics education learning practices that are unsustainable toward cognitive development. It is not always the case where plagiarism occurs because of deliberate cheating. According to, most students plagiarize because they lack understanding of different types of academic plagiarism, and skills to circumvent it [19]. Other causes were outlined as weak language and academic writing skills, saving effort, easy access to online resources, conventional assignments, types of assessment design executed, inadequate digital literacy, short timeframe, saving time, and challenge to balance personal, professional, and academic life [19–21]. The authors studied plagiarism and outlined the causes that align mostly with students' practices, and facilitator practices that align with conventional

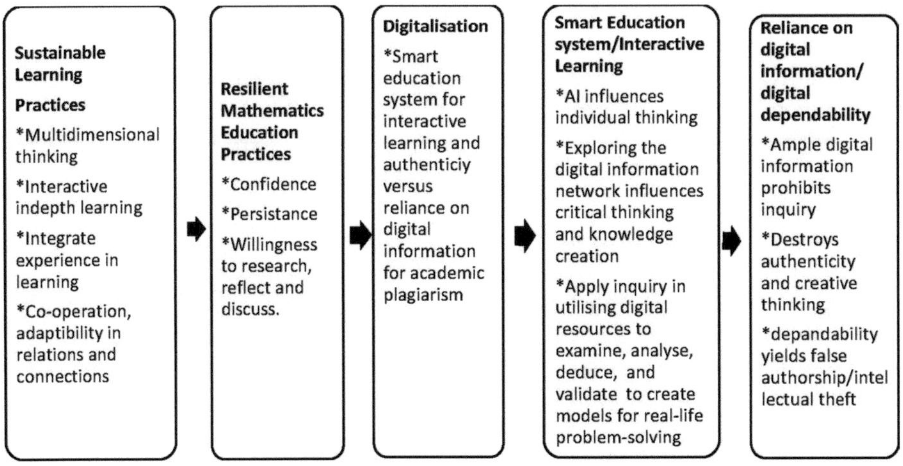


**Figure 1.**
*Effects of sustainable and resilient practices through digitalization. Source: Author.*

assignments and types of assessment design executed. In this chapter, I agree with the outlined causes, however, I emphasize that facilitation practice in the ODeL space needs to be transformed so that it supports students' critical analysis of study material and the online information at their exposure.

### 2.5 Synthesis

Transformative pedagogies aligned with ESD as influenced by digitalization are bound to support sustainable teaching practices to empower students with sustainable learning practices for adaptation in the ever-increasing world of digital information. Facilitation of learning that relies on producing dependable students prohibits the ability to apply sustainable learning practices, therefore, contributing complete reliance on digital information and ultimately lack of academic integrity in knowledge creation. **Figure 1** denotes the effects of sustainable and resilient practices through digitalization. In addition, the impact of digital dependability is outlined.

Sustainable learning practices inculcate skills, such skills build resilience characteristics such as confidence, persistence, and willingness to research, reflect, and discuss (**Figure 1**). Attaining sustainable and resilient learning practices yields sustainable digitalization that contributes smart education system for interactive learning and authenticity. Lack of sustainable and resilient practices produces reliance on digital information enhancing digital dependability and academic plagiarism.

## 3. Theory of the digital age

This report aligns the pragmatist view of inquiry with the sustainability and resilience of mathematics education practices. That is, subjective and objective practices combine to balance the act of inquiry. In narrating my experiences in the online classroom, I apply a pragmatic stance that sustainable mathematics education is experimental, should contribute to change toward society and environment; and enable those who learn to operate actively at cooperative levels [7, 22]; and along the digital resources to solve common problems encountered. Considering this, subjective-objective social and individual cognitive networks remain essential in the establishment of sustainable resilient mathematics education practices. The pragmatic inquiry into learning mathematics should be enhanced by considering connectivism as a theory of the 4IR, that is, a theory of the digital age as discovered by Siemens (2004). Connectivism aligns with sustainability in the social context that is digitally orientated as it capitalizes on students' abilities to "live, work and thrive in the interconnected community" [2]. The implications of the connectivism theory are that the objective of teaching based on the connectivism theory is to stimulate knowledge networks through modeling [2]. The theory of the digital age plays an essential role in network creation. I considered network creation from two points of view, that is, social networks and mental or cognitive networks. Connectivism theory asserts that acquiring knowledge is distributive, that is, it is everywhere through networks of connections established among society members, between individuals, organizations, and technology as a link to all [23]. In addition, the author argues that the characteristics of a successful network are connectivity, openness, autonomy, and diversity. Connection networks differ, some can be local connections, and some can go as far as world connections [23]. In such connections information is extensive and individuals can harvest as much information as they can. In terms of mental networks, connectivism as a theory of the mind bases natural connections on patterns that are both distributive and associative [23]; distributive in the neural system of the brain, and associative, where there is complementary interaction between two or more neurons. Within the social and mental or cognitive networks, several principles support connectivism (**Table 1**).

Furthermore, Siemens 2005 developed a connectivism framework that emphasizes the essence of internet technology in shaping the students' thinking and in transforming the way learning occurs. The connectivism framework recognizes students as digital natives whose learning depends on autonomy, connectedness, diversity, and openness. Therefore, the current study argues that connectivism is a guiding lens in an ODeL teaching and learning environment where students must be efficient users of digital resources, utilize the same resources to network, build online social relations or learning communities, and they must be able to connect with all sources of knowledge, acquire and build knowledge, and ultimately be able to expand their knowledge and share to contribute knowledge.

- Learning and knowledge rest in diversity of opinions.
- Learning is a process of connecting specialized nodes or information sources.
- Learning may reside in non-human appliances.
- The capacity to know more is more critical than what is currently known.
- Nurturing and maintaining connections are needed to facilitate continual learning.
- The ability to see connections between fields, ideas, and concepts is a core skill.
- Currency (accurate, up-to-date knowledge) is the intent of all connectivism learning activities.
- Decision-making is itself a learning process. Choosing what to learn and the meaning of incoming information is seen through the lens of a shifting reality. While there is a right answer now, it may be wrong tomorrow due to alterations in the information climate affecting the decision.

**Table 1.**
*Principles of connectivism. Source: Ref. [24].*

### 3.1 Sustainability and resilience in the interconnected digital community

In adaptation to social and mental networks for inquiry, the application of sustainable practices for knowledge creation is essential. Sustainable learning practices ensure resilience in learning to enable students to advance sustainable decision-making toward sustainable decision-making toward authentic knowledge creation (**Figure 2**).

In addition, it is necessary to maintain resilience to thrive in the interconnected community of learning. **Figure 2** outlines the resilient learning practices as among others, the development of capacity to know more, thus acquiring more knowledge through research, reflection, and discussion. Such characteristics as those of resilience enable connections and networks to accumulate the necessary knowledge. In essence, the connectivism characteristics support the notion that knowledge is distributive with technology as a link to all, requiring sustainable education practices is imperative through sustainable learning practices for students to advance interactive learning systems.

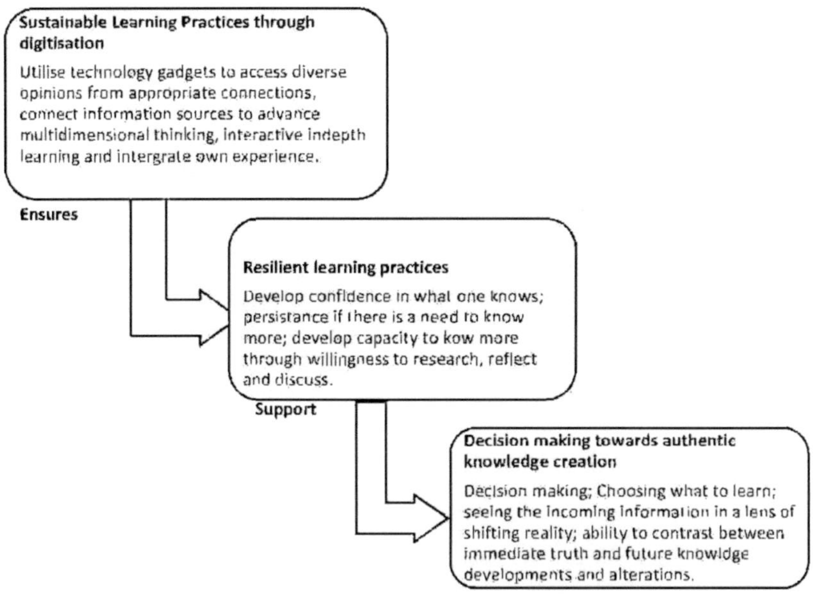


**Figure 2.**
*Sustainability and resilience in the interconnected learning community. Source: Author.*

## 4. Methodology

This report draws from the autoethnographic qualitative case-study inquiry into the ODeL mathematics education students' interactive learning process. A case study in this chapter takes the form of a story that is enhanced by theory and practices aligned with the researcher's experiences. In my story of analysing a case of interactive learning in ODeL learning space, I share the self-observation notes I have drafted from the students' practices in the interactive classroom; in addition, my notes are supported by analyses of students' peer interactions in the interactive classroom, as well as inquiries directed through email to me as the facilitator.

Autoethnography designates a qualitative research methodology utilized by researchers whose interest lies in narrative descriptions and evocations of the lived experience ([25], p. 8). In addition, autoethnography involves the author as a researcher crafting creative narratives shaped out of the author's personal experiences within a culture and addressed to varied academic audiences. This report is based on the author's experience as a mathematics teacher, facilitator, mathematics education practitioner and researcher in a blended teaching context. That is, a practitioner in both face-to-face as well as in open distance e-learning contexts.

The research field encompasses the interactive learning situation in an ODeL context, including the students and the learning encounter. In autoethnographic research the researchers' life experiences are the primary source of information, therefore, several ways can be incorporated into the data collection process [26]. The autoethnographic researchers immerse themselves in the research field and record everyday occurrences in an in-person or online community ([27], p. 3). For example, data can be collected through (1) self-observations by taking ethnographic field notes; (2) self-reflective data from the autoethnographic researcher's journal of reflections related to the research; (3) use of pertinent and accessible data such as artifacts, documents, photographs, letters, and diaries [26]. In this autoethnographic research, data is collected from the interactive learning session; notes I have written from my lived experience in facilitating interactive learning, and commentaries in an ODeL interactive learning context. Triangulation for quality control [26], was achieved in this research through several forms of inquiry into the case, mainly self-observation, analysing notes I have collected, and commentaries into the students' online interactions and students' individual queries seeking individual support to work and thrive in the interactive learning process.

Analysing data from autoethnographic study can be drawn from known qualitative analysis methods, for example through general descriptive qualitative research, narrative strategies of analysis, ethnographic research analysis, and more [26]. I draw upon descriptive qualitative research analysis strategy and narrative thematic analysis in this chapter of data analysis. The thematic structure incorporated encompasses reports on occurrences in the interactive classroom, explanations, and descriptions of events. To apply ethics in autoethnographic research, it is essential the researcher focuses on own experiences and feelings, rather than characterization; and anonymity and confidentiality through using pseudonyms must be maintained [26]. I base my arguments on my classroom experiences; there is no character in reference; the students are not characterized, and their names, qualification, specific module name, and code are not revealed in this chapter. **Table 2** reveals my autoethnographic engagement.

| | |
|---|---|
| Methodology and approach | A qualitative case-study research inquiry into the ODeL learning process. |
| The ODeL Mathematics Education Facilitator | The autoethnographic researcher. |
| The research area | Interactive learning situation involves the mathematics education student and the interactive learning encounter. |
| Data collection | Data is derived from the facilitator's notes and recollection of lived experiences and encounters in the interactive learning environment. |
| Reflexive writing | A heuristic process where new insights emerge. |
| The case study | A story that is theory-driven and that enhances theory. |

**Table 2.**
*Qualitative, autoethnographic study.*

The reflexive writing of my lived experience encompasses a heuristic process, where prompts are used to arrive at new insights and judgment. I have drawn from my personal experience to describe, analyse, and interpret the ODeL mathematics education practice; and connect my insight to self-identity, traditions, and shared meanings [25].

## 5. Findings and discussion

I have been a life-long learner in mathematics and mathematics education, also, my orientation as a teacher has been on mathematics and related subjects. Therefore, I understand when students share the difficulty of studying mathematics and would want the teacher to be the knowledgeable other whom they must imitate in every step of problem-solving. Furthermore, I have read across research in mathematics education that criticizes traditional teaching as the cause of failure in achieving the learning outcomes in diverse content areas in mathematics. Continual reliance on the teacher and exposure to rote learning, contribute to plagiarism at a later stage of studying. When the teacher can no longer play the know-it-all role, students use existing material and social networks to plagiarize. Even to this day, mathematics education practices are encouraging rote learning that is sustainable for a short period but cannot sustain knowledge for long-term memory. Resilience in learning mathematics is a factor that needs attention, to alleviate the challenges of short-term knowledge for promotion while knowledge cannot be sustained for contribution in development of real-life context to meet the human needs and wants. The case study findings are based on discussions about social and cognitive networking in an online classroom. I also discuss the shortcomings that transpire from an interactive learning system.

### 5.1 Social and cognitive networking in an online classroom

ODeL learning facilitation encompasses both closed practices that support individual learning and open practices that encourage learning networks through online collaboration and connections. Mostly, closed teaching practices that focus on individual students include fixed material like a direct study guide and prescribed textbooks with memory-related assessments. However, an open teaching system encourages networking where a learning group collaborates to explore concepts together to attain group competency which yields individual competency [28]. Furthermore, to enhance cognition, open teaching supports students to explore using diverse materials where they evaluate the excess information that exists in relation to the content at their exposure. This enables them to judge and make decisions about what they need to know, and what they already know, and determine new knowledge that must be declared.

To facilitate a learning network in an interactive classroom, I developed content-based discussion forums where all students were encouraged to participate through mark allocation, where they all had an equal chance to throw in ideas about content-related matters. Discussion forums are important in online classes to enhance interactions among students [29]. The social networking in an online classroom that I engaged students in had an instruction that students must complete some content-based activities as (1) individuals and post activities in the forum; and some activities as (2) a team, collaborating to advance cooperative learning and read other groups' posts and comment on the posts. Students were not grouped by the facilitator but had to individually network within the module site to find a team to work with. The criteria for mark allocation in group work were (1) belonging to a group/finding a group, (2) cooperative skill collaboration to complete the activities; (3) posting teamwork—all activities completed and posted; and (3) participating in the classroom discussion—individually reading three posts and commenting. The aim of a group form for networking was to enable students to share ideas and to learn from one another through collaboration in a specific group and through networking in the whole classroom. Individual posts were meant to assess (1) the student's ability to access information individually, (2) their confidence to post their own ideas on the forum platform, and (3) cognitive networking abilities through finding and reading additional material to advance in-depth learning and integration of own experience.

#### *5.1.1 Sustainable and resilient practices through digitization*

Not all students can thrive in an interactive classroom though utilizing relevant gadgets to network and access diverse opinions to structure individual interactive depth learning for alignment with individual experiences. A total of 280 students enrolled and were part of the interactive online learning. However, 39% (110) of students did not post any individual work, were not traced in any group, they did not participate completely in the discussion forum or interactive learning. These students were found to have participated only in written assignments that demanded no sharing of information through the classroom social network. In such assignments, the only source was found to be the material uploaded as a study guide and a prescribed book. In-depth learning was found to be lacking where students rely only on the material developed by the facilitator. The evidence was reliance on online material uploaded which prohibited IBL; lack of authenticity and creative learning and encouraged false authorship. Most students did not account for nor alert me of their challenges, other than one student who shared her frustration in a direct email to me stating: *I understand the instructions of how the activities are done, but right now I am struggling to add my work in the discussion forum let alone create a group*. Though I managed to guide the only student who *shared* her frustrations with me, I was concerned about the 109 students who were not sharing any challenge through any accessible platform, and who were nowhere to be found on the online platform. I had to conclude that perhaps they might be having gadget problems, digital literacy challenges, or a lack of confidence and persistence to identify themselves with the online community.

Of the 280 students who participated 61% (170) participated in either both group and individual activities or partially, in one activity. **Table 3** shows the record of those who fully or partially participated in the interactive learning session.

Students (37%) worked hard to utilize the online interactive learning platform, to share ideas within the network, and to learn from the information shared by other students. This is relatively a major percentage in the group that participated through individual and group interaction. In the utilization of digital resources to participate in the interactive learning platform, 30% of students could not post attachments to display the graphics/pictures and diagrams they were supposed to share. This has shown that students still need digital literacy skills to partake fully in interactive learning, moreover, in an ODeL context. However, students had shown resilience through sharing what they could to be part of the online community. Within this 30% that were willing but experiencing challenges, some used email mode of communication to seek help from the facilitator. **Table 4** outlines the students' clarity-seeking

- 12 (7%) students did not post individual work but belonged to groups.
- 44 (26%) students completed the individual work but belonged to no group. 51 (30%) experienced some challenges and could not post attachments to display the graphics they were supposed to share.
- Only 63 (37%) of those who participated in the blog managed to successfully post all tasks including graphic attachments; and participated in groups.

**Table 3.**
*Students' participation in the interactive session.*

- *I do not understand if we must type our work and upload it; if we must upload, how do we attach pictures of drawings?*
- *thanks for the clarity on how to post the assignment, but how do we post the diagrams?*
- *I do not understand clearly in terms of drawings; how are we going to draw; do we browse images and upload or how are we going to do it?*

**Table 4.**
*Students' challenges toward interactive online learning.*

questions to enhance their knowledge of how to operate gadgets for participation in the interactive online learning platform.

The connectivism traits require efficient usage of technology to learn and share information and expand own knowledge. Inquisitiveness remains a basic character that drives an individual to develop persistence to want to know more. The students had shown resilient learning practices as they were willing to share their authentic, sketches, diagrams, and pictures.

In some instances, students have preferences, that is, work better as individuals than in a group. I have realized this from the 26% of students who were not belonging to groups but completed all individual activities and shared them on the social platform. The students contributed to the network but seemingly lacked collaborative and teamwork skills. On the contrary, there were students who could participate in a group and their work posted on the interactive platform based on group efforts (7%). Students display cooperative learning skills and, ability to thrive in teamwork, however, lack confidence in what they know as individuals. Students could not persevere through a need to know more from their peers through network criticism and comments. In the 26% that participated partially, no reasons were given for their failure to fully engage in the interactive classroom.

#### *5.1.1.1 Critical peer analysis*

Integration of students' experience toward interactive learning accompanied by resilience through confidence in what one knows was evident in critical analysis of posted comments on peers. Comments have shown that within the network, competent students in diverse parts of the activity are able to share their expertise. Students alerted others of activities that were not well done. **Table 5**, outlines comments based on critical analysis and geared toward peer assistance.

The comments outlined in **Table 5** were exposed for all to read. Firstly, the students who posted comments like those in **Table 5** indicated that they are able to make decisions regarding what they learn, the ability to contrast among chunks of knowledge and how to apply; and see information learned as a lens of transformation.

- *Well done, your work is neat and well structured, however, you have left out activity 1.1.*
- *You made a numbering error. Your activity 1 answer should be activity 2 answer.*
- *Your work is good but information on drawing is missing. You have not included any diagrams as you are referring to them in the activity.*
- *Your explanation of visualization is good, also the example that you gave that learner learn by seeing, is good. However, you did not include any models for learners to see. Maybe you could use wood blocks of a square, rectangle, and circle. You could make learners see, and maybe invite others to demonstrate with the blocks to show a square, rectangle, and other figures.*

**Table 5.**
*Interactive peer critical analysis.*

Secondly, students who were part of the interactive classroom and could read comments were able to expand their knowledge in the subject.

### *5.1.2 How interactive learning increase sustainable and resilient learning practices*

In relation to connectivism, interactive learning becomes successful when the online learning environment is characterized by connectedness, authenticity, openness, and diversity. The mentioned characteristics are possible to achieve when the interactive class facilitator enforces assessment or completion of activities that would need maximal usage of digital gadgets in networking, to learn through connecting, building, and expanding. **Figure 3** shows the visual model of student's interaction in an online interactive class for sustainable practices in relation to social and cognitive networking.

In relation to utilizing digital resources to access information, 61% have shown to have relevant gadgets and are able to perform some activity in an interactive online classroom, though the interaction or participation level was different (Cf **Table 1**). The students were active members of the digital society within their interactive classroom. In essence, a graded content blog motivated students and they were able to participate in their majority.

Reading others' posts contributed toward knowledge improvement whereas peer feedback contributed to individual learning. Students learn to critique and analyse others' work and to apply critical analysis and decision-making toward their learning. Group motivation and competency have been shown to enhance individual motivation and competency. Students were able to practice research and investigation skills to gather information to complete tasks in a strive to obtain allocated grades. Though more students were focused on obtaining allocated grades, sustainable and resilient practices were acquired through their participation in an interactive classroom. Ability to answer and post all questions shows that students read widely and were able to access information. Metacognition is another important factor that seemed to have developed as students engaged in groups. Students were aware of how they learned as they had to play a part in a group and were given the chance to determine their own way of learning. Authenticity is achieved, as students cannot plagiarize other student's work and post on the same platform. Active engagement in open learning is essential to circumvent plagiarism. In essence, the student gained knowledge that they can incorporate into the wide spectrum of online information and learned how to incorporate the available and easily accessible online information into their own experiences to create their own knowledge. I aver in this chapter that students who are

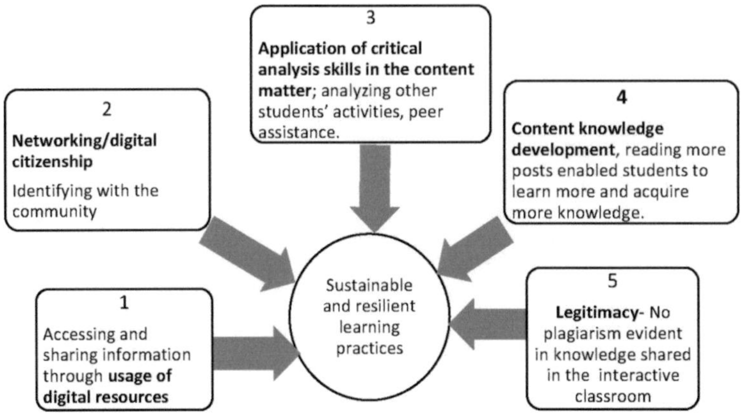


**Figure 3.**
*Visual model for interactive learning.*

not inquisitive, who do not search for information and analyse it critically, and who cannot cope in social and cognitive networks resort to the only available source and resort to plagiarism which is a major challenge in the current digital era.

Inclusivity is fully achieved through engaging students in both closed and open online activities. Students who cannot cope with closed questions and individual work are included in open methods of assessment through connectivism. **Table 6** outlines the characteristics that the online facilitator and learning to support sustainable and resilient 4IR learning practices that can equip the future workforce of the industry 5.0.

## 5.2 Shortcomings that emanate from interactive learning classroom

While other students' comments show deep understanding of concepts and enlighten others, other students still comment for marks. A full mark could not

| 4IR characteristics of online facilitation and learning | Effect on the 5IR space. |
|---|---|
| Connectedness | An element of digitization.<br>Connects individuals to ample knowledge, to the world of knowledge and students advance knowledge integration. |
| Inclusivity | Group identity and active online citizenship afford all a chance to belong, to learn from others, and to enlighten others through peer support. |
| Self-regulated learning | Skills are attained through peer influence. Firstly group competency, group determination, and group cognition, then motivation to self-regulation, leading to individual competency, individual determination, and individual authentic cognition. |
| Peer support | Should be maximized to create a supportive online interactive learning environment. |
| Peer feedback | Yields deep knowledge of concepts substantive conversation and deep understanding that contribute toward intellectual quality. |

**Table 6.**
*Sustainable and resilient ODeL facilitation and interactive learning practices.*

be allocated to a student who does not apply a critical analysis skill, for example, for comments like *well done*; *you have done such a good work*. In large classes, some students refrain from participating, looking at the 39% (110) students who did not participate at all in the assessment that required sharing work through the discussion forum. Such students relied on other assessments for their marks. This shows that if all assessments were based on open learning, students would be compelled to be part of the interactive classroom. There are students who seemed not to be confident as individuals but managed to work with the group and obtained a group mark while individual marks were lost. Quality of performance is still an issue that still needs attention from the tutor. Group work in other groups was not showing rigor, for example, a group discussed a concept only in one sentence or uploaded incorrect solutions to some problems. Though there are shortcomings realized, further research on total engagement of students in open learning is still necessary, to alleviate the problem of plagiarism that occurs through closed learning and adherence to only uploaded sources for acquiring knowledge. Sustainable and resilient ODeL facilitation and interactive learning practices as in **Table 6**, are necessary toward supporting authentic learning in the 4IR era to build resilience and sustainability that is necessary for the industry 5.0 competency.

## 6. Conclusion

Authentic learning through critical inquiry, triggers creativity and critical thinking. These are attributes that align with 4IR practice to advance sustainable education practices necessary for industry 5.0. In addition, the attributes that are aligned with academic norms and values ensure ethical practices and positive responses to digitalization. The students who learn in an ODeL institution are full-time on gadgets to build social and cognitive connections. Essentially, module facilitators in any ODeL context, including the mathematics education context, should strive to engage students to live, work, and thrive in an online classroom; and to let them connect to a wide range of knowledge received through social and cognitive networks based on ethical, sustainable, resilient practices to create own, new, and authentic knowledge.

## Author details

Motshidisi Masilo
University of South Africa, Pretoria, South Africa

*Address all correspondence to: masilmm@unisa.ac.za

## References

[1] Kassim A. 4IR, 5IR, Society 5.0, and values in education. IIUM Journal of Educational Studies (Arabic). 2023;**11**(1):1-2

[2] Downes S. Connectivism. Asian Journal of Distance Education. 2022;**17**(1):58-87. DOI: 10.5281/zenodo.6173510

[3] Su CS, Díaz-Levicoy D, Vásquez C, Hsu CC. Sustainable development education for training and service teachers teaching mathematics: A systematic review. Sustainability. 2023;**15**(10):8435

[4] Egana del Sol PA. Education for sustainable development: Strategies and key issues. In: Quality Education. Cham: Springer International Publishing; 2020. pp. 258-272

[5] Friesen S, Scott D. Inquiry-based learning: A review of the research literature. Alberta Ministry of Education. 2013;**32**:1-32

[6] Trna J, Trnová E. Inquiry-based science education in science and technology education as a connectivist method. In: Proceedings of the 8th International Conference on Education, Samos, Greece. Greece: Research and Training Institute of East Aegean; 2012. pp. 831-837

[7] Masilo MM. Implementing inquirybased learning to enhance grade 11 students' problem-solving skills in Euclidean geometry [doctoral dissertation]. South Africa: The University of South Africa; 2018. Available from: http://hdl.handle.net/10500/24966

[8] Luo T, Arcaute K, Muljana PS. Integrating inquiry-based learning into engineering education: A case study. Innovations in Education and Teaching International. 2023;**60**(6):836-847

[9] Arends RI. Learning to Teach. 9th ed. New York, NY: McGraw-Hill; 2012

[10] Johnson AD. Designing 'authenticity' in digital learning environments. Journal of Interactive Technology and Pedagogy. 2016;**9**:12-39

[11] Johnston-Wilder S, Lee C. Developing mathematical resilience. In: BERA Annual Conference. England: University of Warwick; 1-4 Sep 2010. pp. 1-17

[12] Bejinaru R. Impact of digitalization on education in the knowledge economy. Management Dynamics in the Knowledge Economy. 2019;**7**(3):367-380

[13] Sousa RD, Karimova B, Gorlov S. Digitalization as a new direction in education sphere. In: E3S Web of Conferences. Vol. 159. France: EDP Sciences; 2020. p. 09014

[14] Shahroom AA, Hussin N. Industrial revolution 4.0 and education. International Journal of Academic Research in Business and Social Sciences. 2018;**8**(9):314-319

[15] Marion G, Lawson D. An Introduction to Mathematical Modelling. Edinburgh: Bioinformatics and Statistics Scotland, University of Bristol; 2008

[16] Uzunboylu H, Tezer M, Yildiz EP. The effects of the authentic learning approach with a course management system (moodle) on students' mathematics success and online authentic learning self-efficacy. Educational Research Review. 2020;**15**(11):679-689

[17] Durandt R, Blum W, Lindl A. Fostering mathematical modelling competency of South African engineering students: Which influence does the teaching design have? Educational Studies in Mathematics. 2022;**109**(2):361-381

[18] Haleem A, Javaid M, Qadri M, Suman R. Understanding the role of digital technologies in education: A review. Sustainable Operations and Computers. 2022;**3**:275-285

[19] Sadruddin MM. Exploring the causes of plagiarism among post graduate research students—A phenomenological case study approach. Journal of Education and Educational Development. 2021;**8**(2):296-318. DOI: 10.22555/joeed.v8i2.443

[20] Doró K. Why do students plagiarize? EFL undergraduates' views on the reasons behind plagiarism. Romanian Journal of English Studies. 2014;**11**(1):255-263. DOI: 10.2478/rjes-2014-0029

[21] Hafsa N. Plagiarism: A global phenomenon. Journal of Education and Practice. 2021;**12**:3. DOI: 10.7176/JEP/12-3-08

[22] Ozmon HA. Philosophical Foundations of Education. 9th ed. United Kingdom: Pearson; 2012

[23] Goldie JGS. Connectivism: A knowledge learning theory for the digital age? Medical Teacher. 2016;**38**(10):1064-1069. DOI: 10.3109/0142159X.2016.1173661

[24] Siemens G. Elearnspace. Connectivism: A Learning Theory for the Digital Age Elearnspace.Org. USA; 2004. pp. 14-16

[25] Poulos CN. Essentials of Autoethnography. Washington, DC: American Psychological Association; 2021. DOI: 10.1037/0000222-001

[26] Cooper R, Lilyea B. I'm interested in autoethnography, but how do I do it. The Qualitative Report. 2022;**27**(1):197-208

[27] Adams TE, Herrmann AF. Good autoethnography. Journal of Autoethnography. 2023;**4**(1):1-9

[28] Masilo M. Exploring the effect of a community of inquiry on geometry education studies in open distance learning. The International Journal of Science, Mathematics and Technology Learning. 2021;**29**(1):17

[29] Keleş U. Writing a "good" autoethnography in educational research: A modest proposal. The Qualitative Report. 2022;**27**(9):2026-2046